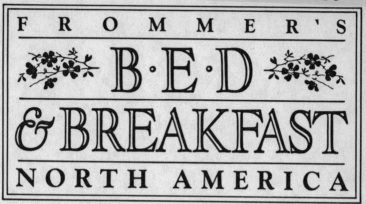

FROMMER'S

B·E·D

& BREAKFAST

NORTH AMERICA

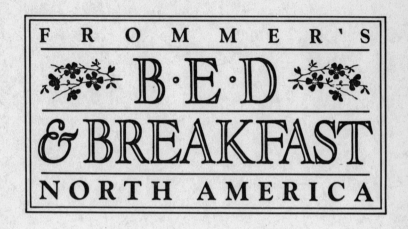

FROMMER'S
B·E·D
& BREAKFAST
NORTH AMERICA

BY HAL GIESEKING

REVISED EDITION

Published by Prentice Hall Press
A Division of Simon & Schuster, Inc.
Gulf + Western Building
One Gulf + Western Plaza
New York, NY 10023

ISBN 0-13-071672-3

Manufactured in the United States of America

CONTENTS _____

PART I

Introducing Bed & Breakfast   11

1   Bed & Breakfast—The *Friendly* Revolution in Travel   13

2   How to Find Bed & Breakfasts   21

3   How to Be a B&B Guest   27

4   B&Bs Abroad   30

5   How to Operate a B&B Home   49

PART II

Directory of B&B Reservation Services and Selected B&B Inns in North America   59

NATIONAL AND REGIONAL B&B RESERVATION SERVICES   61

THE NORTHEASTERN STATES   67

     Connecticut / 69
     Maine / 72
     Massachusetts / 80
     New Hampshire / 95
     New York / 101
     Rhode Island / 113
     Vermont / 116

THE MIDDLE ATLANTIC STATES   129

     Delaware / 131
     District of Columbia / 132
     Maryland / 133

New Jersey / 135
North Carolina / 137
Pennsylvania / 142
South Carolina / 151
Virginia / 158
West Virginia / 164

THE GREAT LAKES AREA   167

Illinois / 169
Michigan / 170
Ohio / 173
Wisconsin / 175

THE NORTHWEST & GREAT PLAINS   179

Idaho / 181
Iowa / 182
Minnesota / 184
Montana / 185
North Dakota / 186
Oregon / 187
South Dakota / 191
Washington / 192

THE SOUTHEASTERN STATES   197

Alabama / 199
Florida / 202
Georgia / 206
Kentucky / 211
Mississippi / 213
Tennessee / 214

THE SOUTHWEST & SOUTH CENTRAL AREA   219

Arkansas / 221
Colorado / 222
Kansas / 228
Louisiana / 229
Missouri / 234
New Mexico / 236
Oklahoma / 238
Texas / 239

CALIFORNIA & THE WEST   243

    Arizona / 245
    California / 248
    Utah / 265

ALASKA & HAWAII   267

    Alaska / 269
    Hawaii / 271

CANADA   273

    British Columbia / 275
    Nova Scotia / 276
    Ontario / 277
    Québec / 280

PART III
The 100 Best B&B Homes in
North America   283

READER'S NOMINATION FORMS FOR B&B
HOMES AND INNS   335

INDEXES   339

    General / 339
    Attractions / 342
    Schools and Colleges / 355

Special Thanks to—

Eleanor Berman, for helping to judge the "100 Best B&Bs"; André Corbin, who was of immense help in the preparation of the section on B&B inns; Irene Kleinsinger, Blythe-Foot Finke, Laura Schachinger, and Kit Young, who came through under deadline pressure; and most of all to the men and women who have started B&B reservation services and to the hosts and hostesses of B&B homes—they are entrepreneurs who have brought a new spirit of friendship to travel and hospitality in North America.

Introducing
Bed & Breakfast

1

BED & BREAKFAST—

The *Friendly* Revolution in Travel

- Travel across the U.S. and Canada, and stay in a B&B home for as little as $20 to $40 a night—breakfast included. Or over $150 for a B&B suite with a spa and swimming pool.
- Get "inside" tips from your hosts on the area's best restaurants, shops, stores, sightseeing attractions.
- Make friends as you travel and become "part of the neighborhood" rather than paying guests at a hotel, welcomed only by an occasional bellman looking for a tip or a desk clerk who may not be able to find your reservation.
- Participate in activities with your host, which can range from shopping the local stores to sailing and lakeside picnics.
- Rather than staying in a cold, impersonal hotel with stain-resistant plastic furnishings, you may wake up in a colonial bedroom filled with antiques.

Many travelers in North America are waking up to the bed-and-breakfast way of travel.

There are now over 10,000 bed-and-breakfast homes operating in the U.S., and the number is climbing almost daily. Many of the states I surveyed reported that the B&B movement was growing so fast they had trouble keeping any list of homes current.

Small wonder. Travelers have discovered what incredible bargains B&B homes can be. The cost of a hotel room in the U.S. has climbed to an average of $55 a night, with many rooms in major cities topping $150 to $200 per night. The B&B homes offer comfortable, homelike lodgings for as little as $15 to $35 per night per single, $20 to $50 per night double. It's true that you can also spend over $100 a night for some B&B rooms, but these are luxury exceptions in choice scenic locations, often with swimming pools, spas, and many other amenities.

But the real reason that the B&B way to travel has caught on is the sheer *friendliness* of many of the hosts. Vacationers and travelers are weary of the impersonality, coldness, and rudeness of many travel personnel. They are tired of passing through some of the most hospitable areas of North America, and meeting no local person other than a bellman or hotel cashier. People who have become B&B hosts are often outgoing and friendly, and they take real joy in welcoming others into their homes and communities.

This welcome shows up in many ways.

In some California B&Bs you may be greeted on arrival with good local wine and cheeses. In many homes the hosts serve far more than the typical continental breakfast (juice, roll, coffee/ tea). They introduce their guests to the local specialties. Not simply bacon and eggs but sourdough pancakes, English scones, fresh-fruit platters, smoked meats, blueberry coffee cake, New England clam cakes, creamed cod on toast, and many other luscious regional surprises you'd never find on a hotel breakfast menu!

Many of the hosts don't treat you like paying guests at all. Stay a few nights and you can practically become part of the family, gathering for cocktails around the fire in the evening with your hosts or even joining them for birthday parties and special local events. The stories I have gathered since I started researching this book indicate just how often hosts go out of their way to make their guests feel welcome.

Many hosts provide laundry facilities. Others will act as your sightseeing guides. Some with small boats or even yachts take guests out on lakes, rivers, and oceans. Many will pick up guests at airports, or bus and train stations. One host provides night-gowns and toothbrushes for guests whose luggage may have been lost by the airline. Many are happy to lend you bicycles for local touring, and give you maps, brochures, directions to inter-esting sightseeing. Still others give you membership cards to local country clubs, tennis clubs, swimming pools, etc. And when you want some company, they are often happy to oblige with breakfast or end-of-the-day conversations. As I said, this is a *friendly* revolution in travel.

Imagine the advantages of learning firsthand where the best restaurants are—from people who have lived in an area for years. You can learn what are the best times to visit Walt DisneyWorld, which are the least crowded roads for New England leaf watching, which local stores are having sales. In these imperfect times, you also learn which local areas have high crime rates and should be avoided.

The hosts themselves are often fascinating people. Here is a random list of their occupations that I discovered in researching B&B organizations across North America: journalists, investment bankers, linguists, painters, musicians (many), tennis pros and buffs, a world-renowned expert on scotch whisky, doctors, lawyers, teachers (many), gardeners, and gracious widows, widowers, divorced people who love to cook and entertain.

You know the hotel chain that proudly advertises "no surprises." Well, B&B homes are full of surprises, often very nice ones. When you check into some hotels, you know there's going to be a standard-size bed, a TV set, a scratch-proof, mar-proof dresser, and often the same graphics on the wall from hotel to hotel. But your room in a B&B home may have a cannonball bed from colonial times, a working fireplace, family antiques that span the centuries, and often original artwork on all of the walls. The homes themselves are often unique. A number of B&B homes are listed on the National Historic Register. Others are not really houses at all but houseboats and yachts in which the hosts welcome you to a floating B&B. One B&B is a sailboat in the San Juan Islands of Washington State. Another is a spectacular solar-designed home with a 360° view of a canyon. There are also working ranches, Boston town houses, New York luxury apartments, and remote Canadian farmhouses.

THE B&B EXPERIENCE

Here are some of the B&B homes and experiences other travelers have encountered recently.

Fireplaces and Forest Views in Wisconsin

In Door County, Wisconsin, you could swap stories with a retired host of a radio/TV show, in a lakeside redwood and native-stone house. The view is spectacular, perched 300 feet above Green Bay. Beautiful grounds are all around you, with flower gardens and modern sculpture blending into evergreen forests. There are two guest rooms for B&B visitors. The first has a fireplace. The homemade continental breakfast is served in a glassed-in porch overlooking the water. The hosts' topics of conversation include music, literature, and gardening.

Ghostly B&B in Louisiana

The Myrtles is a beautiful old (1796) plantation on U.S. 61 near St. Francisville, Louisiana. There are supposedly creaks and groans in the night, possibly the wanderings of Revolutionary War hero Gen. David Bradford. But in the morning you waken to a good southern-style breakfast, and can sit on the long veranda.

The Thomas Huckins House, 1705—in Cape Cod, Mass.

A recent B&B guest reported, "This gray shingled colonial is located at 2701 Main Street in Barnstable, a charming old Cape Cod village. It is the home of Burton and Eleanor Eddy, who have spent four years transforming their historic home from a wreck to a showplace. The house has the original wide floorboards, five fireplaces, and cubbies and crannies everywhere. The guest room downstairs has a walk-in fireplace and wood paneling painted Williamsburg blue, and is beautifully decorated with a blue paisley comforter on the bed, a big comfortable wing chair, an antique chest, a collection of German steins on the shelf over the fireplace and a cubby filled with Burt's hand-carved birds (so appealing I bought one).

"The private bath, which is super-size, is in tan and green with handsome brass fittings, and on a brass openwork shelf, a collection of old advertising tins; a wooden container that once held chewing gum is now filled with fancy soaps.

"They are an intelligent and very interesting couple. He's a retired army career man. They've lived all over the country and in Germany. During their longest stint in one place she got a master's at the University of Kansas and taught history there. This was really like visiting lovely people in an extraordinary home. The accommodations were quite private, even to the separate entrance to hall to front door so you didn't have to go through the rest of the house to come and go. Even breakfast was exceptional—fresh-fruit cup and homemade waffles."

Opera Star's Georgia Hideaway

Travel writer Vivian Holley visited Arden Hall, a B&B home built as a farmhouse in 1880 in Marietta, Georgia. She reports, "It's a two-story frame structure painted gray-green with dark-green shutters and a red door. Marietta is an Atlanta suburb some 25 miles north of the city and home of the Kennesaw Mountain National Battlefield Park of Civil War fame. The house is on the National Register of Historic Places.

"It's furnished with antiques, Oriental rugs, and objets d'art collected in the owners' travels. Guests have the run of the house, including the warm, comfortable kitchen, which has been modernized but retains the original pine cabinets with white porcelain knobs. The three guest bedrooms, each with bath, are meticulously decorated down to the last needlepointed pillow. One of the rooms is done in pink; its curtained double bed boasts an eyelet dust ruffle, plump pillows, and a comforter covered with tiny pink bows. Since the room's decor is feminine, the owner keeps some masculine trappings handy for a quick change for male guests. The owner's friend, opera star Roberta Peters, frequently occupies this room and her autographed photo hangs on the wall. Each room has heavily lined 'blackout' draperies for late sleepers."

As you can see, not your typical motel modern decor.

Philadelphia Party

Recently a young doctor from Milwaukee visited Philadelphia. He had sufficient travel funds to stay at a fashionable center-city hotel for about $80 per night, or at a motel near the airport for about $45 a night. Instead, he chose a B&B private home for only $19 a night.

But the cost savings were only part of the story. He enjoyed a breakfast *in bed* of melon, fresh croissants with butter and jam, and hot coffee. (It was all delivered on a tray to his door.) That evening he joined his hostess and other guests at a going-away dinner party for a young foreigner (also a B&B guest) returning home.

ABOUT THIS BOOK

As you can see, B&B travel is not your typical run-of-the-mill travel. Of course you could get a bad B&B—a poorly maintained house, surly people, a stale roll for breakfast. But I've personally encountered all of these problems in modern, expensive hotels, and you probably have too.

B&B travel can be more fun and more personal and more relaxing than any kind of traveling you've ever done before. You can meet and make new friends all over the country and the world. You can also save a lot of money.

Talking about savings, think about this. Next time you and your spouse or friend have breakfast in a top hotel, add up the *total* cost, including the tip to the waiter and local sales tax. That cost alone may just about equal the cost of a typical bed-and-breakfast for two in many parts of the country.

This guidebook was written to help you make the most of your next trip. It contains one of the most comprehensive listings and descriptions of North American B&B reservation services ever published. Many of these services pre-inspect every single home on their list. I surveyed them *twice*—with a span of one year between each survey—to help ensure that I was including the most stable and long-lasting services of this fledgling cottage industry. Some asked if they had to pay to be included in this guidebook. I told them "of course not." My only criteria for their inclusion was how well they were serving the traveling public.

I found many of these reservation-service organizations to be extremely conscientious, personally *pre-inspecting* the B&B homes included in their lists.

This guidebook also contains a listing of some special B&B inns that have come to my attention, my selection of the "100 Best B&B Homes" in North America, plus useful information for your next visit to a B&B overseas.

So come join the *friendly* revolution in travel—bed-and-breakfast. You're going to like it!

ANSWERS TO SOME COMMON QUESTIONS ABOUT B&B TRAVEL

Q. *Is B&B travel a new idea?*

A. Not at all. It's one of the oldest. In the 11th century, when monks and other pilgrims were walking to Rome or other holy sites, they frequently stopped overnight at private farms, monasteries, and homes. After breakfast in the morning, they were on their way—the first B&B guests.

In recent years the B&B movement has spread throughout much of Europe. Europeans frequently stop at homes with "Bed & Breakfast" or "Zimmer Frei" (room free) signs posted on the front lawn.

In the American depression years of the 1930s, "tourist homes" sprang up all over the countryside. For as little as $2 you could have a modest room and sometimes an equally modest breakfast.

However, the current B&B movement is much different. While there are still many modest homes offering a room and breakfast, the quality of most accommodations (and breakfasts) is light-years ahead of early tourist homes.

Q. *I get confused. I see B&B signs on hotels*

A. It is confusing. Many small inns have taken to calling themselves bed-and-breakfast places. These can be very pleasant, and over 200 of them are listed in this guidebook. But when I say "B&B" I'm talking about a room in a private home with at least a continental breakfast served to guests.

Q. *Why should I make a reservation through a B&B reservation-service organization? I see lists of individual B&B homes in books and brochures.*

A. You can, of course, make your own reservations directly with a B&B home. Some of these I've seen can be very good. However, because of zoning and other problems with neighbors, often the best B&B homes *never* appear in any public list. The only way you can book them is through a reservation-service organization.

The best of these organizations *pre-inspect* all prospective B&B homes before listing them.

Some of these organizations can occasionally be hard to reach. Many are small "mom and pop," or sometimes just "mom," operations. They have a list of B&Bs, a telephone, and an answering machine. Sometimes you may not be able to reach them until after 6 p.m. at night because the owners of the service work during the day. However, with a little persistence, you can usually get through. Almost all of the organizations I have included in this guide have been in existence at least one year. I surveyed most of them *twice,* with a span of one year in between.

Q. *Can I use a B&B home for business travel?*

A. Of course—B&Bs are ideal for business travelers who want to reduce costs. The reservation-service organizations included in this directory have listed many of the major corporations that are located near their B&B homes.

B&B homes are also ideal for parents visiting children at college, single women relocating to a new community, skiers, vacationers visiting specific scenic attractions, national parks, and other recreation areas, and everyone who's tired of paying high hotel costs and sometimes getting second-class, impersonal treatment.

Q. *Can I travel with a pet?*

A. Some B&B homes, especially in rural areas, do allow well-behaved dogs and cats to stay with their owners. Always ask about this, however, when you make your reservation. I know of one cat owner who stayed in B&B homes all over the state of Colorado with Tabby joining him for breakfast every morning.

If you are allergic to dogs or cats, be sure to ask if any are in residence in the B&B home before you make your reservation.

Q. *Are there any disadvantages to B&B travel?*

A. Yes. There can be a lack of privacy. Sometimes you and your spouse or friend want to be alone together on vacation; the conversation of even a well-meaning hostess may be more than you want. You also may have to wait in line for a shared bathroom, just like at home if you have a large family. You also may feel guilty staying too long in the shower when you know that others are waiting.

You also may find a few B&B homes that are disappointing. Barbara Notarius, president of Bed & Breakfast USA Ltd., reported on her visit to one: "I recently went out on an appointment to visit one prospective B&B for my network. I arrived at the appointed time. The place was beautiful from the outside, handmade by a custom cabinetmaker, very rustic and nestled in the woods by a running stream just outside a desirable country community. When I rang the bell, a woman came to the door and stared at me. I asked for the woman of the house from whom I had the first inquiry many weeks previously. The woman looked at me a bit bewildered and said 'No,' and just stood there. So I asked for the husband who had given me detailed directions only a few days before. Again this woman said 'No,' and continued to look at me. I finally said, 'Who are you? When will the family be back?' Her response was that she was a tenant and the family had had a spat the day before. The wife had left and [the woman] thought the husband had gone off flying shortly before I arrived. Since they obviously had forgotten about the appointment, I asked to have a look at the house anyway. She didn't mind, so in I went. Furniture was practically nonexistent, filth was everywhere, and even the room this woman was renting had only a sleeping bag over a piece of foam, no sheets."

Moral: It's a pretty good idea to have the B&B home inspected and approved by the reservation organization *before* you pull into the driveway.

2

HOW TO FIND BED & BREAKFASTS

- Many of the most fascinating B&B homes never advertise or post a B&B sign.
- New sources of B&B information are springing up almost every week.

This book is the key to hundreds of the better B&B homes throughout the U.S. and Canada.

Why "better"?

Because most of the most luxurious or interesting or historic B&B homes won't risk angry confrontations with their neighbors by posting a "Bed & Breakfast" sign on their lawn or advertising in a local publication. Even B&B homes that have received free publicity from a well-meaning reporter have encountered problems from zoning boards, health boards, and sometimes a whole block of people who have exaggerated fears about a "business" operating in the neighborhood.

Also, many B&B hosts feel much more secure if any prospective guests are screened by a reliable reservation-service organization. Otherwise they would be opening their homes to total strangers right off the street.

That's why so many of the really great B&B homes *never* are advertised or publicized. Some of these homes have swimming pools, country antiques and fireplaces in every room, and beautiful grounds. The way to find them is to call one of the reservation organizations listed in this book.

Use the unique *B&B Finder* cross index at the back of this guide. For example, if you are parents of a son at Atlanta University, you could simply turn to the "Schools and Colleges" section and find which reservation agencies offer B&B accommodations near this school. If you want to attend a Shakespeare play at the Stratford Festival in Ontario, Canada, turn to the "Attractions" section for your B&B reservation service. If you are a business person tired of the plastic sameness and $100+ price tags of many hotels, check the reservation listings for a home in the city or area you plan to visit. This service can be particularly valuable for women travelers who enjoy the security and comfort of a home environment when they're out of town.

If you ever do get stuck and can't contact a reservations organization operating in the area you want to visit, there are several alternatives.

First, you can look in the local Yellow Pages phone directory. Reservation services and individual bed-and-breakfast homes will be listed under a new, separate "Bed & Breakfast" heading.

You can also write ahead to local chambers of commerce and state tourism offices (their addresses are listed in this guidebook). Many are now beginning to offer free lists of B&B homes or brochures about individual homes and farms.

Tourist information booths along state highways are also beginning to carry B&B brochures and information.

When you're visiting a resort area, stop in the local tourist office. Some can tell you about local availabilities, and may even be able to book you into a B&B on the spot.

In some rural areas (where neighbors are more tolerant or friendly), you will see "Bed & Breakfast" signs in front of some homes.

You also can now get information about B&B accommodations from the American Automobile Association. In a newsletter to other AAA clubs, the National Travel Department of AAA wrote, "Due to the rapid growth of interest in bed-and-breakfast facilities, we decided to review our method for presenting B&B data to AAA Clubs. In the future, in order to ensure that members receive current information pertaining to reputable B&B referral services, we will provide a listing of only those B&B referral services which screen their listings. In this way, the listing provided to clubs will reflect AAA's concern for property cleanliness, hospitable hosts, and ethical operations." (*Note:* AAA really meant "reservation"—not "referral" agencies.)

As the B&B movement keeps growing (and in some areas it's starting to roar along, picking up new momentum with each day), you'll find more and more sources of information.

For information about finding bed-and-breakfast accommodations in foreign countries, Chapter 4, "B&Bs Abroad," contains a complete list of foreign tourist offices and their addresses, usually good sources of basic information before you go. You'll also learn how seasoned travelers overseas keep an eye peeled for "Zimmer Frei" and "chambre d'hôte" signs to find some delightful B&Bs along their way.

When you're traveling in North America, take this guidebook along. It can introduce you to B&Bs all over the U.S. and Canada through a network of reservation-service organizations. It's among the friendliest, most inexpensive ways to travel today.

Want to stay in a B&B inn? You'll find a list of special ones that have come to my attention (listed by state following the B&B reservation-service information in Part II).

Want to stay in one of the finest B&B homes in North America? See Part III, "100 Best B&B Homes in North America." You can even become one of our judges in selecting the "100 Best" for the next edition of this book.

STATE TOURIST OFFICES

Many state tourist offices can supply you with names and addresses of some outstanding B&B homes and inns in their area, as well as good state maps and other travel information. Here is a complete list.

Alabama Bureau of Publicity &
  Information
532 S. Perry St.
Montgomery, AL 36130
  Toll free 800/ALA-BAMA

Alaska State Division of Tourism
Pouch E
Juneau, AK 99811
  907/465-2010

Arizona State Office of Tourism
1480 E. Bethany
Phoenix, AZ 85014
  602/255-3618

Arkansas Division of Tourism
One Capitol Mall
Little Rock, AR 72201
  501/371-7777

California Office of Tourism
1121 L St.
Sacramento, CA 95814
  916/322-1396

Colorado Office of Tourism
1313 Sherman St., Rm. 500
Denver, CO 80203
  303/866-3045

Connecticut Dept. of Economic
  Development, Tourism
  Division
210 Washington St.
Hartford, CT 06106
  203/566-2496

Delaware State Travel Service
99 Kings Hwy.
Dover, DE 19901
  302/736-4271

Florida Division of Tourism
107 W. Gaines St., Rm. 505
Tallahassee, FL 32301
  904/488-5606

Georgia Tourist Division
P.O. Box 1776
Atlanta, GA 30301
  404/656-3594

Hawaii Visitors Bureau
2270 Kalakaua Ave., Suite 801
Honolulu, HI 96815
  808/923-1811

Idaho Travel
State Capitol Building, Rm. 108
Boise, ID 83720
  Toll free 800/635-7820

Illinois Office of Tourism
310 S. Michigan
Chicago, IL 60604
  312/793-4732

Indiana Tourism Development
  Division
1 N. Capitol Ave.
Indianapolis, IN 46204
  317/232-8870

Iowa Tourism & Travel Division
600 E. Court Ave.
Des Moines, IA 50309
  515/281-3100

Kansas Division of Travel
  Marketing
503 Kansas Ave., 6th Fl.
Topeka, KS 66603
  913/296-2009

Kentucky Department of
  Economic Development
Capitol Plaza Tower
Frankfort, KY 40601
  502/564-4930

Louisiana Office of Tourism
P.O. Box 94291, Capitol Station
Baton Rouge, LA 70804
  504/925-3853

Maine Publicity Bureau
97 Winthrop St.
Hollowell, ME 04347
  207/289-2423

Maryland Office of Tourism
  Development
45 Calvert St.
Annapolis, MD 21401
  301/269-2686

Massachusetts Dept. of
  Commerce & Development
100 Cambridge St.
Boston, MA 02202
  617/727-3201

Michigan Travel Bureau
P.O. Box 30226
Lansing, MI 48909
  Toll free 800/248-5700

Minnesota Tourism Bureau
419 N. Robert St.
St. Paul, MN 55101
  612/296-2755

Mississippi Dept. of Economic
  Development, Division of
  Tourism
P.O. Box 849
Jackson, MS 39205
  601/359-3414

Missouri Division of Tourism
308 W. High St.
P.O. Box 1055
Jefferson City, MO 65102
  314/751-4133

Montana Promotion Bureau
Department of Commerce
Helena, MT 59620
    406/449-2654

Nebraska Travel & Tourism
    Division
P.O. Box 94666
Lincoln, NE 68509
    402/471-3111

Nevada Tourism Commission
600 E. Williams
Carson City, NV 89710
    702/885-4322

New Hampshire Office of
    Vacation Travel
105 Loudon Rd., Box 856
Concord, NH 03301
    603/271-2666

New Jersey Division of Travel &
    Tourism
P.O. Box CN826
Trenton, NJ 08625
    609/292-2470

New Mexico Tourism & Travel
    Division, Commercial and
    Industrial Dept.
Bataan Memorial Building
Santa Fe, NM 87503
    505/827-5571

New York Division of Tourism
230 Park Ave., Suite 1155
New York, NY 10169
    212/949-8429

North Carolina Travel & Tourism
    Division
430 N. Salisbury St.
Raleigh, NC 27611
    919/733-4171

North Dakota Tourism
    Promotion Division
Capitol Grounds
Bismarck, ND 58505
    Toll free 800/437-2077

Ohio Office of Travel & Tourism
P.O. Box 1001
Columbus, OH 43216
    614/466-8844

Oklahoma Tourism & Recreation
    Dept.
505 Will Rogers Building
Oklahoma City, OK 73105
    405/521-3981

Oregon Tourism Division
595 Cottage St.
Salem, OR 97310
    Toll free 800/547-7842

Pennsylvania Bureau of Travel
    Development
416 Forum Building
Harrisburg, PA 17120
    Toll free 800/237-4363

Rhode Island Dept. of Economic
    Development
7 Jackson Walkway
Providence, RI 02903
    Toll free 800/566-2484

South Carolina Dept. of Parks,
    Recreation & Tourism
1205 Pendleton St., Suite 113
Columbia, SC 29201
    803/758-2536

South Dakota Division of
    Tourism
P.O. Box 6000
Pierre, SD 57501
    Toll free 800/843-1930

Tennessee Department of Tourist
  Development
P.O. Box 23170
Nashville, TN 37202
  615/741-2159

Texas Tourist Development
  Agency
P.O. Box 12008, Capitol Station
Austin, TX 78711
  512/475-4326

Utah Travel Council
Council Hall, Capitol Hill
Salt Lake City, UT 84114
  801/533-5681

Vermont Travel Division
134 State St.
Montpelier, VT 05602
  802/828-3236

Virginia Division of Tourism
202 N. 9th St., Suite 500
Richmond, VA 23219
  804/786-2051

Washington Tourism Division
101 Gen. Administration
  Building
Olympia, WA 98502
  206/753-5600

Washington Convention and
  Visitors Association
1575 I St. NW, Suite 250
Washington, DC 20005
  202/789-7000

West Virginia Travel
  Development Division
1900 Washington St. East
Charleston, WV 25305
  304/348-2286

Wisconsin Division of Tourism
123 W. Washington Ave.
P.O. Box 7970
Madison, WI 53707
  608/266-7621

Wyoming Travel Commission
Frank Norris, Jr., Travel Center
Cheyenne, WY 82002
  307/777-7777

TERRITORIES

Guam Visitors Bureau
P.O. Box 3520
Agana, Guam 96910
  671/646-5278

Mariana Visitors Bureau
P.O. Box 861
Saipan, Mariana Islands 96950
  6-7327

Puerto Rico Tourism Company
P.O. Box 44350, Old San Juan
  Station
San Juan, PR 00905
  809/721-2400

Virgin Islands Division of
  Tourism
1667 K St. NW, Suite 270
Washington, DC 20006
  202/293-3707

3

HOW TO BE A B&B GUEST

- Use a reservation-service organization that pre-inspects the homes on its lists.
- Some B&B homes offer free pick up at airports and train and bus stations for travelers without cars.
- Use our B&B PHONE BOOKING FORM to help you get the B&B home that best matches your needs and pocketbook.

While enjoying the hospitality and warmth of a typical B&B home may be as easy as saying "Pass the strawberry preserves," finding the right home for you and your family may require a little effort and advance planning.

First, I strongly recommend that you use a reservations service rather than taking pot luck as you drive along the road or call a home that you've seen listed in a book. Any reservation service worth the fee that it usually receives from each rental (from the B&B host, not from you) will inspect the homes on its list. Or at a very minimum the service will quickly drop any homes that guests have complained about frequently.

It's true that you may occasionally find a gem on your own simply by stopping at a "Bed & Breakfast" sign. But the odds are against you because many of the best B&B homes aren't listed.

I've repeated this warning in other parts of this guide because I truly believe that booking your B&B home through an established reservation-service organization is the simplest, safest, and ultimately the most satisfying way.

However, before you call any reservation service, you should write down your basic needs. In many cases the reservation service will send you a free or low-cost brochure that describes the homes and locations available. You then phone or write the reservation service after you've made the selection. You will usually be required to confirm the reservation by a minimum payment of the first night's rental. Some services may require full payment in advance.

After you have a confirmed reservation from the reservation service, always call the host. This is a very important call because it will be your first contact with this very important person. You can begin to establish a friendship with that first call. Have a map handy so you can ask specific questions about the most direct route to the B&B home. (This is very important—I have been stranded at night in some remote rural areas looking for "the second road on the right.")

Many B&B hosts offer pickup services to carless travelers, free or at a small fee. If you arrive by plane, bus, or train, you may be able to have the host meet you at the airport or station.

It is always a good practice (and often required) that you pay the host any balance due for your entire B&B stay when you arrive. This also saves problems when you check out if the host is away.

Ask about the use of a house key, particularly if your host works and you want access to the house and your room during the day. You may be required to post a key fee.

Ask all about the use of the house and grounds. Some hosts give you kitchen privileges and allow you to fix your own breakfast whenever you're ready. One B&B guest surprised her host by making strawberry pancakes for her husband and the whole host family. "They were pleased," she said later. "But you could tell this wasn't their typical breakfast. They really thought I was serving them dessert."

There may be recreation facilities/equipment in the house and on the grounds—TV sets, stereos, barbecue pits, volleyball nets, swimming pools, sleds, etc. Find out if you're permitted to use them. Many hosts are happy to oblige.

In the house itself, is smoking permitted in your room? In certain areas? Or forbidden throughout the house. Do you have access to the family room, the living room, and the laundry facilities?

Never hesitate to ask if you need certain comfort items—an extra blanket for the bed, extra towels, etc. Some rooms have individual air conditioners or temperature controls. Ask for a demonstration of how to regulate them.

The host may give you a written set of "house rules." Follow them and treat the house as you would your own. Clear communication and common courtesy are the bases for a successful and happy B&B homestay.

Always sign the guestbook when you leave, with any personal comments about what you liked about the visit and your hosts. It's a great keepsake for the hosts. It also can lead to Christmas cards, social notes, and just possibly, a lifelong friendship.

4

B&Bs ABROAD

- Sleep in a French country château in a room with one whole wall a fireplace, with a medieval timbered barn and green mountains right outside your three windows. Cost? About $20 a night for two, breakfast in an antique-filled kitchen included.
- Bed and breakfast in a Cyprus monastery high atop a craggy mountain—at no charge (a small donation is appropriate).
- Help herd a flock of the unique black sheep and sightsee glaciers. Then come home to a warm welcome on a B&B farm in New Zealand.

What can you and the ambassador from Australia, the secretary of finance from Denmark, and the former prime minister of the Netherlands have in common?

You can all stay in a chambre d'hôte in Normandy, France, for about $20 a night. That is the cost for two people, who like the world statesmen, elect to stay in the 16th-Century farmhouse in the village of Commes as the guests of the Leroys.

All of the statesmen named above did just that, and signed the family's guestbook which is overflowing with notes of thanks, friendship, and photographs from all over the world.

The house is an ancient delight with huge sunny rooms filled with country antiques from different periods of French history. Madame Leroy may welcome her guests with some of the Calvados region's famous apple cider and apple cake. Not only apple orchards flourish in this rich Normandy soil. It is said to be so rich that a farmer thrusting a stick into the ground in the morning will find it filled with leaves in the afternoon. You may have trouble swallowing that local claim, but certainly not Madame Leroy's glorious breakfasts. On a typical country morning she may serve eggs, corn flakes, fresh pan bread, the freshest butter you've ever spread on bread, and homemade jams. You have your choice of café au lait (coffee with hot milk), tea, or chocolate. The source of all these fresh dairy products will probably come in view during the day when a herd of cows leaves the 16th-century barn right across the courtyard.

Then the day is yours to explore Normandy. During the summer you may want to head to the nearby beaches. The Leroy farm is also close to the D-Day landing areas and the Normandy American Cemetery. Near the farmhouse a signpost will direct you to Bayeux. You will want to take a full day to explore the 11th-century cathedral and, of course, see the Bayeux Tapestry in the former Bishop's Palace. This magnificent 11th-century work of art is misnamed. It's not really tapestry but embroidery: colored wools on linen. Shown under glass, it depicts 58 historic scenes with astonishing perspective and freshness. Or you may decide to follow the plump red apple "route du Cidre" signs to ancient farmhouses where making the tart, bracing apple cider is a Normandy art. If you're lucky enough to be a passenger rather than a driver, you may also want to sample the potent Calvados apple brandy made and sold right on the farms.

The whole area offers many great restaurants. After all, this is France. But some B&B guests have learned that one of the very good "restaurants" is much closer to home—right in the Leroys' spacious dining room. For about $8 per person, the Leroys will serve a dinner that consists of soup, salad, meat with vegetables, cheese, and some more of that famous apple cake.

There are some 600 bed-and-breakfast–style homes (chambre d'hôtes) in Normandy. Some are in beautiful country châteaux surrounded by gardens and ponds. Others are in simple rustic farmhouses. All of them have washbasins in the room, include excellent breakfasts in the price, and—with the continuing strength of the dollar in Europe—all are incredible bargains. Prices range from a low of about $10 per night for one person to a little over $25 to $30 for two.

The local tourism office goes all out to encourage the development of these chambre d'hôtes, paying owners 20,000 francs for each room they renovate and rent. No more than five rooms may be renovated, and the tourist office, through the use of its checkbook, helps to control standards and quality.

Said one tourist officer, "We call this 'green tourism'—living in the country and coming in contact with the French people. Personal contact is the key. Travelers, however, should remember that these people are not professional hotelkeepers. Don't expect things a hotel staff might do, such as carry your bags or serve you breakfast in bed. But these French farm people can be so warm and friendly, and they love to meet people."

I personally experienced some of this warmth when I visited another Normandy B&B, Le Manoir du Champ Versant. This château is a 17th-century building that has already been featured in a coffee-table book of great French houses. The hostess is a lovely, animated French woman who speaks no English. But that doesn't matter. She takes you to some of the rooms that are available. One has a huge fireplace that dominates the room, and an equally huge country bed. The room and its antique furniture is a sun-filled joy. The light comes from three windows that look out over the surrounding countryside, a scene which includes an ancient timbered barn, herds of cattle, a large pond, and green hills. On learning that this room cost only about $16 a night for two, I was ready to abandon this guidebook and rent the place for the summer. Unfortunately an American painter who lives on Central Park West in New York City had already seen the view, the bed, and the fireplace and booked it long-term.

While the settings may be rural, the reservations system for these chambre d'hôtes is as modern as the computer in the local Caen office. For more information you could write to the French Tourist Office (see address at the end of this chapter) or directly to the Chambre d'Agriculture, Promenade de Sevigne, 140000 Caen, Normandy, France.

You also can simply look for the green "chambre d'hôte" signs along the roadside. In certain summer months the rooms may already be booked. (Consider the case of the greedy long-term renter, the American painter.) But in spring and fall you have an excellent change of waking up to the smell of hot coffee and warm pan bread emanating from a rich country kitchen, such as that of Madame Leroy. Be sure to sign her illustrious guestbook.

Great Britain is almost the ancestral home of the whole B&B movement. For a number of years American travelers have stopped, slept, and breakfasted in the honey-colored homes of the Cotswolds, in cottages rising right out of the mist of Scotland's Isle of Skye, and in every nook and quaint cranny of London.

Eleanor Berman, author of *Away for the Weekend: New England,* recently was touring Wales with her daughter and stopped at a B&B in Llangollen, Wales, near the River Dee.

She reported, "Llangollen is a charming typical Welsh village of stone cottages, made particularly scenic by a river flowing through the center of town. Church Street parallels the river and runs right into the main shopping street—an ideal location—and Maew Mawr House and its proprietors are right out of central casting. A cozy home and rosy-cheeked, plump, white-haired couple who couldn't have been sweeter or more solicitous.

"Rooms are very big here and look out either at the river or the pleasant street. This isn't decorator decor, but has been done with obvious care. Each room has a color scheme carried through to curtains, linens, and comforters atop each bed. Ours was pale violet. Another nice room was done in pale green. The bathroom was all in blue. Each room has an electric teapot and fixings for coffee or tea.

"Our hostess's first question after we checked in was "What time will you want breakfast?" The meal was the usual hearty English morning fare of a fried egg, sausage *and* bacon, grilled tomato, and toast. The very pleasant dining room looks out at the river. The mantel is covered with postcards from former guests all over the world.

"She then sat down with us and drew a careful map of the most scenic route to follow when we left. Then came out with us to the car park to watch for traffic for me so I could back out without any trouble, knowing I was still uneasy with my gear shift, left-drive car."

The cost at that time? About $16 a night for two, with that breakfast of "sausage *and* bacon" included.

You will also find B&Bs all over Germany and Austria. Most of these can be booked on the spot. You just look for the "Zimmer Frei" sign in front of the houses, and take your pick. You are always welcome to inspect the room before booking.

Surprisingly there are few, if any, B&B homes in Italy. However, you will find a number of moderately priced *pensiones,* which may be located in private homes but are essentially full-time commercial operations. The B&B concept has not yet spread to the Middle East to any great extent, although the Egyptian tourism people are currently considering this idea. Some women in Greece (on the island of Lesbos) are trying to start the first B&Bs in that country.

B&Bs are flourishing in many other parts of the world. In New Zealand you can stay in city and town B&Bs, or join a sheep-raising family on their farm. The country offers a free-wheeling

B&B concept called "Go as You Please" (from October 1 to March 31 each year). You buy a series of vouchers and a book listing all hosts. You call your host at least 24 hours in advance from anywhere along the road. You can travel by rental car, rail coach, air, or even bicycle.

Japan offers something similar to B&Bs. There are homestays in typical Japanese houses, often in rural areas. These are not for the super-comfort seekers. You may sleep on mats in a barely furnished room. Travel writer Jack Adler said, "It may not be for the first-time traveler to Japan. On my visit with my wife we made our own beds and had to bring our own soap and washcloths. But we did prepare meals right in the room, and that was great fun."

If you plan to look for B&B accommodations abroad, you should first write to the country's tourist office in the U.S. Some of these, unfortunately, have a knee-jerk response to many letters and may send you a general brochure that doesn't even mention B&Bs. But others are becoming much more sensitive to this "people's hotel" concept, and will send you very complete information.

You can visit the regional tourist offices when you've arrived. These offices often have lists of area B&B homes, and some may even handle bookings for you.

In Europe a good source of B&B information is often the local bookstore (English-language section). On a recent visit to Paris I found a number of books and directories to B&Bs on the continent, and for many areas of Great Britain. The Europeans long ago discovered the economies and pleasures of the B&B.

FOREIGN TOURIST OFFICES

The tourism departments of various foreign countries and areas with offices in major U.S. cities can be very helpful when you're looking for B&B accommodations abroad. A complete list of these offices is at the end of this chapter.

Here are some of the particularly useful responses to my queries.

Australia (Australian Tourist Commission)

Australia is almost literally bursting with bed-and-breakfast opportunities.

An organization called Bed & Breakfast International plans and books a number of unusual home- and ranchstays. A "homestay" includes your room in a private home. Breakfast is included and dinner may often be booked. You can also stay on a working sheep station or a cattle ranch. All the homes included in the program have been personally inspected by Bed & Breakfast International.

Here are a few of the B&B programs you can choose:

In the "Meet the Aussies" program, you spend four days and three nights with a host family in Sydney, Melbourne, Adelaide, Brisbane, Perth, Canberra, Caires, or a resort or country town. The price depends on the type of room and home you choose and ranges from about $60 to $75. Or you can spend a budget week in Sydney for about $13.50 a night. The organization will attempt to match you with a host who has similar interests.

It's even possible to combine a *flying* tour of the Australian outback with your B&B stay.

Bed & Breakfast International promises this idyllic-sounding vacation: "Imagine an elegant homestead, a large outback ranch, a personality-plus host, wildlife, and not a soul in sight for miles. But charter your host's light aircraft and he will take you to seldom-visited, inaccessible areas plus fabulous Queensland boulder opal country. This is the Australia of wide-open spaces, extensive livestock grazing, artesian water, kangaroos and emus, where man has a constant battle with nature." The cost for a four-day-three-night ranchstay is about $225. Not cheap, but it could be quite an experience.

Did you ever hanker to milk a cow, shear and dip a sheep, or go for long hayrides into the countryside? You can do all this and more on a B&B stay in *Brooklyn*. Yes, Australia has one too. The cost is only about $20 a day and includes *all* meals.

Like New Zealand, Australia also offers self-drive holidays which combine a rental car with stops along the way at B&B homes.

For further information on these and many other B&B accommodations and complete vacations in Australia, write for these free booklets: "Australia Farm Holidays" and "Australian Homestays and Ranchstays." These are available from the Australian Tourist Commission (address at the end of this chapter).

Bed & Breakfast International (Australia)
18–20 Oxford St.
P.O. Box 442, Woollahra
Sydney, N.S.W., Australia 2025
Telex: AA27229

For self-drive holidays—

PT International
1318 SW Troy
Portland, OR 97219

Austria (Austrian National Tourist Office)

When traveling through Austria, keep your eye out for a sign "Zimmer Frei" or simply a sign with a white bed on a green background. These signs are usually hung at the front gate of private homes that offer bed-and-breakfast accommodations. When this sign is on display, it's the equivalent of an American motel sign flashing "Vacancy."

Feel free to stop and ask to inspect the room (advance reservations are extremely rare and usually impossible). If you like the room and the price, take it. The price isn't hard to like—$8 to $15 a night for two people, including a continental breakfast. A single traveler might pay as little as $5 per night.

You should pay your bill when you take the room, in Austrian schillings. Don't expect a private bath—there's often only one bathroom in the whole house. But the rooms are usually very clean, and there is a washbasin in the room with hot and cold water.

Bermuda

On a recent visit to Bermuda, I stopped in the Visitors Service Bureau in Hamilton, about a block from the Princess Hotel. The official greeter gave this advice to anyone looking for B&B in Bermuda: "We have a list of homes that visitors can book by stopping here."

The office also provides this information in letter form:

"More than one hundred families in all parts of the island are registered with the Bermuda Chamber of Commerce. Some offer single or double rooms with or without breakfast. Others offer studio apartments, or one- and two-bedroom guest cottages. The rates are from $15 to $25 per person per day (double occupancy).

"Arrangements can be made by writing to the Visitors Service Bureau, Bermuda Chamber of Commerce, P.O. Box 655, Hamilton 5–31, Bermuda. We must know the exact dates of arrival and departure, number of people in your party, type of accommodation preferred, and the maximum rate per person. We will then book your accommodation and direct you to send a two-day deposit to your host to confirm the room.

"If you prefer to telephone and are prepared to accept a collect call when we have found a suitable home, much time will be saved. Our telephone number is 809/295-1430."

Note: There is one possible disadvantage to staying at a B&B in a remote location. Unless you ride a bicycle or a Moped, you may have real trouble getting around the island. There are no rental cars in Bermuda, and taxis are in short supply—usually available primarily at the airport and around major hotels. You can also call for a taxi, but this can take some time. I was recently stranded for well over an hour in St. Georges, Bermuda, waiting in vain for a taxi I had called.

Bulgaria (Bulgarian Tourist Office)

Mr. Ivan Dimov, director of the Bulgarian Tourist Office in New York, says, "Private boarding houses with bed-and-breakfast or full board are available for tourists in every large town in Bulgaria." All reservations are made through Balkantourist. This organization also offers a wide range of services that include tours and trips for groups and individual tourists, motel or hotel accommodations, booking of minibuses and rent-a-cars.

The address of Balkantourist is 1 Vitosha Boulevard, Sofia 1000, Bulgaria. Attn.: Overseas Department (tel. 84-131, ext. 284; Telex 865–22583 or 865–22584).

Cyprus (Cyprus Tourism Organization)

Cyprus does not have any bed-and-breakfast homes as such, but does have commercial guesthouses. The tourism office also offers an intriguing alternative, bed-and breakfast in a monastery. You can actually stay overnight for three nights without charge (although it is customary to leave a donation at the end of the stay).

For example, you could stay at the Kykko Monastery, perhaps the most famous monastery in the world. The literature reports: "The monastery was founded around A.D. 1100 . . . [and] possesses an icon of the Virgin Mary and Child, believed to have been painted by St. Luke."

You may also want to visit the Stavrovouri Monastery (founded in A.D. 327) and situated high on a peak 25 miles from Nicosia. According to a belief held by many, there is still a fragment of the Holy Cross in the monastery. You can also see a huge wooden cross from 1476, carved with biblical scenes. But couples would not make this a B&B stop. Because of the monastery's strict religious vows, women are permitted to visit only on Sunday. Men traveling alone can stay over on Monday, Wednesday, Friday, and Sunday.

On a drive through Cyprus, you may want to plan your own breakfast picnic. Stop for homemade bread and a jar of the marvelous flavored honey that you can purchase from one of the monasteries.

Czechoslovakia

According to Cedok Travel & Hotel Corporation (the company that arranges almost all travel to Czechoslovakia, "there is no possibility to accommodate travelers in homes on a bed-and-breakfast basis. Nevertheless for people traveling to Europe with a limited budget we have the following suggestions:

"1. Accommodations with two meals daily (MAP) in three-star category hotels owned and operated by CEDOK cost between $37.50 and $52 per double room.

"2. During the summer months, a limited number of student dormitories is available, basically in Prague, Brno, Bratislava, and Olomou, as well as in some other cities. For each season a complete list including addresses is available from our national tourist office. Price is between $12 and $15 per person (double occupancy). Breakfast is usually available in nearby restaurants on an individual basis."

Denmark (The Danish Tourist Board)

B&B homes are available in this delightful country—but the tourist office has no information or lists of them. Your best bet is to stop in one of the local tourist offices when you're traveling through Denmark. These offices can arrange private accommodations.

Egypt (Egyptian Tourist Authority)

Mr. Shawki Hussein, director of the Egyptian Tourist Authority in New York, advises: "Staying with families is hardly practiced in Egypt. However, the Egyptian General Authorities for the Promotion of Tourism is currently exploring the possibilities to provide such means of accommodation."

French West Indies—Guadeloupe, Martinique (French West Indies Tourist Board)

There are no bed-and-breakfast homes in the French West Indies. However, there are alternatives. These are some suggestions from the tourist office.

"On Guadeloupe the Relais-Hôtels de la Guadeloupe are a group of small hotels and inns, some with as few as seven rooms, where guests receive the personal attention of the manager and where room with breakfast can be arranged. The association's address is: Chaine des Relais-Hôtels de la Guadeloupe, Chateaubrun 97180, Sainte-Anne, Guadeloupe, FWI (Telex 919913).

"For visitors wanting a home atmosphere, houses can be rented from Gîtes de France, but this is quite different from B&B. The houses range from modest weekend places to comfortable villas, either in villages or by the sea. Details are available through Mme Marcelle Lautric, c/o Guadeloupe Tourist Office, 5 Square de la Banque, Pointe-à-Pitre, Guadeloupe 97110, FWI (tel. 82-09-30).

"On Martinique La Chaine des Relais de La Martinique is comprised of small hotels, bungalows, and cottages. Some of these properties offer room and breakfast; others, breakfast-making facilities. There is a central reservations service: Petite Hotellerie de la Martinique, Pavillon du Tourisme, rue Ernest-Deproge, 97200, Fort-de-France, Martinique, FWI (tel. 71-56-11)."

Germany (German National Tourist Office)

"Hospitality is especially personalized in private bed-and-breakfast homes throughout Germany offering visitors clean and comfortable rooms from $8 to $16 (U.S.) nightly, per person, including a full breakfast!

"All bed-and-breakfast accommodations are inspected periodically by local tourist boards and must merit approval before being offered to the public. Homes must provide clean and comfortable rooms (some rooms have sinks with hot and cold running water). Bathroom facilities are often shared, although some homes provide a private bath.

"Breakfasts range from hearty to elegant. Guests can count on eggs, freshly baked rolls and bread; plenty of butter, jam, and marmalade; perhaps cold cuts and cheese; and, of course, coffee, tea, and hot chocolate."

After sending all of this helpful information, the tourist office underlined with a heavy yellow pen this point—*"Information on available rooms is only obtainable from local tourist offices"* which are usually within or near the rail terminals in cities. In smaller towns and villages tourist offices are located in or nearby the Rathaus (city hall). A tourist office generally will give a visitor three listings, and also subsequent leads if the visitor isn't satisfied with the first round of inspection. Quite often homeowners will pick up rail travelers who telephone from the tourist offices.

"Bed-and-breakfast rooms are available year round in Germany. There are more choices in popular tourist areas from April through the summer, and many homes in the winter sports areas make rooms available during that season. In larger cities, a number of homes are suitable for business travelers. Accommodations are especially welcomed during periods when trade fairs and conventions are held, and during the peak season when major hotels are booked well in advance.

"Bed-and-breakfast homes accept only cash. Rates are set by the homeowners."

Great Britain (British Tourist Authority)

B&B homes are easy to spot. Just look for the sign "Bed & Breakfast" in the downstairs front windows of many homes. You may also see this sign on posts on the lawn or hanging on the garden gate. Breakfasts are a special treat because they almost always include a hot course such as bacon and eggs, plus toast and coffee or tea and marmalade. In rural areas these products may be just hours from the farm. You can "book a bed ahead" at British Tourist Information Centers (stop before noon to arrange the evening's accommodations). For more information, write the Tourist Authority for their helpful booklet, "Bed & Breakfast in Britain."

India (Government of India Tourist Office)

If you're interested in booking a B&B in India, you should first write the Tourist Office in the U.S. for a list of brochures about the various areas. Mr. S. K. Kachroo then advises that travelers "can write to our offices in India. Their addresses are mentioned in each of the brochures. The local offices which maintain such lists can assist the traveler."

Ireland (Irish Tourist Board)

Catherine Cullen of the Public Relations Department of the Irish Tourist Board wanted to share this information with readers of this guidebook:

"All bed-and-breakfast homes listed in Irish Tourist Board guides have been inspected by our staff and are identified by an 'approved' sign (the word 'Approved' in red, flanked, of course, by two green shamrocks).

"We have a comprehensive listing of all properties called 'Irish Homes.' Travelers may write to us for a copy.

"Reservations may be made by: (a) writing to our reservations department—Central Reservations Service, Dublin Tourism, 14 Upper O'Connell St., Dublin 1, Ireland (tel. 01-747733); (b) as holidaymakers driving through Ireland, they may make reservations at Irish Tourist Board offices which are located in almost every town; or (c) simply asking at a home which displays the 'Approved' sign."

Israel (Israel Ministry of Tourism)

While there have been local programs that allow you to meet with the Israelis in their homes for conversation, B&B programs have lagged behind. The Ministry of Tourism directed my inquiry to Excursions Limited, a U.S. tour company that recently recruited a number of families in Israel as B&B hosts. These homes are part of tours and can't be booked individually. Ms. Phillis P. Caro, president of the organization, said, "The traveler or their travel agent must contact Excursions Unlimited prior to departure for Israel to make the bookings. All Israel Government Tourist Offices, El Al offices, many travel agencies, and most Jewish Community Centers will have brochures." For more information, write Excursions Unlimited, 2 Headley Way, Woodbury, NY 11797.

Japan (National Tourist Office)

Minshuku are the Japanese equivalent of B&Bs. You can stay in a private home, but "creature comforts" are often modest. You may stay in a city apartment or a thatch-roofed cottage and sleep on Japanese mats on the floor. The Japanese National Tourist Organization will supply a list of these minshuku accommodations.

New Zealand (Tourist Office)

"Bed-and-breakfast is booked a little differently in New Zealand than, for instance, in England and Europe," says Diane Moir, marketing officer for the New Zealand Tourist Office in New York.

"One has to book through an agency such as the New Zealand Home Hospitality Ltd., P.O. Box 309, Nelson (tel. 54-85-727; Telex NZ3697 Attn. HOMEHOSP); their services are fully described in the free brochure "New Zealand Bed & Breakfast in Town and Country Homes." Or for a farm stay through the agencies listed on page 122 of the New Zealand Accommodation Guide. [*Note:* This free book is excellent; be sure to ask for it by name.] Both these guides are available to the general public from the tourist office."

"You can book such accommodations, either by writing directly to the agencies, or more easily and efficiently, through a travel agency contacting the New Zealand Tourist Office in San Francisco which handles all internal New Zealand reservations. (This reservation must be made through a travel agent and not by the traveler himself.) The address is: New Zealand Tourist Office, Alcoa Building, Suite 970, Maritime Plaza, San Francisco, CA 94111.

Norway (Handled by Scandinavian National Tourist Offices)

Elin Bolann, director of the Scandinavian Tourist Office, says: "Bed-and-breakfast is mostly only common in the cities. Most types of accommodations in the countryside offer breakfast and dinner. Unfortunately there is no list available of bed-and-breakfast homes in Norway. The best thing to do for travelers is to contact the local tourist offices in Norway, and ask there."

The Philippines (Office of the Tourism Director)

Marilen Paderon writes, "Our office maintains a list of accredited tourist establishments throughout the Philippines. However, our classification does not include bed-and-breakfast homes. We do have a number of inns, pensions, and lodges within Metro Manila and in the provincial areas which would probably be equivalent to your bed-and-breakfast homes in North America. This list is available upon request through our office. Advance bookings may be made directly through our domestic field offices."

Yugoslavia (Yugoslav National Tourist Office)

B&B-type accommodations are available throughout this country, and are even organized and classified by the government. Prices range from $10 to $25, and that upper price limit is along the Adriatic Riviera. The major difference among the categories seems to be how much private time you get in the bathroom: Category 1A provides a room with private bath in a villa-type house; Category I applies to a room with bathroom shared with other guests on the floor; Catetory II ensures a room with bathroom facilities shared with guests and the host family; Category III enables you to stay in a house in one of the old citadels, with bathroom shared with the host families. You will pay a premium of about 30% for stays of less than three nights. The breakfast charge is extra.

To book one of these rooms in advance, you should first get free literature from the Yugoslav Tourist Office in New York, which lists all of the local tourist offices in Yugoslavia. Then you write directly to the office in the area you want to stay. It is not possible to make reservations in the U.S., either through the tourist office or through any tour operators.

However, there is another possibility when you've arrived in Yugoslavia. You can stop at a local tourist bureau or travel agency in any major tourist area and ask to see a list of available private homes. Or when driving down the road, you can look for an appealing home with a "Soba-Simmer-Room" sign outside (meaning they have a room available).

GOVERNMENT TOURIST OFFICES

Antigua Tourist Board
610 Fifth Ave., Suite 311
New York, NY 10020
  212/541-4117

Aruba Tourist Bureau
1270 Ave. of the Americas, Suite 2212
New York, NY 10020
  212/246-3030

Australian Tourist Commission
636 Fifth Ave., 4th Floor
New York, NY 10111
  212/489-7550

Austrian National Tourist Office
500 Fifth Ave.
New York, NY 10110
  212/944-6880

Bahamas Tourist Offices
Ministry of Tourism
Box N-3701
Nassau, Bahamas
  809/322-7500

Barbados Board of Tourism
800 Second Ave.
New York, NY 10017
  212/986-6516

Belgian Tourist Office
745 Fifth Ave.
New York, NY 10151
  212/758-8130

Bermuda Department of Tourism
Church Street
P.O. Box 465
Hamilton, Bermuda
  809/292-0023

Bolivian Consulate General
10 Rockefeller Plaza
New York, NY 10020
  212/586-1607

Bonaire Information Office
1466 Broadway, Suite 903
New York, NY 10036
  212/869-2004

Brazilian Consulate General
630 Fifth Ave.
New York, NY 10020
  212/757-3080

British Tourist Authority
40 W. 57 St.
New York, NY 10019
  212/581-4708

British Virgin Islands Tourist
  Board
370 Lexington Ave.
New York, NY 10017
  212/696-0400

Bulgarian Tourist Office
161 E. 86 St.
New York, NY 10028
  212/722-1110

Canadian Government Office of
  Tourism
235 Queen St.
Ottawa, Canada K1A 0H6
  613/966-4610

Cayman Islands Department of
  Tourism
250 Catalonia Ave., Suite 604
Coral Gables, FL 33134
  305/444-6551

Tourist Office of Chile
c/o Lan-Chile Airlines
Rockefeller Center
630 Fifth Ave., Suite 809
New York, NY 10111
  212/582-3250

China, Republic of, Tourism
  Bureau
1 World Trade Center, Suite
  86155
New York, NY 10048
  212/466-0691

Colombian Government Tourist
  Office
140 E. 57 St.
New York, NY 10022
  212/688-0151

Costa Rica Embassy
2112 S St. NW
Washington, DC 20008

Curaçao Tourist Board
400 Madison Ave., Suite 311
New York, NY 10017
  212/751-8266

Cyprus Tourist Office
13 E. 40 St.
New York, NY 10016
  212/686-6016

Czechoslovak Travel Bureau
10 E. 40 St.
New York, NY 10016
  212/689-9720

Danish Tourist Board
75 Rockefeller Plaza
New York, NY 10019
  212/582-2802

Dominica Tourist Board
Caribbean Tourism Association
20 E. 46 St.
New York, NY 10017
  212/682-0435

Dominican Tourist Information
  Center
485 Madison Ave.
New York, NY 10022
  212/826-0750

Egyptian Tourist Authority
630 Fifth Ave.
New York, NY 10111
  212/246-6960

Finnish Tourist Board
655 Third Ave.
New York, NY 10017
  212/582-2802

French Government Tourist
  Office
610 Fifth Ave.
New York, NY 10020
  212/757-1125

French West Indies Tourist Board
610 Fifth Ave.
New York, NY 10020
  212/757-1125

German National Tourist Office
747 Third Ave.
New York, NY 10017
  212/308-3300

Greek National Tourist
  Organization
Olympic Tower
645 Fifth Ave., 5th Floor
New York, NY 10022
  212/421-5777

Consulate General of Guatemala
57 Park Ave.
New York, NY 10016
  212/686-8513

Haiti Government Tourist Bureau
1270 Ave. of the Americas
New York, NY 10020
  212/757-3517

Hong Kong Tourist Association
548 Fifth Ave.
New York, NY 10036
  212/869-5008

Hungarian Travel Bureau
630 Fifth Ave.
New York, NY 10111
  212/582-7412

India Government Tourist Office
30 Rockefeller Plaza, 15-n.
  Mezzanine
New York, NY 10112
  212/586-4901

Indonesia Consulate General
5 E. 68 St.
New York, NY 10021
  212/879-0600

Irish Tourist Board
590 Fifth Ave.
New York, NY 10036
  212/869-5500

Israel Ministry of Tourism
350 Fifth Ave.
New York, NY 10118
  212/560-0650

Italian Government Travel Office
630 Fifth Ave.
New York, NY 10111
  212/245-4822

Jamaica Tourist Board
866 Second Ave.
New York, NY 10017
  212/688-7650

Japan National Tourist
  Organization
630 Fifth Ave.
New York, NY 10111
  212/757-5640

Jordan Tourist Information
  Center
535 Fifth Ave.
New York, NY 10017
  212/949-0060

Kenya Tourist Office
424 Madison Ave., 6th Floor
New York, NY 10017
  212/486-1300

Korea National Tourism
  Corporation
460 Park Ave., Suite 400
New York, NY 10022
  212/688-7543

Liberian Consulate General
820 Second Ave.
New York, NY 10017
  212/687-1025

Luxembourg National Tourist
  Office
801 Second Ave.
New York, NY 10017
  212/370-9850

Malaysian Tourist Information
  Centre
Transamerica Pyramid, 5th Floor
600 Montgomery St.
San Francisco, CA 94111
  415/788-3344

Mauritius Tourist Information
  Service
401 Seventh Ave.
New York, NY 10001
  212/239-8350

Mexican Ministry of Tourism
405 Park Ave., Suite 1002
New York, NY 10022
  212/755-7261

Monaco Government Tourist and
  Convention Bureau
845 Third Ave.
New York, NY 10022
  212/759-5227

Moroccan National Tourist Office
20 E. 46th St.
New York, NY 10017
  212/557-2520

Netherlands National Tourist
  Office
576 Fifth Ave.
New York, NY 10036
  212/245-5321

New Zealand Tourist Office
Tishman Westwood Building
10960 Wilshire Blvd.
Los Angeles, CA 90024
  213/477-8241

Northern Ireland Tourist Board
40 W. 57 St., 3rd Floor
New York, NY 10019
  212/765-5144

Norwegian National Tourist
Office
75 Rockefeller Plaza
New York, NY 10019
212/582-2802

Pakistan Consulate General
12 E. 65 St.
New York, NY 10021
212/879-5800

Panama Government Tourist
Bureau
2355 Salzedo St.
Coral Gables, FL 33134
305/442-1892

Peruvian Consulate
803 Third Ave.
New York, NY 10017
212/644-2850

Philippine Ministry of Tourism
556 Fifth Ave.
New York, NY 10036
212/575-7915

Polish National Tourist Office
500 Fifth Ave.
New York, NY 10110
212/391-0844

Portuguese National Tourist
Office
548 Fifth Ave.
New York, NY 10036
212/354-4403

Romanian National Tourist
Office
573 Third Ave.
New York, NY 10016
212/697-6971

Scandinavian National Tourist
Offices
75 Rockefeller Plaza
New York, NY 10019
212/582-2802

Senegal Government Tourist
Bureau
Pan Am Building
200 Park Ave.
New York, NY 10166
212/682-4695

Singapore Tourist Promotion
Board
342 Madison Ave.
New York, NY 10173
212/687-0385

Spanish National Tourist Office
665 Fifth Ave.
New York, NY 10022
212/759-8822

Swedish Tourist Board
75 Rockefeller Plaza
New York, NY 10019
212/582-2802

Swiss National Tourist Office
608 Fifth Ave.
New York, NY 10020
212/757-5944

Tanzania Tourist Corporation
201 E. 42 St.
New York, NY 10017
212/986-7124

Togo Information Service
1625 K St. NW
Washington, DC 20006
202/659-4330

Tourism Authority of Thailand
3440 Wilshire Blvd., Suite 1101
Los Angeles, CA 90010
213/382-2353

Trinidad and Tobago Tourist
Board
400 Madison Ave., Suites
712–714
New York, NY 10017
212/838-7750

Turkish Tourism and Information
  Office
821 U.N. Plaza
New York, NY 10017
  212/687-2194

Turks and Caicos Islands Tourist
  Board
Caribbean Tourism Association
20 E. 46 St.
New York, NY 10017
  212/682-0435

Uruguay Consulate
301 E. 47 St., Suite 19A
New York, NY 10017
  212/753-8193

U.S.S.R. (Intourist) Travel
  Information Office/U.S.A.
630 Fifth Ave.
New York, NY 10111
  212/757-3885

Venezuelan Government Tourist
  Bureau
7 E. 51st St.
New York, NY 10022
  212/355-1101

Yugoslav National Tourist Office
630 Fifth Ave., Suite 210
New York, NY 10020
  212/757-2801

Zambia National Tourist Board
235 E. 52nd St.
New York, NY 10022
  212/758-9450

5

HOW TO OPERATE A B&B HOME

- Some hosts make $10,000 and over a year. But the majority earn far less. However, they do make a lot of new friends from around the world.
- Take advantage of possible tax deductions when you use part of your home as a business.
- Expect the unexpected. B&B people have hosted everyone from motion picture and soap opera stars to casual visitors who ask to be married in their home!

A surprising number of people want to become B&B hosts and turn one or two spare rooms in their house into guest rooms. Some are widows, widowers, divorcees, and single people who are burdened by the rising costs and taxes of homeownership. The idea of earning anywhere from $15 to $80 per night for a room (depending on the quality and location of the home) can be very appealing.

Others are simply "empty nesters" whose children have gone off to college or careers and left them with extra rooms and an abnormally quiet house. They like the idea of meeting new people from around the U.S. and the world. Many of these hosts are college professors, doctors, lawyers, world travelers, company presidents, as well as automobile mechanics, shop foremen, secretaries, and bus drivers—a generous cross section of America.

Other people who become B&B hosts are frustrated innkeepers or restaurant owners. Many dream of one day owning their own inn on a mountain or designing their own restaurant serving "new American cuisine." Becoming a B&B host allows a person—at least partially—to satisfy some of these dreams.

However, before you go into this business (and it *must* be a business, not a hobby, if you hope to qualify for possible tax deductions on your house), you should look at the pros and cons with your eyes wide open. You may want to follow Ben Franklin's wise advice. Write down all of the positives you can think of on one sheet, all of the negative factors on another. Then look at both of them together. You may then quickly see what your decision should be.

Here are some things you should consider:

1. Don't expect to make much money. In fact, one B&B association estimated that only about 10% of the B&B homes make a profit at present. However, as every business person knows, "profit" is relative. You might make attractive and useful improvements in your home, such as new carpeting, drapes, furnishings. You might qualify for depreciation of your house (and furnishings) for tax purposes. However, be sure that you really do operate as a business. If the IRS rules that you are pursuing B&B as a hobby, wave good-bye to any tax deductions. That means you have to make *serious* efforts to rent the room regularly.

2. Look at your home objectively. Does (do) your spare room(s) have a good double or twin beds? Are the furnishings in good condition? Is there adequate closet space? Will your guests have access to a private bath, or will the bathroom be shared with the family and other guests? One knowledgeable hostess said, "Always sleep at least once in the room you plan to use for your B&B service. You may be surprised by street noises, or too bright a light in the early morning streaming in the windows—things you would be aware of only if you stayed in your own room." Often one of the key factors in how often the room is rented is the location of your home. If it's in or near a major interstate highway, a major city, scenic attraction, college, hospital, or major corporations, your chances of renting it regularly increase dramatically. Some reservation agencies have told me that a few B&B homes in really remote areas may only be rented about once a year!

3. Poll your whole family. How do they feel about having guests? Remind them that they may lose some privacy in their own home and that they may have to wait in line to use the bathroom. Everyone may have to cooperate to keep the whole house clean (particularly the bathroom) for the arrival of guests. This may be the time for a good family discussion before you make any decision. Do you have a pet? A dog that protects the home by nipping strangers could cost you a lawsuit.

4. Talk with a good lawyer or someone in local government who is familiar with regulations that may govern B&B operations. The real problem is that zoning laws across the country are often very vague about B&B homes. Some zoning laws seem to permit occasional boarders in a home. At other times riled neighbors, who fear that their property value or privacy may be threatened by strangers coming into the neighborhood, may contact the local zoning board for a ruling. Recently one woman in La Jolla, California, began to operate a B&B business in her home. She posted notices locally. Some incensed neighbors brought suit against her. Although she fought the legal action vigorously, her lawyers eventually advised her to close the business. These zoning laws are in flux all over the nation. However, some B&B home-owners are also winning their cases and getting favorable rulings from zoning boards. This is particularly true in states that are actively encouraging the growth of the B&B movement as a way of stimulating more tourism.

Also ask your attorney to check local public health/safety laws/regulations that may apply to any commercial application of your home. For example, some areas may require smoke detectors throughout your home.

5. If you do decide to become a B&B host, you now must decide whether you want to operate independently or want to be connected with a local or national reservation service. *I strongly recommend that you register your home with a reservation service*. If you operate as an independent, you must advertise and promote your home in some ways to attract guests. That could mean putting small ads or generating publicity in local newspapers and magazines. You might even put a small sign in front of your home. Unfortunately all of these activities could raise red flags for your neighbors or local officials. There is another problem. With your phone number on public display in an ad or in one of those books that describes independent B&B homes, you could be subject to unwelcome calls at any time of the day or night. You also would have little opportunity to screen the people who come into your home to spend the night. Instead you would be much better off using a reservation service that does not list your address or phone number in any of their literature. Let the reservation service screen prospective guests. (Before you sign up for any reservation service, ask about their screening activities.) You may want a service that handles all the financial details, even accepting credit-card payments, and forwards a check to you. A service typically charges you a small annual fee to cover administration/advertising costs plus a percentage of each rental (often 20% to 30%). When a service regularly brings you business and conscientiously screens prospective guests, they are more than worth their keep. If the service seems to be choosy about selecting homes for their network and wants to come out for a personal inspection of your home, be thankful! It means, that the service really cares about offering attractive accommodations to the public, and you are in very good hands. Some of the larger services even hold seminars and annual meetings for B&B hosts. This whole business is still in its infancy, and hosts are learning from each other. This guide contains one of the most complete listings of reservation services now operating. Turn to one operating in your area. If none, consider one that offers B&B listings across the U.S.

6. Check your home insurance coverage with your insurance agent. Tell him frankly what you plan to do. Ask what kind of coverage you have and how you would be protected if a paying guest were injured in your home. As the B&B movement grows, the insurance industry is becoming aware of the problems and drafting special new policies. *Warning:* Insurance costs for B&B continue to increase.

I have deliberately listed the most negative factors, not to discourage you but to be sure that you understand that becoming a B&B host is not as simple as deciding you want to do it. That decision involves a commitment, and some careful attention to detail to avoid the pitfalls. However, there can be enormous personal rewards. Many of the stories I have heard from B&B hosts have been heartwarming. One hostess described the young lady who came to their bed-and-breakfast and liked their home so much that she asked to be married there. Other homeowners have met people from around the world who became fast friends. Barbara Notarius, president of Bed & Breakfast USA, Ltd., frequently offers her home as a B&B. She told of her first guest, a retired mining engineer from Australia. He had spent much of his life in remote areas of the world such as New Guinea and had hundreds of stories to tell. Soon Barbara's husband was skipping work so he could drive the guest around town. On another occasion, several of her house guests were musicians. Before they went to bed at night, they gave a chamber concert for Barbara and her family. "What a privilege!" she said.

But hosts also have to learn to be resilient and expect the unexpected. One hostess received a booking from a young woman for two people. When the two women arrived (one an actress who had recently appeared in a successful avant-garde film), they announced that they were gay and wanted to share a double bed. The hostess accommodated them, and had food for conversation at the next eight bridge parties with her friends. (If you operate a B&B home, you have to decide in advance if you will accept unmarried couples, singles, etc. This is another advantage of using a reservation service that knows your preferences.) Joan Brownhill, president of Pineapple Hospitality reservation service in New Bedford, Massachusetts, tells how she selects B&B homes and hosts: "We send out a 'Host Home' preliminary packet which tells of our philosophy as an agency. There is a form to be completed that gives a profile of the prospective host, and answers such basic questions as to whether the host will accept children and pets. Two interviewers then visit the home by appointment to check everything out. If it meets the standards we've set, we sign an agreement with the new B&B home. An annual fee to the agency is collected."

Even when you are listed with an agency and want additional guests, there are a number of ways you could discreetly attract a number of guests:

▪ If you are close to a local college, call or write the personnel office or office of student housing. Describe your home, its location, and room availability. Often visiting parents need an economical place to stay, especially with today's college costs being what they are. There also may be visiting professors or alumni who would welcome a home atmosphere. You might have some very stimulating guests.

▪ Contact the personnel office or corporate travel department of major corporations. Transferees and other visiting employees might make excellent prescreened guests. Women business travelers are particularly receptive to the relaxed B&B concept.

▪ Talk with local real estate agents. They may have out-of-town prospects who need a place to stay while looking for a new home. You'll not only earn extra income by providing hospitality, but you may also be making friends with new neighbors.

▪ Ask previous guests back. When you find particularly appealing and thoughtful guests, invite them back in the summer or winter. Always keep a guestbook and ask them to write their comments. You may be pleasantly surprised how many Christmas/holiday cards you receive from guests who enjoyed your hospitality. *Note:* If your guest originally came from a reservation-service organization, you should ask them to rebook through this organization rather than directly with you. The few dollars you would lose in commission are more than made up by keeping the goodwill of the reservation service that is advertising and generating business for you.

SOME TIPS FOR HOSTS—

"The Gift of Hospitality"

1. Show room and house and give guests an opportunity to unload their belongings.
2. Offer a drink/beverage and see if anything else is needed.
3. Take care of business, such as collecting money, signing the guestbook and contracts, giving a receipt (preferably within 20 minutes of the guests' arrival).
4. Answer questions and mention nearby attractions.
5. Supply guests with an information sheet containing questions and answers about your local area.
6. Collect brochures on sightseeing for your local area, as well as your state, and have them available for guests.
7. Offer a "Sue's Special": picnic basket breakfast in bed.
8. Collect menus from popular restaurants to leave in the guests' room.
9. Make coffee early. Find out when guests arrive what they prefer to drink in the morning. A Thermos of coffee outside the door, so the first cup of coffee can be drunk in bed, is a real treat for the real coffee drinker.
10. Put an umbrella stand with loan umbrellas near the door and tell guests about it.
11. Set up a game corner (garage sales are a wonderful source of these and other handy items).
12. Place extra toilet articles (small sample sizes) in drawers.
13. Use liquid soap in the bathroom so that no guest has to use anyone else's soap.
14. Offer a special guest tray including a fruit bowl, drinking glass, tissues, etc.
15. Have on hand books and magazines for your guests to read.
16. A hair dryer, makeup mirror, and curling iron from a garage sale may be lifesavers for your female guests.
17. Have newspapers on hand.
18. Have a good map on hand.

19. Copy the section of your local map showing your home and circle your house, restaurants, attractions, movies, etc., and run off enough copies so that each guest can take one with him/her.

20. Collect articles from your newspaper's attractions section and keep in a folder easily available to guests. Copies hold up better than newsprint originals.

21. Collect discount coupons from nearby attractions and restaurants for guests.

22. Save fast-food discount coupons too.

23. Leave a note on the guests' desk or bureau telling where they can order take-out pizza. Let them know if it's all right to eat on your deck or patio.

24. Deliver ice water to the guests' room in the evening.

25. Have iced tea available in the refrigerator or let guests know that they can always boil themselves hot water for tea or instant coffee.

26. Help your guests to feel comfortable in your home. Assure them that they should ask if there is something they need—extra towels, more pillows, etc.

27. Copy your special B&B recipes so guests can take them home.

28. Invite guests to watch you do your hobbies/special-interest activities (such as stained glass, pottery, etc.).

29. If you have a historic home, guests may be interested in its history and architecture. Take a course about tracing the history of your home and keep the results of your work accessible.

30. See if the historical society or other town group has a walking tour of the community published that your guests can take.

31. Be sensitive to your guests' need for privacy and space. Don't ever make a guest feel that he's there to amuse you. Be available for those who want to talk but in touch enough to recognize when a guest just wants to be left alone.

32. B&B attracts a lot of folks looking for romance. If your setting is conducive to this, encourage it. Offer guests some privacy in front of the fireplace, put out a decanter with a little after-dinner liqueur, etc. Flannel sheets are wonderful in cold climates.

33. Let your guests get to know you as an individual—your way of life, your part of the country.

(Suggestions from *Rocky Mountains–Bed & Breakfast* hosts, reprinted with the permission of Kate Peterson and Barbara Notarius)

COMMONLY ASKED QUESTIONS ABOUT HOSTING

Q. *How much should I charge for the room?*

A. The rate depends on several factors. The most important is location. Even a modestly furnished room in a modest house that is close to a popular ski slope can often command a premium rate. The condition of the room, its furnishings, and the general appearance of your home also should be considered. If the room has a private bath instead of a shared bath, you can also charge more. However, you want to be sure that the rate you charge is competitive and doesn't drive business away. Check the rates of other B&B homes in your area. Also, find out the rates of local hotels and motels. Your rate should generally be lower than hotel rates. Travelers expect B&B rates to be bargains.

Q. *What about income tax deductions?*

A. If your home is only used for B&B hosting 14 or fewer nights per year, you may not have to pay any income tax on what you make. However, if a room in your home is rented more than 14 nights a year, then you would have to declare all income. You would also be entitled to deductions that could range from depreciation on your furnishings, fees paid to reservation-service organizations, stamps, phone calls, etc. You also may be able to claim depreciation on your house and a percentage of certain housecleaning/home maintenance costs. You should make (and report) a profit at least two out of every five years or the government may claim your B&B operation is a hobby—not a business—and disallow any business deductions. *Note:* You may be unable to deduct some smaller expenses as a result of the newly revised federal tax law. To avoid problems, work with a good accountant who can help you interpret the current IRS rules.

Q. *Should I tell my neighbors I operate a B&B home?*

A. No. Not unless you are a would-be Perry Mason anxious to plead your case before a local zoning board.

Q. *Should I charge sales tax?*

A. Check with local authorities about this. It may be necessary for you to get a tax number and collect sales tax on all B&B

rentals. Don't follow the human tendency to just keep mum about any rentals or income. You could become liable for back taxes and penalties.

Q. *I have to leave for work early in the morning. How can I fix breakfast for guests or give them access to the house should they return while I'm away?*

A. You could leave breakfast ingredients in the refrigerator and give your guests kitchen privileges for a do-it-yourself meal. Some hosts also give their guests a key, charging a "key fee" of $5 or $10 (which is refunded when the guest returns the key). For your own security, you may give the guest a key only to the regular lock, not a deadbolt lock, if you have one. You then have the security of locking the deadbolt without worrying about any unreturned keys that might be floating around.

Q. *What about the possibility of theft? I am letting strangers into my home.*

A. Theft could happen. However, at least so far, B&B guests seem to be an unusually honest group of people. In talking with B&B hosts, I have yet to hear of an incident where a guest has taken as much as a teaspoon. (In contrast, talk with any major-city hotel, which regularly loses a large quantity of towels and room-service silverware and linen in the luggage of departing guests.) You would want to use some common sense in protecting your personal belongings. If your guests have active children, you might want to store away any obvious breakables. You also can get an extra measure of security by having all prospective guests screened by the reservation-service organization. Many of these organizations ask guests for personal references.

Q. *Should I print a "brochure" on my B&B home?*

A. It really isn't necessary. You might want to do a simple letter on your stationery which describes your home and the breakfast you serve, tells of any "house rule" restrictions (such as no smoking, no pets, etc.), and gives directions to your home. Offset print a quantity and send some to your reservation-service organization. Or mail one to the guest who calls and asks for directions or more information.

Q. *Will I make much money as a B&B host?*

A. As I've said before, you probably *won't* make a high income as a host. However, I have been told of hosts who make $10,000 or more a year. Others who are close to scenic attractions, major cities, resort areas, etc., reliably make several hundred extra dollars each month. One hostess recently used her B&B earnings to pay for an all-expense safari in Africa. But there are also some B&B homes in remote locations that are only rented as little as once a year. As the real estate people love to say about selling a house, the three most important factors are location, location, and location.

A LAST NOTE

Much of your reward of being a B&B host will come from meeting other people. Kate Peterson, coordinator of Bed & Breakfast Rocky Mountains, shared this letter she had received from one of her new hosts:

Dear Kate,

Clyde and I just wanted to let you know how delighted we are with our first experience hosting bed-and-breakfast travelers. The couple from Houston left just this morning. I know we have made new friends. They were so comfortable with us that they have already decided to return in June to stay. It's amazing to me that they have even referred some of their friends to us—all this in just the last few days. Yesterday was really special. It was my birthday. When I got home in the afternoon, they had a birthday card and a delicate dried-flower arrangement waiting for me. I was truly touched. Kate, we want to thank you for making this opportunity possible for us and for others. We are looking forward to the next bed-and-breakfast travelers we can serve.

Sincerely,
Fairley

These are the *real* rewards of becoming a B&B host.

Directory of B&B Reservation Services and Selected B&B Inns in North America

SPECIAL NOTE TO READERS

Be sure to check the "B&B Bonuses" section of each reservation-service listing. This is designed to give you an edge over other people calling the same reservation service. It describes some of the B&B homes that the services themselves consider their most appealing. Ask about them. Also you will learn about special services available from many B&B hosts for the asking.

National and Regional B&B Reservation Services

AMERICAN HISTORIC HOMES BED & BREAKFAST

P.O. BOX 336, DANA POINT, CA 92629

Offers B&B Homes In: 500 locations throughout the United States.
Reservations Phone: 714/496-6953
Phone Hours: 9 a.m. to 5 p.m. Monday to Friday
Price Range of Homes: $25 to $65 single, $35 to $85 double
Breakfast Included in Price: Continental or full American . . . some specialties are cinnamon rolls, freshly ground coffee, smoked meats, fresh-baked breads, and "recipes from the Gold Rush days in Mother Lode Country"
Brochure Available: For $1 (includes listings)
Reservations Should Be Made: 2 weeks in advance (last-minute reservations accepted if possible)

B&B Bonuses

You may choose to stay in an estate built in 1693 and occupied by the Marquis de Lafayette as his headquarters; a Federal-style home circa 1827 on the old Boston Post Road that includes a secret room under a trap door in the library for slaves escaping north; a lighthouse on the National Register of Historic Places; an opulent estate with a full view of San Francisco Bay three blocks from Fisherman's Wharf; a carriage house in Washington, D.C., two miles from the White House. There are Queen Anne Victorians, Georgians, colonial plantations, and Cape-style homes available throughout the country.

BED & BREAKFAST HOSPITALITY

P.O. BOX 2407, OCEANSIDE, CA 92054

Offers B&B Homes In: Major cities and rural areas across the U.S., Hawaii, New Zealand, Australia, Israel, Ireland, England, Scotland, France, Bermuda, Iceland, South Africa
Reservations Phone: 619/722-6694
Phone Hours: 9 a.m. to 6 p.m. Monday to Saturday; no holidays

Price Range of Homes: $18 to $95 single, $36 to $110 double
Breakfast Included in Price: Continental or full American . . . most hosts serve home-baked breads and muffins, fresh fruit in season, and farms serve their own eggs and produce
Brochure Available: Free. International Directory is $10, including tax and handling (this also covers fee for those who wish to join this organization).
Reservations Should Be Made: 2 weeks in advance for the U.S.; 6 weeks for international (last-minute reservations accepted if possible)

B&B Bonuses

The listings include sheep ranches in Australia; castles and manor houses in England; rural Irish village homes; kibbutz/monastery in Israel; beach areas in California, Florida, Hawaii, etc.; ski areas; fresh- and saltwater fishing areas; San Francisco Victorian homes; and many renovated and restored homes in the U.S., Europe, and other countries.

Occasional extras are airport and train pickups, gourmet picnic lunches and evening meals, sherry and high tea, sightseeing tours, horseback riding, restaurant and theater reservations.

BED & BREAKFAST INTERNATIONAL— SAN FRANCISCO

151 ARDMORE RD., KENSINGTON, CA 94707

Offers B&B Homes In: San Francisco and all areas of tourist interest in California, including Los Angeles, Monterey Peninsula, San Diego, Wine Country, coastal and mountain regions; also, Seattle, Las Vegas, New York City, and Hawaii
Reservations Phone: 415/525-4569
Phone Hours: 8:30 a.m. to 5 p.m. Monday to Friday, till noon on Saturday
Price Range of Homes: $30 to $95 double; single is $6 discount on double rate
Breakfast Included in Price: Full American . . . the famous sour-dough bread is served in many of the San Francisco host homes
Brochure Available: Free
Reservations Should Be Made: 2 weeks in advance preferred

B&B Bonuses

Hosts live in modern apartments in city centers, in Victorian mansions, California Mediterranean-style homes on quiet, tree-lined streets, mountain chalets, beach houses, and a houseboat in Sausalito.

THE BED & BREAKFAST LEAGUE, LTD.
3639 VAN NESS ST. NW, WASHINGTON, DC 20008

Offers B&B Homes In: Washington, D.C.; Annapolis, Baltimore, New York City, San Francisco
Reservations: 202/363-7767
Phone Hours: 9 a.m. to 5 p.m. Monday to Thursday, to 1 p.m. on Friday
Price Range of Homes: $30 to $55 single, $45 to $65 double
Breakfast Included in Price: Continental . . . juice, roll or toast, coffee
Brochure Available: Free if you enclose a stamped, self-addressed no. 10 envelope
Reservations Should Be Made: 3 weeks in advance (accepts last-minute reservations when possible)

Scenic Attractions Near the B&B Homes: All of the attractions of the nation's capital, including the White House, Smithsonian museums, National Gallery of Art
Major Schools, Universities Near the B&B Homes: Georgetown, George Washington, American

B&B Bonuses
In one Washington, D.C., B&B the host will let you give a party in the parlor of a huge Victorian mansion on Capitol Hill. Invite your senators and business friends into a room with 11-foot ceilings and marble fireplaces. Or perhaps you would like to stay in a 43-foot boat moored in the Washington Channel. The private cabin has a double bunk and private head with shower. When the weather is sunny, you have breakfast on deck.

BED & BREAKFAST REGISTRY LTD.
P.O. BOX 8174, ST. PAUL, MN 55108

Offers B&B Homes In: 47 states, Canada, Mexico, the Caribbean, and Great Britain
Reservations Phone: 612/646-4238
Phone Hours: 9 a.m. to 6 p.m. Monday to Friday (sometimes on Saturday, depending on need and season)
Price Range of Homes: $20 to $145 single, $25 to $200 double

Breakfast Included in Price: Most hosts serve a continental-plus breakfast: "The breakfast varies by region, and our hosts have their own family recipes which add something special to our guests' visits."
Brochure Available: Free. Complete Host Directory available for $9.95 plus $1.50 for shipping.
Reservations Should Be Made: Advance reservations are encouraged.

B&B Bonuses

A B&B home to ask for in New Orleans: an antebellum mansion. It's on the National Register of Historic Places and has authentic fixtures and furnishings with a magnificent parlor and dining room.

Want to give someone the gift of a stay at a B&B? "Because You Are Someone Special" gift certificates are available from this service. They can be used at 400 locations in North America.

BED & BREAKFAST SOCIETY INTERNATIONAL

307 W. MAIN ST., SUITE 2, FREDERICKSBURG, TX 78624

Offers B&B Homes In: All over the U.S., Canada, England, Ireland, Europe, and 18 other countries
Reservations Phone: 512/997-4712
Phone Hours: 24 hours daily
Price Range of Homes: $35 to $100 single or double
Breakfast Included in Price: Continental or full American . . . "Gourmet or unique breakfasts are increasing, as the hosts get away from purely simple continental breakfasts."
Brochure Available: "Bed & Breakfast World Directory & Guidebook" available for $6 plus $1.50 first-class postage
Reservations Should Be Made: As soon as possible (last-minute reservations are also welcome)

Scenic Attractions Near the B&B Homes: Information on area attractions available when the guest books

B&B Bonuses

When visiting Germany, you can stay at a beautiful B&B inn at the foot of Liechtenstein Castle. There's a large brook on the property filled with trout. The hostess provides riding horses and speaks many languages.

CHRISTIAN BED & BREAKFAST OF AMERICA
P.O. BOX 338, SAN JUAN CAPISTRANO, CA 92693

Offers B&B Homes In: 350 cities all over the U.S.
Reservations Phone: 714/496-7050
Phone Hours: 8 a.m. to 5 p.m. Monday to Friday, plus weekend evenings from 6 to 9 p.m.
Price Range of Homes: $15 to $40 single, $20 to $55 double
Breakfast Included in Price: Continental or full American . . . specialties offered in some areas, such as high English tea served on 100-year-old china in prize-winning table setting
Brochure Available: For $1
Reservations Should Be Made: 2 weeks in advance (last-minute reservations accepted if possible)

B&B Bonuses
   Their many host homes throughout the country include farms, ranches, oceanfront apartments, historic homes, and estates. Regional sightseeing and cultural tours, windsurfing and sailing excursions, picnic lunches, skiing, live music, and airport pickups are some of the extras frequently offered.

COHOST, AMERICA'S BED & BREAKFAST
P.O. BOX 9302, WHITTIER, CA 90608

Offers B&B Homes In: Northern and Southern California and in many other states
Reservations Phone: 213/699-8427
Phone Hours: 8 a.m. to 9 p.m. daily, or anytime on answering machine
Price Range of Homes: $20 to $70 single, $25 to $75 double
Breakfast Included in Price: Full breakfast . . . CoHosts specialize in regional foods, such as a typical Mexican breakfast with huevos rancheros and tortillas, or country biscuits and gravy with ham and eggs, or eggs Benedict and fruit compotes
Brochure Available: $1 if you send a stamped, self-addressed no. 10 envelope
Reservations Should Be Made: 2 weeks in advance (last-minute reservations accepted if possible)

B&B Bonuses

You could enjoy the hospitality of a Spanish-speaking, world-traveled bachelor who collects art and photographs. Or ask about the home of the former owners of a popular restaurant; they offer breakfast with succulent crêpes and pastries. If you have children, you may want to stay at a home with large bedrooms in a quiet neighborhood near Disneyland and Knott's Berry Farm; the hosts will welcome you back with tea or wine and cheese after your day.

For a moderate fee, arrangements can be made to take guests to and from airports by limousine. Many hosts are eager to provide sightseeing trips to the guest's choice of destinations. The reservation agency advises: "Our rates do not fluctuate with seasons or special events."

The Northeastern States

Connecticut / 69
Maine / 72
Massachusetts / 80
New Hampshire / 95
New York / 101
Rhode Island / 113
Vermont / 116

CONNECTICUT

B&B Reservation Services

NUTMEG BED & BREAKFAST
222 GIRARD AVE., HARTFORD, CT 06105

Offers B&B Homes In: Connecticut (125 homes)
Reservations Phone: 203/236-6698
Phone Hours: 9 a.m. to 5 p.m. Monday to Friday
Price Range of Homes: $35 to $70 single, $40 to $85 double
Breakfast Included in Price: Continental or full American . . . many homes serve full breakfast, often featuring nut breads and croissants
Brochure Available: $2.50 for a complete directory
Reservations Should Be Made: 2 weeks in advance (last-minute reservations accepted if possible)

Scenic Attractions Near the B&B Homes: Mystic Seaport, Sturbridge Village, etc. (guests are advised of attractions in the area before arrival)
Major Schools, Universities Near the B&B Homes: Yale, Wesleyan, Trinity, Coast Guard Academy, Hotchkiss, Kent, Pomfret, Lakeville, Choate, Rosemary Hall, Wallingford and Miss Porter's Farmington prep schools

B&B Bonuses
Ask for the country home at the entrance to Penwood Forest. You can jog, ski, swim, and hike in the area. There are "11 goats which cut the grass and answer to their names." Long-term accommodations are available for business people who are relocating (with price adjustment).

BED & BREAKFAST, LTD.
P.O. BOX 216, NEW HAVEN, CT 06513

Offers B&B Homes In: Connecticut
Reservations Phone: 203/469-3260
Phone Hours: 5 to 9 p.m. Monday to Friday, plus weekend mornings

Price Range of Homes: $35 to $45 single, $45 to $65 double
Breakfast Included in Price: Continental or full American . . . varies with individual home
Brochure Available: Free if you send a stamped, self-addressed no. 10 envelope
Reservations Should Be Made: 1 week in advance (last-minute reservations accepted if possible)

Scenic Attractions Near the B&B Homes: New Haven Coliseum, Long Wharf Theater, Powder Ridge ski area, Shubert Theater, Connecticut shore, Mystic Seaport, Peabody and British Art Museums, antique shops, historic country villages
Major Schools, Universities Near the B&B Homes: Yale, Wesleyan, Southern Connecticut State, Albertus Magnus, Hopkins, Choate, Milford Academy, Hamden Hall, Coast Guard Academy, Taft

B&B Bonuses

One of the homes is a grand Victorian in-town residence that has been on the local house tour for three years. It is filled with antiques as well as contemporary touches, is near beaches and Yale, and convenient to highways I-95 and I-91.

Knowledgeable and helpful hosts offer a welcome cocktail or tea, fresh fruit and chocolates, menus from local restaurants, and a friendly "home away form home" atmosphere.

COVERED BRIDGE BED & BREAKFAST
P.O. BOX 701, NORFOLK, CT 06058

Offers B&B Homes In: Goshen, Kent, Sharon, Norfolk, Litchfield, Lakeville, and other towns in the northwest corner of Connecticut; the Berkshires—Lenox, Great Barrington, Sheffield, Stockbridge, Williamstown—in Massachusetts; Shaftsbury in Vermont; East Haddam and Essex in southern Connecticut
Reservations Phone: 203/542-5944
Phone Hours: 9 a.m. to 8 p.m. daily
Price Range of Homes: $40 to $100 single, $45 to $120 double
Breakfast Included in Price: Continental . . . juice, roll or toast, coffee
Brochure Available: Free
Reservations Should Be Made: 2 weeks in advance (last-minute reservations accepted if possible)
Scenic Attractions Near the B&B Homes: Tanglewood Music Festival, Williamstown Theater, Jacob's Pillow, Sharon Playhouse,

Appalachian Trail, white-water canoeing, skiing, antiques, Lime Rock car racing, state parks, White Flower Farm
Major Schools, Universities Near the B&B Homes: Williams, Bennington, Simon's Rock at Bard, Hotchkiss, Kent, Salisbury, Berkshire, Indian Mountain Gunnery, Taft

B&B Bonuses

Your choice of working farms, with mountain views and ponds, Victorian estates, and Cape Cods. Some guest rooms have fireplaces; ask for one when you call. Some hosts speak several languages.

B&B Inns

THE INN AT CHESTER
318 W. MAIN ST., CHESTER, CT 06412

Reservations Phone: 203/526-4961
Description: The inn was built during the war years of 1776–1778. There are 48 bedrooms and baths filled with antiques, period pieces and oriental rugs. Now completely restored, it's a beautiful inn.

Nearby Attractions: Parks, summer theaters, river activities
Special Services: Tennis, exercise room, fireplaces, sauna, large and small conference rooms
Rates: $80 double

COPPER BEACH INN
MAIN STREET, IVORYTON, CT 06442

Reservations Phone: 203/767-0330
Description: This is a gracious home in a woodland setting. There are four guest rooms in the main house and nine additional rooms in the old carriage house.
Amenities: Fresh fruit, cold cereals, muffins, juice, coffee or tea

Nearby Attractions: The seaport town of Essex with charming old sea captains' homes, an old railroad, Gillette Castle, the Goodspeed Opera House, local beaches

Special Services: The inn's limo will pick up guests at local marinas, airports, and the Amtrak stations.
Rates: $70 to $125 double in high season (May through October)

HOMESTEAD INN AND MOTEL

5 ELM ST., NEW MILFORD, CT 06776

Reservations Phone: 203/354-4080
Description: All the rooms in this 140-year-old Victorian inn have been recently renovated. The front porch overlooks the town green. Rooms in the motel are also available to guests.
Amenities: Expanded continental breakfast

Nearby Attractions: Lake Waremug, Indian Archeological Institute, two wineries
Special Services: Innkeeper in residence 24 hours a day for your convenience
Rates: $38 to $41 single, $44 to $50 double

MAINE

B & B Reservation Services

BED & BREAKFAST OF MAINE

32 COLONIAL VILLAGE, FALMOUTH, ME 04105

Offers B&B Homes In: Maine
Reservations Phone: 207/781-4528
Phone Hours: 6 to 11 p.m. plus 24 hours daily via an answering machine
Price Range of Homes: $25 to $45 single, $35 to $70 double
Breakfast Included in Price: Full American . . . "We encourage hosts to serve hearty breakfasts. At least fresh breads and real butter; blueberry pancakes are popular and fresh fruit cups or jams."
Brochure Available: $1
Reservations Should Be Made: 2 weeks in advance

Scenic Attractions Near the B&B Homes: Daily cruise to Nova Scotia, clam bakes, lobster festivals, craft shows, foliage tours, art festivals, island cruises, coastal resort activities
Major Schools, Universities Near the B&B Homes: U. of Maine, Bates, Maine Maritime, Northeastern, Westbrook, Bowdoin

B&B Bonuses

One 1800s farm has a canoe available on its own lake and offers their picnic area for guests to bring back lobsters to cook in the yard. Another host invites guests out for an island boat trip in good weather; others offer babysitting. One has a sauna, and several homes have game rooms.

BED & BREAKFAST DOWN EAST, LTD.

BOX 547, MACOMBER MILL ROAD, EASTBROOK, ME 04634

Offers B&B Homes In: Maine, statewide; including Acadia National Park, Mt. Desert Island area, coastal, inland, rural, western lakes and mountains
Reservations Phone: 207/565-3517
Phone Hours: 8 a.m. to 8 p.m., plus any day at any reasonable hour
Price Range of Homes: $30 to $50 singles, $35 to $80 double
Breakfast Included in Price: Most hosts give guests a choice between continental and full American . . . some specialties served are blueberry scones, popovers, and "toad-in-a-hole"
Brochure Available: $3 for 45-page directory
Reservations Should Be Made: At least 2 weeks in advance (last-minute reservations accepted if possible)

Scenic Attractions Near the B&B Homes: Acadia National Park, Jackson Laboratory, Bar Harbor, scenic coastal areas, historic sites, museums, hiking trails; ski areas
Major Schools, Universities Near the B&B Homes: U. of Southern Maine, Portland, Gorham, Colby, Waterville, Bates, Lewiston, Bowdoin

B&B Bonuses

Ask for the Portland condo in an old-world brick building. Or stay on an unspoiled island in Penobscot Bay, swim in the ocean, and feast on fresh-caught seafood. Or stay in a "cottage" at Bar Harbor and maybe have a game of chess or tennis with the owner.

B&B Inns

TOWN MOTEL AND GUEST HOUSE
12 ATLANTIC AVE., BAR HARBOR, ME 04609

Reservations Phone: 207/288-5548
Description: Combining old-fashioned comfort with modern convenience, the guest rooms have pull-chain "johns," marble sinks, and period furniture.

Nearby Attractions: The rocky coast of Maine, fishing, swimming, golf, tennis
Special Services: Color TV
Rates: $25 single, $46 to $66 double

NORSEMAN INN
P.O. BOX 50, BETHEL, ME 04217

Reservations Phone: 207/824-2002
Description: This 200-year-old building complex sits on four acres of land in the western foothills of Maine.
Amenities: Full breakfast with fruit of the season, as available

Nearby Attractions: Excellent hiking and camping facilities
Special Services: Activity room, living room with large fireplace, lounge with bar service
Rates: $40 single, $50 double, in winter; $30 single, $40 double, in summer

BLUEHILL FARM COUNTRY INN
P.O. BOX 437, BLUE HILL, ME 04614

Reservations Phone: 207/374-5126
Description: An old turn-of-the-century farm situated at the foot of Blue Hill Mountain, all its rooms overlook 48 acres of field, pond, and woods.
Amenities: Squeezed orange juice, fruit of the season, local Camembert cheese on fruit plate, their own granola, cereals, fresh-baked muffins, breads, or popovers—all served with fresh-ground coffee

Nearby Attractions: Acadia National Park, Kneisel Music Camp, Blue Hill Fair
Special Services: Snowshoeing and skiing
Rates: $35 single, $45 double, in summer; $30 single, $40 double, in winter

TOPSIDE
MCKOWN HILL, BOOTHBAY HARBOR, ME 04538

Reservations Phone: 207/633-5404
Description: A historic sea captain's house furnished with antiques—all rooms have a private bath and a refrigerator.

Nearby Attractions: Reid State Park, Carousel Music Theater, Boothbay Dinner Theater, golf, boatrides
Rates: $80 single, $90 double, in summer; $50 single, $65 double, in spring and fall

WHITEHALL INN
52 HIGH ST., (P.O. BOX 558), CAMDEN, ME 04843

Reservations Phone: 207/236-3391
Description: This 1834 building has operated as an inn since 1901. Edna St. Vincent Millay stayed here. The inn is furnished with antiques and Oriental rugs. The porches have rocking chairs for the guests.
Amenities: Full country breakfast and dinner included

Nearby Attractions: Camden State Parks, many accessible islands
Special Services: Swimming pool, tennis courts
Rates: $65 single, $115 double, in summer

CHEBEAGUE INN BY THE SEA
P.O. BOX 492, CHEBEAGUE ISLAND, ME 04017

Reservations Phone: 207/846-5155
Description: This old-fashioned inn sits high on a hill overlooking the ocean and a golf course. Rooms have been recently renovated and have private baths. The inn has a wrap-around porch and the

Great Room has both books and a piano available to guests. Access is by ferry only.
Amenities: Full breakfast

Nearby Attractions: L. L. Bean's, Camden, Portland, Casco Bay
Special Services: Mopeds and bicycles available, croquet, golf
Rates: $80 double in summer, $67 double in winter

LINCOLN HOUSE COUNTRY INN
LINCOLN HOUSE, DENNYSVILLE, ME 04628

Reservations Phone: 207/726-3953
Description: Built in 1787, this four-square colonial sits on 95 acres overlooking the Dennys River. The building has been carefully restored and has earned a place on the National Register of Historic Place.
Amenities: Full country breakfast; dinner is included.

Nearby Attractions: Campobello Island, Roosevelt International Park, Moosehorn National Wildlife Refuge, Cobscook State Park, Reversing Falls
Special Services: Salmon fishing, whale watching, swimming, tennis
Rates: $65 double

CRAB APPLE ACRES INN
RTE. 201, THE FORKS, ME 04985

Reservations Phone: 207/663-2218
Description: This 1835 farmhouse on the Kennebec River has seven guest rooms and two shared baths. There are quilts on all beds and a wood-burning stove in the kitchen.
Amenities: Complimentary continental breakfast is served.

Nearby Attractions: White-water rafting on the Kennebec River, Fall Foliage Festival (package trips available), canoeing, hunting, fishing, cross-country skiing
Special Services: They will make full arrangements for your rafting trips.
Rates: $40 double.

THE GREEN HERON INN

OCEAN AVENUE, (P.O. DRAWER 151), KENNEBUNKPORT, ME 04046

Reservations Phone: 207/967-3315
Description: Built in 1908 on an inlet of the Kennebunk River, 300 yards from the ocean, this inn has no two rooms alike.
Amenities: Besides the usual breakfast fare, the inn serves Swiss potato patties, Golden Buck, Zimmies, and fish cakes.

Nearby Attractions: Colonial village with historic houses, Trolley Museum, theme parks and amusement centers
Special Services: Bus or plane pickup, bicycles
Rates: $24.50 to $33.50 single, $35 to $44 double

THE WINTER'S INN

P.O. BOX 44, KINGFIELD, ME 04947

Reservations Phone: 207/265-5421
Description: This gracious old mansion sits above the town cemetery where the old monuments look down on three graceful curves of the Carrabassett River. The architect/owner restored this old Victorian with care and furnished it in the proper style, right down to the stuffed armadillo over the fireplace in the parlor, mid-18th-century portraits, and Egyptian knicknacks.
Amenities: Breakfast features stuffed French toast, quiche, omelets, homemade preserves

Nearby Attractions: Sugarloaf, Robert Trent Jones golf course, white-water rafting, tennis court
Special Services: Swimming pool
Rates: $70 to $90 double in fall, $50 to $70 double in winter and summer

PUFFIN INN BED & BREAKFAST

97 MAIN ST., OGUNQUIT, ME 03907

Reservations Phone: 207/646-5496
Description: This 150-year-old sea captain's home, tastefully decorated with period furniture, is set on landscaped grounds abounding with flowers.
Amenities: Continental breakfast

Nearby Attractions: Perkins Cove, Ogunquit Playhouse, Rachel Carson Wildlife Preserve, Marginal Way (a footpath along the rocky coast)
Special Services: Guidance in planning your day and a local map
Rates: $45 to $50 double

THE FARMHOUSE INN

RTE. 4 (P.O. BOX 496), RANGELEY, ME 04970

Reservations Phone: 207/864-5805
Description: Originally built by one of Rangeley's first settlers, this 1850 farmhouse has country suites, consisting of a sitting room, dining room, common room, and large porch. A large porch overlooks Rangeley Lake.
Amenities: Full farm breakfast

Nearby Attractions: Rangeley Lake State Park, Saddleback Mountain, skiing
Special Services: Common room with pool and Ping-Pong tables, and a cupboard full of games, puzzles, and books.
Rates: $45 to $70 double

CRAIGNAIR INN

CLARK ISLAND ROAD, SPRUCEHEAD, ME 04859

Reservations Phone: 207/594-7644
Description: The inn is set in a tiny town of 100, formerly a granite quarry, overlooking the ocean and Clark Cove.
Amenities: Full breakfast with fruit from the garden, eggs, bacon, sausage, muffins, cereal, coffee and tea

Nearby Attractions: Lighthouse, ferry to offshore islands, Montpelier (Gen. H. Knox's home)
Special Services: Pickup service, swimming in an old quarry
Rates: $38 single, $58 double, in summer; $34 single, $51 double, in winter

EAST WIND INN AND MEETING HOUSE

MECHANIC STREET (P.O. BOX 149), TENANTS HARBOR, ME 04860

Reservations Phone: 207/372-6366
Description: An authentic coastal inn, the three-story frame building, with a wrap-around porch, is located at the water's edge. It's

furnished with period antiques, and singles, doubles, and suites are available.

Nearby Attractions: Farnsworth Art Museum, Owls Head Transportation, ferry to Monhegan Island, Vinalhaven and Islesboro, antique shops, lighthouses, and movie theaters
Special Services: A passenger sailing vessel leaves from the wharf daily
Rates: $50 to $100 double in summer, $44 to $90 double in winter

KAWANHEEINN LAKESIDE RESORT
LAKE WEBB, WELD, ME 04285

Reservations Phone: 207/585-2243
Description: The main lodge has a large stone fireplace capable of taking four-foot logs; on the second floor are 14 comfortable bedrooms. Eleven cabins face the lake, and can accommodate from two to seven guests; Each cabin has a living room with a stone fireplace, one or two bedrooms, a private bath, and a screened porch.

Nearby Attractions: Mount Blue, and Tumbledown and Bald Mountains
Special Services: Lake for swimming or boating
Rates: $38 double in summer

DOCKSIDE GUEST QUARTERS
HARRIS ISLAND ROAD (P.O. BOX 205), YORK, ME 03909

Reservations Phone: 207/363-2868
Description: On a peninsula jutting out into the harbor at York, the main lodge was an early seacoast homestead. Four contemporary multi-unit cottages and a dining room building complete the complex. The furnishings of the public rooms include antiques, ship models, and choice marine paintings. Most bedrooms have their own bath and direct access to the porch or lawn.
Amenities: Buffet-style continental breakfast served on the oceanside porch

Nearby Attractions: The center of York Village is a National Historic District and the buildings are open to the public.
Special Services: Marina, boat rentals, special yachting excursions
Rates: $39 to $67 double

B&B Reservation Services

FOLKSTONE BED & BREAKFAST
P.O. BOX 931, BOYLSTON, MA 01505

Offers B&B Homes In: Worcester County
Reservations Phone: 617/869-2687
Phone Hours: 9 a.m. to 1 p.m. Monday to Friday, and also on many weekends
Price Range of Homes: $30 to $65 single, $30 to $65 double
Breakfast Included in Price: Continental (juice, roll or toast, coffee) or full American with specialties such as beef or chicken hash, homemade English muffins, omelets to order, pancakes with seasonal fruits and berries
Brochure Available: For $1
Reservations Should Be Made: 2 weeks in advance (last-minute reservations accepted when possible)

Scenic Attractions Near the B&B Homes: Sturbridge Village, Worcester Science Center, Higgins Armor Museum, Horticultural Society
Major Schools, Universities Near the B&B Homes: U. Mass. Medical School, Clark U., Worcester Polytech, Anna Maria College, Atlantic Union College

B&B Bonuses ———————————————————
  Ask for the 1752 working farm. Guests have their run of the farm, and swim in the trout-stocked pond from a sandy beach. One host in Graffton provides terrycloth robes for guests and champagne for special occasions.

BED & BREAKFAST, BROOKLINE/BOSTON
P.O. BOX 732, BROOKLINE, MA 02146

Offers B&B Homes In: Boston proper (including Beacon Hill, Back Bay, Brookline, Cambridge), Cape Cod, Nantucket Island, Gloucester, and other Massachusetts areas
Reservations Phone: 617/277-2292

Phone Hours: 10 a.m. to 4 p.m. Monday to Friday
Price Range of Homes: $40 to $50 single, $50 to $65 double
Breakfast Included in Price: Continental breakfast can include homemade jams such as "Beach Plum" on Cape Cod, cranberry muffins, croissants, cereal, "Anadama bread"; several hosts serve full breakfasts.
Brochure Available: Free. For accommodations lists, send $1 and a stamped, self-addressed no. 10 envelope.
Reservations Should Be Made: Any time—"first come, first served"

Scenic Attractions Near the B&B Homes: All of Boston's attractions are minutes away by subway; the Museum of Fine Arts, Gardner Museum, and Fenway Park are especially convenient to several of the host homes.
Major Schools, Universities Near the B&B Homes: Harvard, Boston U., Tufts, Simmons, Wheelock, plus centers for international visitors and studies

B&B Bonuses

Ask about the gracious homes of exclusive Beacon Hill, Back Bay, Brookline, and Cambridge, and the turn-of-the-century brick rowhouse in Boston. Several hosts speak foreign languages, and many have extended extra care and hospitality to people visiting patients in nearby hospitals. Children can usually be accommodated.

GREATER BOSTON HOSPITALITY

P.O. BOX 1142, BROOKLINE, MA 02146

Offers B&B Homes In: Boston, Cambridge, Newton, Needham, Wellesley, Winchester, Marblehead, Salem, Swampscott, Charlestown, Belmont, Brighton, Massachusetts
Reservations Phone: 617/277-5430
Phone Hours: 24 hours daily
Price Range of Homes: $30 to $60 single, $40 to $90 double
Breakfast Included in Price: Full American, which may include homemade peach preserves and scones, hot chocolate, buttermilk pancakes, bagels with smoked salmon and cream cheese, croissants . . . and a vegetarian/macrobiotic home serves fresh carrot juice, rice muffins with tofu cream cheese, hot oatmeal, apple-pear crunch, brown rice, tea or coffee.
Brochure Available: Free
Reservations Should Be Made: 2 weeks in advance (last-minute reservations accepted if possible)

Scenic Attractions Near the B&B Homes: Boston Symphony, Boston Pops, Boston Ballet, Christian Science Church, Kennedy Library, Museum of Fine Arts, Isabella Stuart Gardner Museum, Faneuil Hall, Quincy Market, Freedom Trail, Chinatown, Beacon Hill, N.E. Aquarium
Major Schools, Universities Near the B&B Homes: Harvard, M.I.T., Boston U., Boston College, Emmanuel, Lesley, Pine Manor, Northeastern, Simmons, Wellesley, Massachusetts College of Art, New England Conservatory, Tufts, Babson, Brandeis

B&B Bonuses

A red-brick Georgian carriage house is located on a cul-de-sac in a fine old Boston residential area. Each guest room is on a separate floor with private bath and glass doors opening onto a large patio, where you can breakfast in summer.

Among the interesting hosts are a former concert pianist who frequently plays for guests, and a world-renowned expert on scotch whisky. Some little extra touches given here and there are maps of the area, candy, fruit, and mints, late-afternoon wine and cheese, and an available washer and dryer.

BED & BREAKFAST—CAMBRIDGE AND GREATER BOSTON
73 KIRKLAND ST., CAMBRIDGE, MA 02138

Offers B&B Homes In: Cambridge, Boston, Cape Cod
Reservations Phone: 617/576-1492
Phone Hours: 9 a.m. to 6 p.m. Monday to Friday; on Saturday from 2 to 6 p.m.
Price Range of Homes: $39 to $66 single, $55 to $80 double (prospective guests must join this B&B's organization for a $6 fee)
Breakfast Included in Price: Full American (juice, eggs, toast, coffee)
Brochure Available: Free
Reservations Should Be Made: 3 weeks in advance (last-minute reservations accepted when possible)

Scenic Attractions Near the B&B Homes: Boston's Freedom Trail, Museum of Fine Arts, John F. Kennedy Library, Museum of Science, Fogg Museum, Gardner Museum, Longfellow Home, Boston Harbor, Boston Symphony and Boston Pops
Major Schools, Universities Near the B&B Homes: Harvard, M.I.T., Boston U., Tufts, Simmons

B&B Bonuses _____

A number of hosts will arrange to pick up guests at the railroad and bus stations and provide tours

CHRISTIAN HOSPITALITY

636 UNION ST., BLACK FRIAR BROOK FARM, DUXBURY, MA 02332

Offers B&B Homes In: The New England States, also in Florida
Reservations Phone: 617/834-8528
Phone Hours: 9 a.m. to 9 p.m. Monday to Saturday
Price Range of Homes: $25 to $50 single, $35 to $55 double
Breakfast Included in Price: Continental or full American
Brochure Available: Free if you send a stamped, self-addressed no.10 envelope
Reservations Should Be Made: 2 weeks in advance (can accept some last-minute reservations)

Scenic Attractions Near the B&B Homes: Historic homes of Boston, the Plymouth and Cape Cod areas, White Mountains and Green Mountains
Major Schools, Universities Near the B&B Homes: Boston College, Gordan College, Stonehill

B&B Bonuses _____

You can stay in one of the oldest B&B homes in the U.S., a 1708 home in Duxbury. Hosts can arrange to pick up guests at Logan Airport in Boston.

BED & BREAKFAST IN MINUTEMAN COUNTRY

8 LINMOOR TERRACE, LEXINGTON, MA 02173

Offers B&B Homes In: Lexington, Concord, Cambridge, Newton, and Brookline, in Massachusetts
Reservations Phone: 617/861-7063
Phone Hours: 9 a.m. to 5 p.m. Monday through Friday
Price Range of Homes: $35 and up single, $40 and up double
Breakfast Included in Price: Continental or full American—it varies according to each individual home
Brochure Available: Free
Reservations Should Be Made: 2 weeks in advance (last-minute reservations accepted if possible)

Scenic Attractions Near the B&B Homes: Historic Lexington-Concord area, homes of Emerson and Hawthorne, Walden Pond, Thoreau Lyceum, museums, beaches, canoeing on the Concord River
Major Schools, Universities Near the B&B Homes: Cambridge, Harvard, M.I.T., Boston U.

B&B Bonuses

Many homes are within easy drive of Harvard, M.I.T., Boston U., etc. Enjoy breakfast in the greenhouse of an 1884 Victorian home, or browse among the antiques and handcrafted articles in a colonial home enhanced by a woodland setting. "Our families are truly exceptional. Gracious, warm, and friendly, each has something special to offer. Many of our hosts are local history buffs, and welcome the opportunity to share their knowledge and enthusiasm with you."

HOST HOMES OF BOSTON

P.O. BOX 117, NEWTON, MA 02168

Offers B&B Homes In: Greater Boston area, primarily Newton and Brookline; also Cambridge, Somerville, Cape Cod, Marblehead, and other Massachusetts areas
Reservations Phone: 617/244-1308
Phone Hours: 8:30 a.m. to 5 p.m. Monday to Friday, to noon on Saturday (or an answering machine with same-day callback)
Price Range of Homes: $35 to $52 single, $45 to $62 double
Breakfast Included in Price: "Hearty" continental (may include home-baked muffins, scones or croissants, bran and yogurt, fresh fruit) or full American (depending on the host or day of the week)
Brochure Available: Free
Reservations Should Be Made: 2 weeks in advance (late reservations accepted if possible)

Scenic Attractions Near the B&B Homes: "All of the cultural, recreational and educational offerings of Boston." This includes the Fine Arts Museum, Museum of Science, Freedom Trail, Faneuil Hall and Quincy Market, Boston Symphony, Lexington and Concord, and Old Sturbridge Village.
Major Schools, Universities Near the B&B Homes: Boston College, Boston U., Harvard, Simmons, Brandeis, Tufts, M.I.T., Wellesley College, Pine Manor, Babson, Northeastern, New England Conservatory

B&B Bonuses

You may want to stay in a brownstone in Back Bay. Or choose a renovated colonial in Chestnut Hill's old estate area (great for guests with children). There's also a large airy lakeside stucco in Newton, a Victorian on a hill in Somerville, or a renovated colonial farmhouse with swimming pool in Framingham. One private home in historic Sandwich on Cape Cod is perfect for families with small children who need babysitters.

NEW ENGLAND BED & BREAKFAST, INC.
1045 CENTRE ST., NEWTON CENTRE, MA 02159

Offers B&B Homes In: Boston and other special places in New England
Reservations Phone: 617/498-9819 or 617/244-2112
Phone Hours: 10 a.m. to 10 p.m. daily (498-9819 is a 24-hour service)
Price Range of Homes: $30 to $45 single, $40 to $57 double
Breakfast Included in Price: Continental (juice, roll or toast, coffee)
Brochure Available: Free
Reservations Should Be Made: 2 weeks in advance (last-minute reservations accepted if possible)

Scenic Attractions Near the B&B Homes: All Boston attractions, sand and dunes of Cape Cod, mountains and streams of New Hampshire and Maine, rolling hills of Vermont, Freedom Trail, historic Concord and Lexington, theaters and museums
Major Schools, Universities Near the B&B Homes: Harvard, Boston College, Boston U., Berkeley School of Music, Lesley, Northeastern, La Salle, Bentley, Brandeis

B&B Bonuses

All host homes are located in safe, convenient neighborhoods near public transportation to the city. Friendly hosts provide extra care, such as inviting a couple and their 7-year-old son to Christmas brunch with 20 other private house guests last Christmas. Frequently hosts drive guests to the airport, bus stops, and hospitals.

PINEAPPLE HOSPITALITY, INC.

100 COTTAGE ST., NEW BEDFORD, MA 02740

Offers B&B Homes In: Massachusetts, Rhode Island, Connecticut, Maine, New Hampshire, Vermont
Reservations Phone: 617/990-1696
Phone Hours: 8 a.m. to 7 p.m. Monday to Friday 9 a.m. to noon, Saturdays
Price Range of Homes: $33 to $65 single, $45 to $95 double
Breakfast Included in Price: Continental
Brochure Available: "Directory of host homes and small inns for all New England" for sale at $4.50 (includes $2.50 rebate coupon for first night's booking)
Reservations Should Be Made: 2 weeks in advance (24-hour last minute surcharge)

Scenic Attractions Near the B&B Homes: Attractions throughout New England

ORLEANS BED & BREAKFAST ASSOCIATES

P.O. BOX 1312, ORLEANS, MA 02653

Offers B&B Homes In: Cape Cod, from the Harwiches to Truro
Reservations Phone: 617/255-3824
Phone Hours: 8 a.m. to 8 p.m. Monday to Friday (also accepts calls on weekends and holidays)
Price Range of Homes: $40 to $80 single, $40 to $80 double
Breakfast Included in Price: Expanded continental (juice and fruit in season, home-baked breads), some hosts are gourmet cooks and do large omelets, French toast, etc.
Brochure Available: For $1
Reservations Should Be Made: 3 weeks in advance (last-minute reservations accepted when possible)

Scenic Attractions Near the B&B Homes: Cape Cod National Seashore, beaches, museums, art galleries, antique and crafts fairs

AROUND PLYMOUTH BAY, INC. B&B

P.O. BOX 6211, PLYMOUTH, MA 02360

Offers B&B Homes In: Plymouth, Sandwich, Falmouth, Kingston, and other areas near Plymouth

Reservations Phone: 617/747-5075
Phone Hours: 8 a.m. to midnight Monday to Friday (also accepts calls on weekends and holidays)
Price Range of Homes: $40 to $50 single, $45 to $75 double
Breakfast Included in Price: Full American with such regional specialties as cranberry muffins
Brochure Available: Free
Reservations Should Be Made: 2 weeks in advance (last-minute reservations accepted when possible)

Scenic Attractions Near the B&B Homes: Plimoth Plantation, Plymouth Rock, many historical homes that are open to the public
Major Schools, Universities Near the B&B Homes: Massachusetts Maritime Academy, Bridgewater State College, Harvard, M.I.T.

B&B Bonuses

  Ask for the Place home, which is within walking distance of two of Plymouth's best beaches, where you'll stay in a huge bedroom, beautifully furnished. Some hosts will arrange to meet guests at the bus terminal, and provide sightseeing tours.

BE OUR GUEST, BED & BREAKFAST
P.O. BOX 1333, PLYMOUTH, MA 02360

Offers B&B Homes In: Plymouth and the neighboring towns of Hingham, Scituate, Kingston, Duxbury, Middleboro, Marshfield, and Canton
Reservations Phone: 617/837-9867
Phone Hours: 8:30 a.m. to 10:30 p.m. daily
Price Range of Homes: $32 to $45 single, $40 to $65 double
Breakfast Included in Price: "Continental breakfast is served, but most hosts serve a good healthy breakfast . . . pancakes and blueberries, zucchini bread (homemade vegetables from garden), and croissants are the favorites."
Brochure Available: Free
Reservations Should Be Made: 2 weeks in advance preferred, but will try to make reservations the same day as your arrival in town

Scenic Attractions Near the B&B Homes: Plimoth Plantation, the Mayflower ship, Plymouth Rock, Cranberry World, Commonwealth Winery, Edaville Railroad, Plymouth Wax Museum, historic homes, beaches, state parks, whale watching, deep-sea fishing, sailing
Major Schools, Universities Near the B&B Homes: Bridgewater State College, and all major Boston schools, colleges, and universities within 30 to 60 miles

B&B Bonuses

In a setting reminiscent of *On Golden Pond,* a house paneled in knotty cedar throughout, with a center chimney fireplace and cathedral ceiling, affords splendid views of the pond. If you prefer ocean views, you can stay at an elegantly decorated Dutch colonial, with decks off every room. From an invitation to dinner with the family to baby-sitting the children and letting them watch *Star Wars* on the home video, to fixing a guest's car that had broken down, hosts have gone beyond the call of duty many times.

BED & BREAKFAST CAPE COD

P.O. BOX 341, WEST HYANNISPORT, MA 02672

Offers B&B Homes In: Cape Cod
Reservations Phone: 617/775-2772
Phone Hours: 8:30 a.m. to 5 p.m. daily
Price Range of Homes: $32 to $50 single, $40 to $105 double
Breakfast Included in Price: Continental or full American . . . home-grown specialties such as native berry preserves and homemade bread and muffins are often served
Brochure Available: Free
Reservations Should Be Made: 2 or 3 weeks in advance (last-minute reservations accepted if possible)

Scenic Attractions Near the B&B Homes: Cruises to Martha's Vineyard and Nantucket, Heritage Plantation, Sandwich Glass Museum, Cape Cod National Seashore, Audubon Sanctuary, Cape Playhouse, Melody Tent, Falmouth Playhouse, golf courses, deep-sea fishing, lake trout fishing, sandy beaches
Major Schools, Universities Near the B&B Homes: Woods Hole Oceanographic Institute, Cape Cod Community College, Cape Cod Conservatory of Music and Art, Boston universities and colleges (1½-hour drive)

B&B Bonuses

Like to stay in a 200-year old country inn, completely restored, in Barnstable? Hyannisport offers a 100-year-old farmhouse restoration overlooking a freshwater pond. Walk to Hyannisport sites, Hyannis, and the Melody Tent. A Chatham carriage house overlooks a freshwater pond with an ocean view as a backdrop; A nationally known artist is your hostess. In Sandwich Village you could stay in an old sea captain's house.

BED & BREAKFAST FOLKS

73 PROVIDENCE RD., WESTFORD, MA 01886

Offers B&B Homes In: Boston, Concord, Lexington
Reservations Phone: 617/692-3232
Phone Hours: 8 a.m. to 10 p.m. Monday to Friday; also on weekends and holidays
Price Range of Homes: $40 to $60 single, $45 to $65 double
Breakfast Included in Price: Full American . . . specialties are apple pie and fresh-tapped maple syrup
Brochure Available: Free
Reservations Should Be Made: 2 weeks in advance (also attempts to accept last-minute reservations)

Scenic Attractions Near the B&B Homes: Concord, Lexington, Walden Pond, ski areas

B&B Bonuses

Monthly discounts are available to corporations, and guest memberships (one time) to a health club.

BERKSHIRE BED & BREAKFAST HOMES

P.O. BOX 211, WILLIAMSBURG, MA 01096

Offers B&B Homes In: Sturbridge area; Pioneer Valley (Springfield, Northampton, Amherst); also in Berkshire Country, eastern New York, southern Vermont, southern New Hampshire
Reservations Phone: 413/268-7244
Phone Hours: 9 a.m. to 7 p.m. Monday to Friday, on Saturday to 1 p.m.
Price Range of Homes: $30 to $55 single, $35 to $85 double
Breakfast Included in Price: Continental or full American   some hosts will also prepare gourmet dinners
Brochure Available: Free; directory of hosts also available for $3
Reservations Should Be Made: 2 weeks in advance; at least one month in advance for choice housing during the Tanglewood concert season

Scenic Attractions Near the B&B Homes: Basketball Hall of Fame, Sturbridge Village, Deerfield Village, Tanglewood, Jacob's Pillow, Mohawk Trail, downhill and cross-country ski trails
Major Schools, Universities Near the B&B Homes: Williams Col-

lege, U Massachusetts, Amherst, Smith, Mount Holyoke, Hampshire, Western New England, North Adams State

B&B Bonuses

Ask for the 1780 fully restored colonial that is on the Historical Register, furnished in American and English antiques.

HAMPSHIRE HILLS BED & BREAKFAST ASSOCIATION

P.O. BOX 307, WILLIAMSBURG, MA 01906

Offers B&B Homes In: The hills of western Massachusetts
Reservations Phone: 413/634-5529
Phone Hours: After 6 p.m.; each home must be phoned directly; obtain numbers from the brochure or call the above number.
Price Range of Homes: $25 to $30 single, $35 to $50 double
Breakfast Included in Price: Continental or full American, which can include such regional specialties as maple syrup, farm-fresh eggs, and homemade blueberry muffins
Brochure Available: Free if you send a stamped, self-addressed no. 10 envelope
Reservations Should Be Made: 2 weeks in advance (last-minute reservations accepted if possible)

Scenic Attractions Near the B&B Homes: William Cullen Bryant Homestead, Historic Deerfield, DAR State Park, Chesterfield Gorge, Jacob's Pillow Dance Festival, Tanglewood Music Center, Williamstown Theater, Sterling Clark Museum, cross-country and downhill skiing, hiking trails, cycling, canoeing, tennis, golf
Major Schools, Universities Near the B&B Homes: Smith, Amherst, Hampshire, Mount Holyoke, U. Massachusetts, Deerfield Academy, Eaglebrook Prep

B&B Bonuses

Ask for the number of the 200-year-old farmhouse where you can stroll to a general store and eat a full American breakfast in a country kitchen by a wood stove. The local "alarm clock" may be the "baa" of sheep or the chimes of an antique Seth Thomas clock. Hosts can assist with directions to points of interest and give dining recommendations.

B&B Inns

BAY BREEZE GUEST HOUSE
P.O. BOX 307, BEDFORD, MA 02553

Reservations Phone: 627/275-7551
Description: Located on Cape Cod Bay at Monument Beach, Bay Breeze has several comfortable rooms that overlook the beach.

Nearby Attractions: Shawmet National Park, Sandwich Glass Museum, Heritage Plantation
Special Service: Boat rides on the Cape Cod Canal, deep-sea fishing
Rates: $25 single, $30 to $35 double, in summer

DEERFIELD INN
THE STREET, DEERFIELD, MA 01342

Reservations Phone: 413/774-5587
Description: Located in the center of Historic Deerfield on The Street with 12 beautifully restored museum homes; the inn has 23 guest rooms with period furnishing, private baths, and air conditioning.

Nearby Attractions: Historic Deerfield with extensive collections of paintings, prints, furniture, silver, ceramics, textiles, and other decorative arts
Special Services: Private function rooms; bakery and restaurant on premises
Rates: $75 to $80 double

BREAD & ROSES
RTE. 71, NORTH EGREMONT, MA 01230

Reservations Phone: 413/528-1099
Description: Bread & Roses is a renovated 1800s farmhouse with a wrap-around porch. The guest rooms are a later addition and all have private baths.
Amenities: Full breakfast with Grand Marnier French toast

Nearby Attractions: Tanglewood, The Mount, Jacob's Pillow, Berkshire Theater, tennis, golf, swimming
Special Services: Concierge
Rates: $85 double

SHIPS KNEES INN
BEACH ROAD, EAST ORLEANS, MA 02643

Reservations Phone: 617/255-1312
Description: Built over 150 years ago, the inn is a restored sea captain's house that gives you old-style New England lodging surrounded by the charm of yesterday while offering the convenience of today. Many of the guest rooms have beamed ceilings, quilts, and four-poster beds. Several rooms have an ocean view and the master suite has a working fireplace.
Amenities: Continental breakfast

Nearby Attractions: Nauset Beach, Cape Cod National Seashore
Special Services: Swimming pool, tennis
Rates: $36 to $75 double

THE EDGARTOWN INN
56 N. WATER ST., EDGARTOWN, MA 02539

Reservations Phone: 617/627-4794
Description: Originally constructed in 1798 as a home for sea captain Thomas Worth, the inn has been host to Daniel Webster, Nathaniel Hawthorne, and later John F. Kennedy. The inn has seen a number of improvements, such as tile baths, comfortable beds, and maid service; otherwise it has remained largely the same. Altogether there are 12 rooms for guests, some with private bath.
Amenities: Full old-fashioned breakfast

Nearby Attractions: Gay Head, Chappaquiddick, Oak Bluffs, The Tabernacle, Vineyard Haven
Special Services: Patio garden for use of guests
Rates: $65 to $110 double in summer, $28 to $65 double in winter

SEA BREEZE
397 SEA ST., HYANNIS, MA 02601

Reservations Phone: 617/771-7213
Description: A group of Cape Cod–style buildings with weathered shingles, Sea Breeze has some rooms with an ocean view.
Amenities: Juice, cereal, fruit, bagels, muffins, toast, danish or doughnuts, coffee

Nearby Attractions: John F. Kennedy Memorial, boats for Martha's Vineyard or Nantucket, sightseeing boat around the harbor and the Kennedy Compound, three minutes walk to the beach
Rates: $49 to $69 double in summer, $25 to $40 double in winter

---

CANDLELIGHT INN
53 WALKER ST., LENOX, MA 01240

Reservations Phone: 413/637-1555
Description: In the heart of historic Lenox Village, the inn has a turn-of-the-century elegance and is lit by candles and fireplaces.

Nearby Attractions: Tanglewood, Norman Rockwell Museum, Jacob's Pillow, Berkshire Playhouse, skiing, tennis, golf, swimming, boating
Special Services: Weekend entertainment in the piano bar
Rates: $75 to $100 double in summer and fall, $50 to $95 in winter and spring

---

WHISTLER'S INN
5 GREENWOOD ST., LENOX, MA 01240

Reservations Phone: 413/637-0975
Description: This is a French/English Tudor mansion built in 1820 in the heart of the Berkshires overlooking seven acres of gardens and woodlands. Central to the inn is its cozy library and elegant music room.
Amenities: A continental breakfast featuring home-baked blueberry muffins, served on the sun porch and terrace

Nearby Attractions: Miles of riding, hiking, and cross-country ski trails; Tanglewood, Norman Rockwell Museum, Chesterwood,

many historical houses, Jacob's Pillow Dance Festival, a variety of sporting activities
Special Services: Sherry is served on arrival.
Rates: $55 to $150 double in summer, $40 to $120 double in winter

UNDERLEDGE INN

76 CLIFFORD ST., LENOX, MA 01240

Reservations Phone: 413/637-0236
Description: This Victorian mansion has been completely restored and now has 19 rooms, many with fireplaces, and both private and shared baths.
Amenities: Continental breakfast

Nearby Attractions: Tanglewood, Jacob's Pillow, Norman Rockwell Museum, Berkshire Theater
Special Services: Solarium
Rates: $40 to $125 double in summer, $40 to $110 double in winter

THE QUAKER HOUSE INN AND RESTAURANT

5 CHESTNUT ST., NANTUCKET, MA 02554

Reservations Phone: 617/228-0400
Description: This 1847 Quaker-style inn is located in the heart of Nantucket Island's historic district. Each of its seven guest rooms is appointed with antiques and period furnishings.

Nearby Attractions: Nantucket Whaling Museum, dozens of historic homes open for tours, art galleries, sandy beaches, sailing, golf, tennis
Rates: $60 double in summer, $45 double in spring

THE WOODBOX

29 FAIR ST., NANTUCKET, MA 02554

Reservations Phone: 617/228-0587
Description: This is Nantucket's oldest inn, built in 1709. It has period antiques, plus three doubles and six suites, some with working fireplaces. The inn is 1½ blocks from the center of town.

Nearby Attractions: Historic houses, excellent beaches, fishing, swimming
Rates: $95 to $140 double in summer

COLONIAL HOUSE INN
207 SANDWICH ST., PLYMOUTH, MA 02360

Reservations Phone: 617/746-2087
Description: The inn is located between Plymouth Rock and Plimoth Plantation. All accommodations are in early American decor with private bath, TV, and air conditioning.

Nearby Attractions: Plymouth Rock, Plimoth Plantation
Special Services: Swimming pool
Rates: $60 single, $70 double, in summer; $50 single, $55 to $60 double, in winter

---

NEW HAMPSHIRE

B&B Reservation Services

NEW HAMPSHIRE BED & BREAKFAST
R.F.D. 2, BOX 53, LACONIA, NH 03246

Offers B&B Homes In: 40 communities through New Hampshire
Reservations Phone: 603/279-8348
Phone Hours: 10 a.m. to 5 p.m. Monday to Friday
Price Range of Homes: $25 to $45 single, $35 to $65 double
Breakfast Included in Price: Most homes serve full American breakfasts, including organically grown foods, real maple sugar, homemade cheese, and even pies and ice cream! Others serve a continental breakfast.
Brochure Available: For $1
Reservations Should Be Made: 2 weeks in advance (last-minute reservations accepted if possible)

Scenic Attractions Near the B&B Homes: Lake Winnipesaukee, Lake Sunapee, White Mountains, Merrimack Valley, ski areas, arts and crafts shows, historic sites and museums

Major Schools, Universities Near the B&B Homes: Dartmouth, Plymouth State, Colby-Sawyer, Keene State, Tilton Academy, New Hampton School. Holderness, Brewster Academy, St. Paul's and Concord Schools

B&B Bonuses

Each of the homes offers something special, such as a copper bathtub, farm animals, maple sugaring, lakefront and mountain views, tennis courts, swimming pools, private beaches, museum tours, cross-country skiing, or antiques. Some past surprises for B&B guests have included a tour of the lake by boat, picnics, cookouts, special dinners, complimentary cocktail—and, yes, breakfast in bed.

B&B Inns

BREEZY POINT INN & MOTEL

R.F.D. 1, BOX 302, ANTRIM, NH 03440

Reservations Phone: 603/478-5201
Description: Located on a peninsula at Franklin Pierce Lake, the inn started its life as a stagecoach stop for tired travelers. Nowadays besides the comfortably furnished rooms there are both cabins and cottages which are rented by the day or week.
Amenities: Complete breakfast each morning

Nearby Attractions: The home of President Franklin Pierce, Hawthorne College, Steam Town featuring locomotive rides
Special Services: Outdoor cooking facilities and picnic tables
Rates: $30 single, $35 double

THE BRADFORD INN

MAIN STREET (P.O. BOX 40), BRADFORD, NH 03221

Reservations Phone: 603/938-5309
Description: This Federal-style building was opened in 1898 as a hotel. It contains individually decorated rooms, a spacious parlor, a grand staircase, and wide halls.

Amenities: Continental breakfast

Nearby Attractions: Lake Sunapee; Sunapee, Winslow, and Rollins State Parks; Franklin Pierce's home; boat cruises
Special Services: Bus pickup in town, sailing and skating nearby
Rates: $46 to $53.50 double

MOUNTAIN LAKE INN
RTE. 114, BRADFORD, NH 03221

Reservations Phone: 603/938-2136
Description: Built by Bradford's first settler about 15 years before the American Revolution, the inn has country casual furnishings with true period antiques. It's located on 167 acres with trout streams, waterfalls, and a quarter mile of beachfront on Lake Massasecum.
Amenities: Juice, eggs any style, omelet of the day, bacon or country sausage, home-fries, coffee, tea, or milk

Nearby Attractions: 8 miles of Lake Sunapee for seaplane rides, scuba-diving, boat and dinner cruises; three national parks; golf, tennis, racquetball, horseback riding
Special Services: Private beach, cookout areas, swimming, bicycles for guests
Rates: $58.50 double

THE PASQUANEY INN
RTE. 3A, BRIDGEWATER, NH 03222

Reservations Phone: 603/744-2712
Description: This turn-of-the-century country inn on the edge of Newfound Lake has a long front porch facing the lake. Single and double rooms with shared or private bath are available.
Amenities: Full breakfast with specialties that might include funnel cakes or eggs St-Denis

Nearby Attractions: In the center of the state within range of most outdoor attractions
Special Services: Recreational barn, boats, bikes, sandy beach
Rates: $68 double

FRANCONIA INN

RTE. 116, EASTON ROAD, FRANCONIA, NH 03580

Reservations Phone: 603/823-5542
Description: This resort offers quiet country life with mountain views from the Easton Valley. The 29 rooms have been recently redecorated and renovated.

Nearby Attractions: Mount Washington, Cannon Mountain Tramway, Tite Flume, the Old Man of the Mountains, White Mountain National Forest, ski areas, gliding, skiing, sleigh rides, ice skating, golf, biking
Special Services: Pool, hot tub
Rates: $60 to $70 double in summer and fall, $50 to $60 double in spring

---

EDENCROFT MANOR COUNTRY INN

R.F.D. 1, RTE. 135, LITTLETON, NH 03561

Reservations Phone: 603/444-6776
Description: Overlooking the White Mountains, the inn was built in the 1890s and is furnished with antiques and handmade quilts.

Nearby Attractions: White Mountain National Forest, Santa's Village, the ski areas of Cannon, Burke, Franconia, and Bretton Woods
Special Services: Snowmobiles, cross-country skiing
Rates: $35 to $55 double

HIDE AWAY LODGE

TWIN LAKE VILLA ROAD (P.O. BOX 6), NEW LONDON, NH 03257

Reservations Phone: 603/526-4861
Description: This turn-of-the-century inn surrounded by a state forest and brook has well-appointed bedrooms for 24 guests. The spacious living room has a stone fireplace. There is a screened terrace and sunny porches to sit on.

Nearby Attractions: Historic New London, the New London Barn Playhouse, Dartmouth College

Special Services: Airport pickup in Lebanon, tennis, private beach, skiing, golf
Rates: $48 double

SUNNY SIDE INN
SEAVY STREET, NORTH CONWAY, NH 03860

Reservations Phone: 603/356-6234
Description: This converted and expanded 1850s New England farmhouse has casual and comfortable rooms with private or shared bath.
Amenities: Full breakfast

Nearby Attractions: White Mountains, four major downhill ski areas, three golf courses, museums
Special Services: Bus depot pickups
Rates: $20 to $50 single, $30 to $55 double

LAKE SHORE FARM
31 JENNESS POND RD., NORTHWOOD, NH 03261

Reservations Phone: 603/942-5521
Description: A family farmhouse expanded to accommodate guests, it has been under the same family management for 60 years.
Amenities: Full breakfast

Nearby Attractions: Shaker Village, Strawberry Banke Capitol Complex, a variety of outdoor sports
Special Services: Game room, tennis, volleyball, Ping-Pong, badminton, horseshoes
Rates: $41 double in summer, $36 double the rest of the year

THE CAMPTON INN
RTE. 175N, CAMPTON, NH 03223

Reservations Phone: 603/726-4449
Description: An 1855 New England farmhouse, the inn is at the foot of the White Mountains. All rooms are individually decorated with antiques.

Amenities: Breakfast includes homemade muffins, breakfast breads and cakes, eggs, bacon, French toast, and pure maple syrup

Nearby Attractions: White Mountain National Forest, Polar Caves, The Flume, Old Man of the Mountains, Lost River, Squam Lake (filming site of *On Golden Pond*)
Special Services: Guest refrigerator, bus pickup, laundry service
Rates: $20 to $35 single, $30 to $50 double, May through October; $20 to $30 single, $30 to $45 double, in April and May

STAFFORDS-IN-THE-FIELD
P.O. BOX 270, CHOCORUA, NH 03817

Reservations Phone: 603/323-7766
Description: This 1778 inn in a secluded setting is in the English country-house style. Many antiques are used throughout, and there is a herb garden and a large collection of apple peelers.
Amenities: Full country breakfast and gourmet dinner included in rates

Nearby Attractions: The Old Man of the Mountains, Santa's Village, boating, golf, skiing, and mountain climbing
Rates: $80 to $130 double in winter, $70 to $120 double in summer

THE INN AT CROTCHED MOUNTAIN
MOUNTAIN ROAD, FRANCESTOWN, NH 03043

Reservations Phone: 603/588-6840
Description: This 14-room country inn is located at the side of Crotched Mountain. Some of the rooms have fireplaces.

Nearby Attractions: Greenfield State Park, Monadnock State Park, a variety of sports year round
Special Services: Swimming pool, two clay tennis courts
Rates: $40 to $60 double on weekdays, $50 to $70 on weekends

B&B Reservation Services

BED & BREAKFAST U.S.A. LTD.
P.O. BOX 606, CROTON-ON-HUDSON, NY 10520

Offers B&B Homes In: All over New York State
Reservations Phone: 914/271-6228
Phone Hours: 10 a.m. to 4 p.m. Monday to Friday
Price Range of Homes: $20 to $60 single daily, $30 to $135 double daily; $140 to $200 single weekly, $280 double weekly
Breakfast Included in Price: Full American (juice, eggs, bacon, toast, coffee)
Brochure Available: Fee is $2.50 if you send a self-addressed no. 10 envelope with 37¢ stamp.
Reservations Should Be Made: 2 weeks in advance (last-minute reservations accepted if possible)

Scenic Attractions Near the B&B Homes: Sleepy Hollow Restorations, Lyndhurst Castle, Rye Playland, Caramoor Music Festival, Murcoot Park, Boscobel and Hyde Park mansions, Croton Clearwater Revival, Cold Spring antiquing, Baseball Hall of Fame, Howe Caverns, Corning Glass, Saratoga, Vanderbilt Mansion, ice caves, plus the attractions of New York City
Major Schools, Universities Near the B&B Homes: Sarah Lawrence, Iona, Manhattanville, Pace, Vassar, Westchester Community College, SUNY New Paltz, Ithaca College, Cornell U., Hamilton, Colgate, Skidmore, Russell Sage, Rensselaer Polytechnic Institute, Elmira College, Columbia U.

B&B Bonuses

You wouldn't expect to find a 15-room Norman castle within walking distance of shopping and trains, but they have one in New Rochelle. A 200-year-old farmhouse on eight acres boasts a swimming pool, and there is even a 52-foot sailing yacht.

Many hosts enjoy driving into New York City with guests, for a Broadway show or other big-city activities. Interpreters and babysitters are often provided. (This agency charges a $15 booking fee for nonmembers; members pay $25 yearly, and no fee to book.)

HAMPTON BED & BREAKFAST
P.O. BOX 378, EAST MORICHES, NY 11940

Offers B&B Homes In: Eastern part and rural areas of Long Island
Reservations Phone: 516/878-8197
Phone Hours: 10 a.m. to 10 p.m. Monday to Friday (accepts weekend calls)
Price Range of Homes: $40 to $60 single, $60 to $120 double
Breakfast Included in Price: Continental breakfast (juice, roll or toast, coffee); also such regional specialties as homemade blueberry and raspberry muffins
Brochure Available: Free
Reservations Should Be Made: 2 weeks in advance (last-minute reservations accepted if possible)

Scenic Attractions Near the B&B Homes: Historic area with famous Hamptons nightlife, beaches, and golf
Major Schools, Universities Near the B&B Homes: Southampton College

B&B Bonuses
   Some hosts will arrange to pick up guests at the train station. Others have local restaurant information available.

BED & BREAKFAST ROCHESTER
P.O. BOX 444, FAIRPORT, NY 14450

Offers B&B Homes In: Around the Rochester area, and down into the Finger Lakes of New York State
Reservations Phone: 716/223-8510 or 716/223-8877
Phone Hours: 9 a.m. to 9 p.m. or "Any time within reason"
Price Range of Homes: $30 to $40 single, $35 to $55 double
Breakfast Included in Price: Continental, which may include apple muffins, apple oatmeal, German coffee cake, and other specialties
Brochure Available: Free if you send a stamped, self-addressed no. 10 envelope
Reservations Should Be Made: 2 or 3 weeks in advance (last-minute reservations accepted if possible)

Scenic Attractions Near the B&B Homes: Eastman House of Photography, Strong Toy Museum, Genesee Country Museum, Letchworth Park, Sonnenberg Gardens, Lake Ontario, wineries, fishing derbies, scenic Finger Lakes region
Major Schools, Universities Near the B&B Homes: U. of Rochester,

Brockport, Geneseo, St. John Fisher, Rochester Institute of Technology, Nazareth

B&B Bonuses

In a summer cottage on the beach at Keuka Lake, a college professor and his artist wife completed the remodeling of an old grape barn from the early 1800s. Some of the levels feature built-in double-decker beds and a treehouse with screened tent. This is available in July and August only.

Hosts will often pick up at the airport, and drive guests around town.

"This is a great area for auctions, antique shops, and garage sales!"

BED & BREAKFAST LEATHERSTOCKING RESERVATIONS

389 BROADWAY RD., FRANKFORT, NY 13340

Offers B&B Homes In: Eleven-county area of centrral New York, including Utica, Cooperstown, Clinton, and along the Mohawk River Valley
Reservations Phone: 315/733-0040
Phone Hours: 7 a.m. to 9 p.m. daily
Price Range of Homes: $20 to $45 single, $30 to $55 double
Breakfast Included in Price: Full American, with such special treats as blueberry pancakes, rhubarb, zucchini bread
Brochure Available: Free; directory also available for $2
Reservations Should Be Made: 2 weeks in advance (last-minute reservations accepted when possible)

Scenic Attractions Near the B&B Homes: Adirondack Park area, Fort Stanwick, Howe Cavern, Farmers Museum, Baseball Hall of Fame, Utica Brewery
Major Schools, Universities Near the B&B Homes: Colgate, Hamilton, Utica College, Herkimer, Fulton, Cobleskill, St. Elizabeth School of Nursing, SUNY at Marcy, Utica School of Commerce

B&B Bonuses

Want a special experience in a house from the 1880s? Ask for the Jonathan House. This Victorian mansion has solid cherry paneling, crystal chandeliers, and Oriental rugs. You can sleep in a canopied bed. Your hosts are a fascinating couple who are interested in the arts, education, the law, and collecting. The home is located in the Mohawk Valley near Cooperstown.

THE B&B GROUP (NEW YORKERS AT HOME, INC.)

301 60TH ST., NEW YORK, NY 10022

Offers B&B Homes In: Manhattan, and a few from May to December in the Hamptons (Long Island), and Acapulco, Mexico (January to April)
Reservations Phone: 212/838-7015
Phone Hours: 9 a.m. to 4 p.m. Monday to Thursday (not on Friday, Saturday, Sunday, or holidays)
Price Range of Homes: $45 to $65 single, $65 to $75 double ($75 to $200 for apartments)
Breakfast Included in Price: Continental (juice, roll or toast, coffee) in host homes only, not in the apartments
Brochure Available: Free if you send a stamped, self-addressed no. 10 envelope
Reservations Should Be Made: 1 to 2 weeks in advance (no last-minute reservations)

Scenic Attractions Near the B&B Homes: Lincoln Center, United Nations, Theater District, Soho, Greenwich Village, Central Park, Museum Row, New York Academy of Sciences, Cooper-Hewitt Mansion, World Trade Center, Wall Street, South Ferry, South Street Seaport
Major Schools, Universities Near the B&B Homes: NYU, Columbia U., Hunter, Fordham U., Baruch, John Jay

B&B Bonuses

This B&B is very popular with London visitors, having been written up in many of the London papers. It offers convenience to all the excitement of the "Big Apple" to people from all over the U.S. and Canada as well. Apartments are on the prestigious East Side of Manhattan, Greenwich Village, and the up-and-coming West Side, and for those who prefer the summer waterfront, there are some host homes in the Hamptons.

Some hosts take time to show their guests around, and most provide maps and directions to special stores and restaurants in New York City and points of interest in their own areas.

BED & BREAKFAST IN THE BIG APPLE (URBAN VENTURES, INC.)

P.O. BOX 426, NEW YORK, NY 10024

Offers B&B Homes In: New York City (over 500 accommodations)

Reservations Phone: 212/594-5650
Phone Hours: 9 a.m. to 5 p.m. Monday to Friday, on Saturday to 3 p.m.
Price Range of Homes: $30 to $60 single, $45 to $85 double
Breakfast Included in Price: Continental (juice, roll or toast, coffee)
Brochure Available: Free
Reservations Should Be Made: 2 weeks in advance (last-minute reservations accepted if possible)

Scenic Attractions Near the B&B Homes: Broadway theaters, Central Park, skyscrapers, famous restaurants, and all the many other "Big Apple" attractions
Major Schools, Universities Near the B&B Homes: Columbia U., NYU, Pace

B&B Bonuses

From a penthouse apartment in Greenwich Village to a duplex on exclusive Park Avenue, you can live like a real New Yorker. Friendly hosts have provided such personal services as lending guests umbrellas and clothing appropriate for the season.

CITY LIGHTS BED & BREAKFAST, LTD.
P.O. BOX 20355, NEW YORK, NY 10028

Offers B&B Homes In: Manhattan, Brooklyn (Brooklyn Heights, Park Slope)
Reservations Phone: 212/877-3236
Phone Hours: 9 a.m. to 5 p.m. Monday to Friday, on Saturday to noon (answering machine always on)
Price Range of Homes: $30 to $60 single $35 to $75 double
Breakfast Included in Price: Continental with some specials such as croissants, muffins, bagels with cream cheese, cereals, preserves, fruits in season, assorted cheeses on occasion
Brochure Available: Free
Reservations Should Be Made: 2 weeks in advance (last-minute reservations accepted when possible)

Scenic Attractions Near the B&B Homes: New York City and all its attractions, including museums, theaters, parks, restaurants, shopping
Major Schools, Universities Near the B&B Homes: Columbia U., NYU, Fordham, City U., Hunter, Marymount, Yeshiva

B&B Bonuses _____

Some hosts will arrange to purchase theater tickets before you arrive, and can take you on sightseeing tours of the city. Some may also take you to restaurants in different ethnic neighborhoods.

NEW WORLD BED & BREAKFAST LTD.

150 FIFTH AVE., SUITE 711, NEW YORK, NY 10011

Offers B&B Homes In: Manhattan, New York City
Reservations Phone: 212/675-5600 or toll free 800/443-3800
Phone Hours: 9:30 a.m. to 5 p.m. daily; 24-hour answering service
Price Range of Homes: $40 single, $50 to $80 double
Breakfast Included in Price: Continental (juice, roll or toast, coffee)
Brochure Available: Free
Reservations Should Be Made: 2 weeks in advance (last-minute reservations accepted if possible)

Scenic Attractions Near the B&B Homes: All of New York City's attractions—theaters, museums, business districts, Statue of Liberty, etc.
Major Schools, Universities Near the B&B Homes: NYU, Columbia, City College, The New School

B&B Bonuses _____

You can choose from East Side luxury apartments, Greenwich Village "pads," a brownstone duplex, accommodations on an island in the East River, a Soho loft, and apartments overlooking the Hudson and East Rivers. The host roster includes writers, artists, architects, actors, linguists, business people, journalists, etc.

"We specialize in finding clean, safe, and friendly places for single women travelers as well as for travelers attending conventions and trade fairs."

RAINBOW HOSPITALITY

9348 HENNEPEN AVE., NIAGARA FALLS, NY 14304

Offers B&B Homes In: Niagara Falls, Lewistown, Youngstown, Wilson east to Rochester, Buffalo suburbs south to Pennsylvania
Reservations Phone: 716/754-8877 or 716/283-4794
Phone Hours: 9 a.m. to 6 p.m. weekdays, on Saturday to 12:30 p.m.
Price Range of Homes: $20 to $30 single, $30 to $55 double

Breakfast Included in Price: Continental or full American, according to the individual home

Brochure Available: Free if you send a stamped, self-addressed no. 10 envelope

Reservations Should Be Made: 2 weeks in advance (last-minute reservations accepted if possible)

Scenic Attractions Near the B&B Homes: Niagara Falls, Lewistown Art Park, Fatima Shrine, Fort Niagara, Kleinhans Music Hall (Buffalo), four large amusement complexes, lakes, rivers, convention centers, antique and outlet shopping, museums and art galleries, winter sports

Major Schools, Universities Near the B&B Homes: Niagara U., SUNY at Buffalo, Buffalo State, Canisius

B&B Bonuses

Experience the atmosphere of an elegant old Victorian-style home with gables and wrap-around verandas, overlooking the Niagara River toward Canada. The host family can direct guests to nearby cultural or recreational activities of all kinds. "Our hosts are people who have a genuine desire to share their hospitality, rather than simply renting a room." Some "extras" are transportation, sightseeing, babysitting, laundry, sailboat charter, and hosts and hostesses who speak several languages.

BED & BREAKFAST OF LONG ISLAND

P.O. BOX 392, OLD WESTBURY, NY 11568

Offers B&B Homes In: Eastern Long Island Hamptons Beach area, Amagansett, Montauk, Southampton, East Quogue, Garden City, Glen Cove, Seaford, Valley Stream, Syosset, Peconic, Southold, Mattituck, Massapequa

Reservations Phone: 516/334-6231 or 516/334-8499

Phone Hours: 9:30 a.m. to 4 p.m. Monday to Saturday, and some holidays

Price Range of Homes: $40 to $65 single, $50 to $125 double

Breakfast Included in Price: Continental or full American, plus regional specialties like homemade beach plum jam and blueberry muffins, waffles, buttery croissants

Brochure Available: Free if you send a stamped, self-addressed no. 10 envelope

Reservations Should Be Made: 2 weeks in advance (last-minute reservations accepted if possible)

Scenic Attractions Near the B&B Homes: Sag Harbor Customs

House, Whaling Museum, John Drew Theater, Guild Hall Art
Exhibits, Home Sweet Home Museum, Parrish Museum, Shinnecock
Indian Reservation, Halsey Homestead, Montauk Hither Hills State
Park, sport fishing, Watermill Old Mill Museum & Windmill
Major Schools, Universities Near the B&B Homes: Hofstra, Adelphi,
SUNY at Stony Brook, Southampton College, Bowling College,
C. W. Post, Kings Point Marine Academy

B&B Bonuses

A historic 1882 landmark house, designed by famous architect
Stanford White, is filled with old-world craftsmanship like leaded-
glass windows and wood paneling. A floor-to-ceiling fireplace sets
another home apart. A cottage on the bay with its own beach,
pool, and Jacuzzi, offers breakfast in the dining room overlooking
the water.

Guests have enjoyed treats like hot cider, wine, homemade clam
chowder, and coloring books with crayons for the children.

A REASONABLE ALTERNATIVE, INC.
117 SPRING ST., ROOM 6, PORT JEFFERSON, NY 11777

Offers B&B Homes In: Nassau and Suffolk Counties, from Great
Neck to Greenport, from Hempstead to the Hamptons
Reservations Phone: 516/928-4034
Price Range of Homes: $20 and up single, double price depends
on season, area, and amenities.
Breakfast Included in Price: Continental (juice, roll or toast, coffee);
occasional extras and regional specialties provided in some homes
Brochure Available: Free if you send a stamped, self-addressed no.
10 envelope
Reservations Should Be Made: 2 weeks in advance (last-minute
reservations accepted if possible)

Scenic Attractions Near the B&B Homes: Bethpage Recreation
Village, Hargreaves Vineyards, Sag Harbor Whaling Museum, Sag
Harbor Museum and Custom House, game farm and zoo, Fire
Island National Seashore, Montauk Lighthouse, Jones Beach,
Westbury Music Fair, Stony Brook museum complex, Sagamore
Hill, Vanderbilt Planetarium, Sunken Meadow State Park
Major Schools, Universities Near the B&B Homes: Hofstra, Adelphi,
C. W. Post, SUNY at Stony Brook

AMERICAN COUNTRY COLLECTION OF BED & BREAKFAST HOMES AND COUNTRY INNS

984 GLOUCESTER PL. SCHENECTADY, NY 12309

Offers B&B Homes In: Northeastern New York, Vermont, and western Massachusetts
Reservations Phone: 518/370-4948
Phone Hours: 10 a.m. to noon and 1 to 6 p.m. Tuesday to Friday (answering machine always on)
Price Range of Homes: $20 to $80 single, $25 to $90 double (rates in and around Saratoga, N.Y., increase approximately 50% in August, the racing season)
Breakfast Included in Price: Breakfasts range from homemade continental to traditional American. There are also elegant four-course gourmet breakfasts. Many Vermont and New York country breakfasts include maple syrup tapped right on the farm. Special treats include waffled French toast, hot fruit soufflé, and blueberry walnut pancakes.
Brochure Available: Free if you send a stamped, self-addressed no. 10 envelope
Reservations Should Be Made: 3 weeks in advance (over a month in advance during the peak travel seasons)

Scenic Attractions Near the B&B Homes: Several in the Saratoga area, near the Saratoga Race Course, Empire State Plaza in Albany, Baseball Hall of Fame in Cooperstown, Bennington Museum and Battlefield, Hyde Park and the Roosevelt Estate, Shaker Museum, Catskill Game Farm, Tanglewood and Lenox, Massachusetts
Major Schools, Universities Near the B&B Homes: Skidmore, SUNY at Albany and SUNY at Cobleskill, Williams, Smith, Bennington, Middlebury, U. of Vermont, Union College

B&B Bonuses

Ask for the bed-and-breakfast inn in New Marlborough, Massachusetts. It dates back to 1791 and once served as a coach and carriage stop. The dining room, library, and living room all have fireplaces. Mention that you would like a fireplace in your room (one of the four rooms has a nice one). Plush terry robes are provided for guests.

Or stay in the former home of *New York Times* theater critic Brooks Atkinson in Durham, New York. There are pictures and memorabilia of Mr. Atkinson's theater days. The home is now a working dairy farm.

B&B Inns

THE HEDGES
BLUE MOUNTAIN LAKE, NY 12812

Reservations Phone: 518/352-7325
Description: In a historic Adirondack camp with unique architecture, the inn's rooms are furnished with antiques. There are 15 separate cottages set on secluded Blue Mountain Lake.
Amenities: Full breakfast cooked to order

Nearby Attractions: The Adirondack Museum, Adirondack State Park with miles of hiking trails
Special Services: Clay tennis courts, canoes and rowboats, swimming
Rates: $100 to $116 double July to September; in June and October deduct 10%.

THOUSAND ISLANDS INN
335 RIVERSIDE DR., CLAYTON, NY 13634

Reservations Phone: 315/686-3030
Description: Serving the public since 1897, the inn's seven sleeping rooms were remodeled in 1980 with private bath and cable color TV. Most rooms have a view of the St. Lawrence River, and central fire and smoke-detector systems have been installed.
Amenities: Full breakfast with flapjacks, sourdough bread French toast, broccoli and cheese omelet among the specialties

Nearby Attractions: Shipyard Museum, Town Hall Museum, 1000 Island Craft School & Textile Museum, fishing and water sports
Special Services: Scenic boat and airplane tours of the 1000 Islands, fishing charters
Rates: $35 single, $45 double, in summer

THE CECCE GUEST HOUSE
166 CHEMUNG ST., CORNING, NY 14830

Reservations Phone: 607/962-5682

Description: In a Mediterranean setting with rooms designed in period style ("Eastlake," Victorian, Louis XIV), the guesthouse is within walking distance of historic Corning.
Amenities: Continental breakfast

Nearby Attractions: Corning Glass Museum, Rockwell Museum of Western Art, 1796 Patterson Museum, Hammondsport Wineries, Watkins Glen, the Finger Lakes
Special Services: Kitchen and living room available for guests staying 3 days or longer
Rates: $35 single, $40 double

BIG MOOSE INN
BIG MOOSE LAKE, EAGLE BAY, NY 13331

Reservations Phone: 315/357-2042
Description: Single and double rooms are available in this rustic lakeside lodge; up to 40 persons may be accommodated.
Amenities: Continental breakfast

Nearby Attractions: Blue Mountain Museum, Old Forge, Enchanted Forest
Special Services: Cocktail lounge, a variety of summer and winter sports available.
Rates: $32 single, $35 double

SOUTH MEADOW FARM LODGE
CASCADE ROAD, LAKE PLACID, NY 12946

Reservations Phone: 518/523-9369
Description: There are beds for ten in these rooms, built around a living room with fireplace and a piano. The "Honeymoon Cottage" is a converted maple sugar house with a wood stove, where candles provide the only light.
Amenities: Large farm breakfast

Nearby Attractions: Winter Olympic site
Special Services: Cross-country skiing, farm chores to share in, camp rates available.
Rates: $26 single, $52 double, in winter; $23 single, $46 double, the rest of the year

PINE HILL ARMS
MAIN STREET, PINE HILL, NY 12465

Reservations Phone: 914/254-9811 or 914/254-9812
Description: Established in 1882, the hotel lies between two ski centers. The 25 rooms have been completely remodeled and have private baths. The lounge has a large stone fireplace.

Nearby Attractions: Skiing, bicycling, golf, tennis, horseback riding, tubing, fly fishing
Special Services: Hot tub spa and sauna, exercise equipment, swimming pool
Rates: $40 single, $80 double, in winter; $25 single, $35 double, in summer

TIBBITTS HOUSE INN
100 COLUMBIA TURNPIKE, CLINTON HEIGHTS, RENSSELAER, NY 12144

Reservations Phone: 518/472-1348
Description: This 126-year-old farmhouse with an 84-foot enclosed porch has comfortably furnished rooms with shared bath, plus an apartment with an old keeping room with beamed ceiling and a corner, raised-hearth fireplace.

Nearby Attractions: The State Capitol and the Empire State Mall (2 miles away), a 45-mile hiking and biking path along the Hudson and Mohawk Rivers
Special Services: Patio, picnic tables, spacious glass-enclosed porch, ample parking
Rates: $33 single, $35 double

BEEKMAN ARMS
BEEKMAN SQUARE, RHINEBECK, NY 12572

Reservations Phone: 914/876-7077
Description: A haven for the tired traveler since 1776, the inn is appointed with antiques, oaken boards, brown beams, muskets, sabers, pistols, and pipes, plus wonderful old guest rooms.
Amenities: Continental breakfast; there's an excellent restaurant for dinner (make reservations—it's very popular).

Nearby Attractions: The FDR Home and Library at Hyde Park, World War I Aerodrome, Vanderbilt Mansion
Rates: $80 double

WASHINGTON IRVING LODGE
RTE. 23A (P.O. BOX 544), TANNERSVILLE, NY 12485

Reservations Phone: 518/589-5560
Description: The original section of this country lodge was built in 1869.
Amenities: Full breakfast in summer, continental buffet or full breakfast in winter

Nearby Attractions: Hunter Mountain ski area, site of summer festivals
Special Services: Swimming pool, tennis court
Rates: $25 to $30 per person double in winter (two-night-minimum package holiday weekends); $20 to $25 per person double in summer

---

RHODE ISLAND

B&B Reservation Services

BED & BREAKFAST OF RHODE ISLAND, INC.
P.O. BOX 3291, NEWPORT, RI 02840

Offers B&B Homes In: Rhode Island and Massachusetts
Reservations Phone: 401/849-1298
Phone Hours: 9 a.m. to 5 p.m. Monday to Friday (on Saturday during summer, noon to 5 p.m.)
Price Range of Homes: $30 to $80 single, $45 to $110 double
Breakfast Included in Price: Juice, fresh fruit, home-baked goods, tea and coffee. About 30% of the hosts serve a full breakfast, many of which are gourmet (Belgian waffles, quiche, fruited specialties, oven pancakes).
Brochure Available: Free; a host directory is also available for $2.
Reservations Should Be Made: 2 weeks in advance (last-minute reservations accepted when possible, but guests may not always stay in the desired area)

Scenic Attractions Near the B&B Homes: Newport mansions and historic homes, yachting and sailing center, Colt State Park (Briston), lighthouses and windmills, Slate Mill (Pawtucket), Providence's historic East Side, ocean beaches

Major Schools, Universities Near the B&B Homes: Brown, Rhode Island College, Providence College, Rhode Island School of Design, Johnson & Wales, U. of Rhode Island, Bryant, Salve Regina, St. George's School, Portsmouth Abbey

B&B Bonuses

Want to live in the 18th century for a few nights? Ask for the home built in 1710 in East Greenwich. It's furnished with antiques and has five working fireplaces. There are wide-plank floors and stenciled walls. The large sleeping room has a ship's-cabin ceiling. The bathroom has been rustically decorated with panels from the house's attic, complete with old newsprint as wallpaper.

CASTLE KEEP BED & BREAKFAST REGISTRY

44 EVERETT ST., NEWPORT, RI 02840

Offers B&B Homes In: Aquidneck-Newport, Middletown, and Portsmouth, Rhode Island
Reservations Phone: 401/846-0362
Phone Hours: 8 a.m. to 8 p.m. daily in season
Price Range of Homes: $40 single, $45 to $80 double
Breakfast Included in Price: Continental to full American, and various special dishes, at the hosts' discretion
Brochure Available: Free
Reservations Should Be Made: 2 weeks in advance, 3 weeks in summer (last-minute reservations accepted if possible)

Scenic Attractions Near the B&B Homes: Naval War College, Topiary Gardens, at least five major boat shows a year, and the summer "cottages" of the rich and famous of yesteryear, yours to explore on fabulous Bellevue Avenue
Major Schools, Universities Near the B&B Homes: St. George's, Portsmouth Abbey prep schools, Salve Regina, Roger Williams

B&B Bonuses

Besides the largest collection of restored colonial homes in America, Newport is famous for its fine beaches and harbors. One host home is a spectacular Victorian mini-mansion replete with old-world charm, and another more modern home is right on the National Historic Seashore with seven miles of ocean at your front door. Fully furnished apartments are also available for weekly or monthly rental.

GUEST HOUSE ASSOCIATION OF NEWPORT

P.O. BOX 981, NEWPORT, RI 02840

Offers B&B Homes In: Newport only
Reservations Phone: Each home on their list must be called directly for reservations; call 401/846-5444 for other information
Price Range of Homes: $35 to $120 single, $35 to $120 double
Breakfast Included in Price: Continental (juice, roll or toast, coffee)
Brochure Available: Free
Reservations Should Be Made: 2 weeks in advance in winter, a month or more in summer or fall (last-minute reservations accepted if possible)

Scenic Attractions Near the B&B Homes: National Historic Landmarks, Victorian "gilded age" mansions, Touro Synagogue (first in America), Cliff Walk, beaches, wharf dining and shopping areas
Major Schools, Universities Near the B&B Homes: Naval War College, Salve Regina, St. George's Prep, St. Michael's, Portsmouth Abbey

B&B Bonuses

All the guesthouses in the association have historical significance, and most were built in the mid-19th century and have been furnished with antiques and period pieces. "The Wayside," a Georgian mansion on famed Bellevue Avenue, has a private pool; the "Brinley Victorian" has two parlors and a library; and "The Cliffside," near Cliff Walk and the beach, boasts an elaborately carved Victorian center staircase.

B&B Inns

WILLIAM FLUDDER HOUSE

30 BELLEVUE AVE., NEWPORT, RI 02840

Reservations Phone: 401/849-4220 or 401/846-2229
Description: With four rooms on the "Walking Tour of Newport," the inn is a short walk to the waterfront for shopping and some of Newport's finest restaurants. Note that breakfast is not served.

Nearby Attractions: Million Dollar Drive and the stately "cottages" of Newport, the Newport Folk Festival, the Tennis Museum
Rates: $40 single, $50 double, in summer; $30 single, $40 double, in winter

HARBORSIDE INN

CHRISTIES LANDING, NEWPORT, RI 02840

Reservations Phone: 401/846-6600
Description: At this harborside inn just off Newport's historic
Thames Street, each suite features a wet bar, refrigerator, color TV,
sleeping loft, and deck.
Amenities: Continental breakfast

Nearby Attractions: The harbor, Newport's famous mansions and
beaches on Cliff Walk and Ocean Drive
Special Services: Meeting rooms available
Rates: $105 to $145 double in summer, $50 to $85 double in
winter

VERMONT

B&B Inns

THE EVERGREEN

SANDGATE ROAD, ARLINGTON, VT 05250

Reservations Phone: 802/375-2272
Description: Set in the Green Mountains, the inn can accommodate
40 guests in comfortable rooms surrounded by spacious lawns.
Amenities: Full breakfast served to guests

Nearby Attractions: Bennington Museum, Southern Vermont Art
Center, Dorset Playhouse, Skyline Drive
Special Services: Bus pickups, kitchen open in the evening for
cookies and cakes, coffee or tea
Rates: $26 to $30 single, $52 to $60 double, in summer; $23 to
$27 single, $46 to $54 double, in fall

COLONIAL GUEST HOUSE

ORCHARD ROAD (R.R. 1, BOX 0163), BENNINGTON, VT 05201

Reservations Phone: 802/442-2263

Description: This 100-year-old restored New England colonial home provides seven bedrooms, some with private bath, for guests. There are two parlors with books and periodicals available.
Amenities: Continental breakfast with fruit and cereal

Nearby Attractions: Middleton Place, Drayton Hall, Magnolia Gardens, Historic Summerville
Special Services: Heated pool, admission to Middleton Place Gardens
Rates: $95 to $130 double in winter, $70 to $95 double in summer

GREENHURST INN
R.D. 2, BOX #60, BETHEL, VT 05032

Reservations Phone: 802/234-9474
Description: This 1890 inn, listed on the National Register of Historic Places, is located in the geographic center of Vermont. It has eight fireplaces, a library of 3,000 volumes, and a Victrola and piano in the parlor.
Amenities: Choice of juice, hot muffins, quick bread, fresh fruit, and Colombian coffee

Nearby Attractions: Mountains, ski areas, outdoor sports
Special Services: Perrier in every room, mints on your pillow, game cupboard, electric blankets
Rates: $40 to $60 double

THE BLACK BEAR INN
MOUNTAIN ROAD, BOLTON, VT 05477

Reservations Phone: 802/434-2126 or 802/434-2920
Description: In a unique mountaintop setting, many of the inn's rooms enjoy mountain views from balconies, and all rooms have private bath and color TV. Guests are welcome to enjoy all the sports and recreation facilities of the Bolton Valley Resort.

Nearby Attractions: Shelburne Museum, many ski areas
Special Services: Outdoor heated pool
Rates: $89 double in summer and fall, $59 double in winter

VILLAGE INN OF BRADFORD

MAIN STREET, (U.S. 5), BRADFORD, VT 05033

Reservations Phone: 802/222-9303
Description: Built in 1826, this inn is a mix of several styles, Federal/Victorian outside, colonial/Victorian inside. Rooms and a suite with private or shared bath are available.
Amenities: Continental breakfast during the week, full breakfast on Sunday

Nearby Attractions: Connecticut River, golf course, historic restored mill, waterfall, horses, canoeing
Rates: $35 single, $40 to $60 double

TULIP TREE INN

CHITTENDEN DAM ROAD, CHITTENDEN, VT 05757

Reservations Phone: 802/483-6213
Description: In this gracious, rambling country house, a variety of antiques furnishes the ten guest rooms. The paneled den has a stone fireplace.
Amenities: Full breakfast served

Nearby Attractions: Green Mountain Forest, hiking trails, Killington (for skiing), canoeing, fishing for trout and salmon, golf
Special Services: Game room for chess and backgammon, hot tub, swimming pool
Rates: $38 per person

ECHO LEDGE FARM INN

Vt. 2, EAST ST. JOHNSBURY, VT 05838

Reservations Phone: 802/748-4750
Description: "The Dwelling House of Phineas Page" was built in 1793. Rooms have been freshly papered or stenciled, and have private baths.

Nearby Attractions: Maple Grove Museum and Factory, Fairbanks Museum and Planetarium, most outdoor sports
Rates: $50 double in fall, $36 double in summer

THE HIGHLAND LODGE

CASPIAN LAKE, GREENSBORO, VT 05841

Reservations Phone: 802/533-2647
Description: This restored 1820s farmhouse is situated just above Caspian Lake in Vermont's Northeast Kingdom. The rooms and cottages are tastefully decorated and afford good views of the mountains. A large porch overlooks the perennial gardens.
Amenities: Full breakfast using local eggs, maple syrup, and fruits

Nearby Attractions: The Green Mountains, complete range of outdoor sports
Special Services: Playroom, tennis courts, changing room and towels, canoes, rowboats, and paddleboat available for guests
Rates: $47.50 to $65 single, $85 to $110 double

MOUNTAIN MEADOWS LODGE

RTE. 1 BOX 3, KILLINGTON, VT 05751

Reservations Phone: 802/775-1010
Description: This converted 130-year-old farmhouse and barn can accommodate 40 guests in summer. Most of the large rooms have private baths. The lodge is set on a 110-acre lake in a country setting.
Amenities: Full Vermont home-style breakfast

Nearby Attractions: Summer theater
Special Services: Swimming pool, tennis and golf nearby
Rates: $58 single, $96 double, April to November; $38 single, $65 double, November to May

NORDIC INN

RTE. 11, LANDGROVE, VT 05148

Reservations Phone: 802/824-6444
Description: The inn is surrounded by the Green Mountain National Forest. It features five individual guest rooms, a solarium, and a restaurant.
Amenities: Juices, home-baked biscuits and sweet breads, fresh fruits, coffee, tea, and hot chocolate are served in summer; a full breakfast with Swedish pancakes and Vermont products is served in winter

Nearby Attractions: Hapgood Pond; Bromley Alpine Slide; Hildene, Bromley, Magic and Stratton Mountain ski areas; Dorset and Weston Summer Theaters; ice skating and horse-drawn sleigh rides
Special Services: Cross-country skiing in 12 miles of groomed trails, rentals and instruction available
Rates: $125 double, Modified American Plan (breakfast and dinner included), December through March; $45.50 double, European Plan (B&B), May to December

BLUE GENTIAN LODGE

MAGIC MOUNTAIN ROAD, LONDONDERRY, VT 05148

Reservations Phone: 802/824-5908
Description: The 14 rooms all have private bath and color TV. The lounge with fireplace and the playrooms are available for guests.

Nearby Attractions: Ski areas, golf, tennis
Special Services: Outdoor pool
Rates: $51 single, $64 double, November to April; $35 single, $44 double, April to November

BLACK LANTERN INN

RTE. 118, MONTGOMERY, VT 05470

Reservations Phone: 802/326-4507
Description: This restored colonial building was built in 1802 as a stagecoach inn. The old brick building is less than ten miles from the Canadian border. The rooms are decorated with antiques, and the suite has a Jacuzzi and a fireplace.

Nearby Attractions: Jay Peak ski area, Hazen's Notch Cross-Country Ski Center, covered bridges
Special Services: Swimming, tennis
Rates: $45 to $75 double in fall and winter, $40 to $65 double in spring and summer

NORTH HERO HOUSE

CHAMPLAIN ISLANDS, NORTH HERO, VT 05474

Reservations Phone: 802/372-8237

Description: This is a small country inn overlooking Lake Champlain. All rooms have private bath, and lake-view accommodations have screened porches to view Mount Mansfield across the lake.

Nearby Attractions: Burlington, Shelburne Museum, Stowe, Trapp Family Lodge, fishing, sailing, waterskiing, tennis, skiing
Special Services: Sauna, game room
Rates: $31 to $67 double in summer and fall

THE INN AT NORWICH
225 MAIN ST. (P.O. BOX 908), NORWICH, VT 05055

Reservations Phone: 802/649-1143
Description: The building, an inn since 1779, has 28 guest rooms each with private bath, telephone, and cable TV. Some of the rooms have canopied, rice-carved four-poster beds, while others are furnished with brass bedsteads.

Nearby Attractions: Swimming, hiking, fishing, canoeing, antiquing, downhill and cross-country skiing
Rates: $60 to $91 double

VALLEY HOUSE INN
4 MEMORIAL SQUARE, ORLEANS, VT 05860

Reservations Phone: 802/754-6665
Description: Built in the 1800s, the inn has a large porch going halfway around the building. There are 20 rooms in the inn, with a cocktail lounge facing the common.
Amenities: Old-fashioned breakfast served

Nearby Attractions: Old Stone House Museum, three lakes within a three-mile radius, 18-hole golf course
Special Services: Live entertainment every Friday night
Rates: $21 single, $30 double, April to October; $19 single, $26 double, October to March

CASTLE INN

P.O. BOX 157, PROCTORSVILLE, VT 05153

Reservations Phone: 802/226-7222
Description: This large stone castle built in 1904 contains elaborate public rooms like the Great Hall, with the family coat-of-arms carved into the woodwork; the library, where cocktails are served; and the Governor's Game Room with its carved ceiling. The guest rooms are done up in the style of the period.
Amenities: Rates include a full breakfast from the menu and dinner

Nearby Attractions: Black River Museum; Calvin Coolidge's Birth-place; Woodstock and Queechee Gorge; Robert Todd Lincoln's home, "Hildene"; major ski areas
Special Services: Swimming pool, clay tennis courts, bicycles, hot tub and sauna
Rates: $140 double, June to October; $100 double, December to April

HARVEY MOUNTAIN VIEW FARM AND INN

ROCHESTER NORTH HOLLOW, ROCHESTER, VT 05767

Reservations Phone: 802/767-4273
Description: The inn was the subject of a full-page article by Noel Perrin in the *New York Times* describing living on a farm and pet-ting and feeding the animals as a unique kind of vacation. Besides accommodations in the inn there is a two-bedroom chalet rented from Saturday to Saturday.
Amenities: Besides a full farm breakfast, dinner is included in the rates

Nearby Attractions: Lake Dunmore, ski areas with gondola and Alpine Slide, tennis courts, Texas Falls with nature walk
Special Services: Bus pickup, swimming pool, a pond for fishing, animals to interact with, a pony to ride, lawn games
Rates: $36 to $42 double

GREEN MOUNTAIN TEA ROOM AND GUEST HOUSE
RTE. 7 (P.O. BOX 400), SOUTH WALLINGFORD, VT 05773

Reservations Phone: 802/446-2611
Description: This former stagecoach stop was built in 1792. There are five guest rooms. The colonial house is on eight acres of land bordering Otter Creek.

Nearby Attractions: Green Mountain National Park, Appalachian Trail, ski areas, fishing, canoeing
Rates: $12 to $14 single, $20 to $24 double

KEDRON VALLEY INN
RTE. 106, SOUTH WOODSTOCK, VT 05071

Reservations Phone: 802/457-1473
Description: The building has been operating as an inn for over 150 years. The guest rooms have canopied beds, Franklin stoves, fireplaces, and private baths.
Amenities: Full country breakfast

Nearby attractions: Billings Farm, a working dairy farm with a museum of early farm implements; Calvin Coolidge's Birthplace
Rates: $75 to $115 single, $80 to $120 double, in winter; $65 to $105 single, $70 to $110 double, in summer

SCARBOROUGH INN
RTE. 100 HC65 #23, STOCKBRIDGE, VT 05772

Reservations Phone: 802/746-8141
Description: This restored 1780 farmhouse is full of Chippendale, Sheraton, and other antiques, pewter, and Haviland china.
Amenities: Full country breakfast

Nearby Attractions: Long Trail and Queechee Gorge, Norman Rockwell Museum, Berkshire Playhouse
Special Services: Airport pickup
Rates: $35 to $50 double, September to March; $30 to $45 double, April to August

BUTTERNUT INN AT STOWE
MOUNTAIN ROAD (R.D. 1, BOX 950), STOWE, VT 05672

Reservations Phone: 802/253-4277
Description: This three-diamond AAA bed-and-breakfast country inn is set on 8½ acres of landscaped grounds by a mountain stream. All rooms have private bath and are air-conditioned and furnished with antiques.
Amenities: Breakfast (served poolside when possible) may include omelets, ham steak, quail, French toast with Vermont maple syrup

Nearby Attractions: Mount Mansfield ski resort, gondola ride, Alpine Slide
Special Services: Swimming pool, golf, tennis, horseback riding
Rates: $70 double, June to October; $56 double, December to April

FIDDLERS GREEN INN
MOUNTAIN ROAD (RTE. 108), STOWE, VT 05672

Reservations Phone: 802/253-8124
Description: This country inn in the Green Mountains was built in 1820 and is situated well off the highway next to a babbling brook.
Amenities: Breakfast specialties include home-grown blueberry and juneberry pancakes, Grand Marnier French toast, and cheese, mushroom, and herb omelets

Nearby Attractions: Mount Mansfield, Alpine Slide, gondola ride, tennis, golf, balloon and glider rides
Special Services: Picnic grove
Rates: $28 to $66 double

THE GABLES INN
MOUNTAIN ROAD, STOWE, VT 05672

Reservations Phone: 802/253-7730
Description: The inn was constructed in 1836. Its decor is colonial, furnished with antiques. All the rooms have private baths and an outstanding view of Mount Mansfield.

Nearby Attractions: Mount Mansfield, Recreation Path, cycling

Special Services: Swimming pool, hot tub, tennis, golf
Rates: $75 single, $100 double, December to April; $50 double, June to September

NICHOLS LODGE
P.O. BOX 1098, STOWE, VT 05672

Reservations Phone: 802/253-7683
Description: The inn is a restored farmhouse located on a 365-acre working farm.
Amenities: Full breakfast served during winter and spring

Nearby Attractions: Mount Mansfield, Smugglers Notch, Trapp Family Lodge, Shelburne Museum
Special Services: Swimming pool, shuffleboard, badminton, volleyball, horseshoes, panning for gold in Gold Brook which borders the property
Rates: $46 to $60 double in winter and spring, $22 to $30 in summer and fall

TIMBERHOLM INN
COTTAGE CLUB ROAD, (R.R. 1, BOX 810), STOWE, VT 05672

Reservations Phone: 802/253-7603
Description: The inn has a view of Worcester Mountain. The living room has a large stone fireplace, picture windows, a deck, and family furniture.
Amenities: Full cooked breakfast

Nearby Attractions: Mount Mansfield ski area and State Park, Stowe Village, Trapp Family Lodge, biking, hiking, and tennis
Special Services: Complimentary soup, après-ski
Rates: $42 to $69 double, September to April; $38 to $55 double, May to August

MAD RIVER BARN LODGE
RTE. 17, WAITSFIELD, VT 05673

Reservations Phone: 802/496-3310

Description: This is a traditional Vermont lodge filled with mementos of years gone by and the charm of country living. Rooms are furnished in simple but comfortable style.
Amenities: Continental and full breakfast

Nearby Attractions: Shelburne Museum, Lake Champlain, Audubon Society Nature Center, Rock of Ages Quaries, Alpine Slide
Special Services: Pool, golf, tennis, fishing, soaring, biking
Rates: $46 double, December to April; $28 double, May to November

===

MILLBROOK LODGE
R.F.D. BOX 62, WAITSFIELD, VT 05673

Reservations Phone: 802/496-2405
Description: This Cape-style farmhouse dates to the 1850s. The six guest rooms are decorated with hand-stenciling, antique bedsteads, and handmade quilts. There's a view of the Green Mountains.
Amenities: Full country breakfast including pancakes with fruit, French toast made with anadama bread, real Vermont maple syrup

Nearby Attractions: Some of the finest skiing in the East five minutes away, Sugarbush and Mad River Glen, 100 km of groomed trails for the cross-country skier, golfing, canoeing, soaring, tennis, horseback riding, windsurfing
Special Services: Pickup from airport in Burlington, and pickup from bus and trains can be arranged.
Rates: $60 to $330 single, $110 to $480 double, in winter; $40 to $50 single, $50 to $70 double, in summer

===

MOUNTAIN VIEW INN
R.F.D. BOX 69, WAITSFIELD, VT 05673

Reservations Phone: 802/496-2426
Description: Though built in 1826, the house has been an inn only for the last 40 years. The seven rooms, each with bath, are decorated in the colonial style with antiques, quilts, and braided rugs.
Amenities: Breakfast begins with fruit and coffee or tea, and

continues with bacon, eggs, and toast, or blueberry pancakes, or waffles, with bacon.

Nearby Attractions: Ski areas at Sugarbush, Mad River Glen, and the Long Trail; soaring, tennis, golf, horseback riding; Shelburne Museum, a Morgan horse farm

Rates: $100 double in winter, $90 double in summer

TUCKER HILL LODGE
RTE. 17 (R.D. 1, BOX 147), WAITSFIELD, VT 05673

Reservations Phone: 802/496-3983, or toll free 800/451-4580

Description: The gray clapboard buildings are on a hillside setting surrounded by very elaborate flower gardens.

Amenities: Breakfast includes homemade bread and muffins, local berries, homemade jams, and maple syrup from the innkeeper's trees.

Nearby Attractions: Mad River for fishing and canoeing, Sugarbush and Mad River Glen ski areas, museums, craft galleries, Shelburne Museum

Special Services: Pool, two clay tennis courts, airport pickup, fresh flowers in guest rooms

Rates: $68 double

VALLEY INN
RTE. 100 (P.O. BOX 8), WAITSFIELD, VT 05673

Reservations Phone: 802/496-3450

Description: The first inn built in the Mad River Valley, the all-wood structure is made of native timbers. The parlor has a large stone fireplace.

Amenities: Full breakfast with fresh berries and Vermont maple syrup

Nearby Attractions: Sugarbush Valley ski resort, Historic Waitsfield Village, covered bridges

Special Services: Tennis, golf, soaring, ski packages, private airport

Rates: $92 double, MAP, in winter; $70 double, B&B, in summer

DEERHILL INN
VALLEY VIEW ROAD, WEST DOVER, VT 05356

Reservations Phone: 802/464-3100
Description: In this colonial inn overlooking the Mount Snow and Haystack ski areas, there are three public living rooms and 17 guest rooms with private bath.
Amenities: Full breakfast

Nearby Attractions: The Green Mountains, Marlboro Music Festival, championship golf course
Special Services: Tennis court, pool, golf, skiing
Rates: $80 to $100 double

WINDHAM HILL INN
R.R. 1, BOX 44, WEST TOWNSHEND, VT 05359

Reservations Phone: 802/874-4080 or 802/874-4976
Description: This restored 1825 farmhouse and barn has 15 antique-filled guest rooms and private baths set on 150 acres.
Amenities: Full breakfast and five-course gourmet dinner included in the rates

Nearby Attractions: Townshend State Park; Jamaica State Park; Marlboro Music Center; Stratton, Bromley, and Magic Mountain ski areas; Volvo International Tennis Tournament
Special Services: Sherry in room on arrival, chamber music
Rates: $60 to $70 double in winter, $55 to $65 double in summer

THE WHITE HOUSE OF WILMINGTON
RTE. 9, WILMINGTON, VT 05363

Reservations Phone: 802/464-2135
Description: This turn-of-the-century mansion set high on a hill has eight distinctive rooms with private bath.
Amenities: Full breakfast and dinner included in the rates

Nearby Attractions: The Historic Molly Stark Trail, Bennington, lakes, horseback riding
Special Services: Pool, sauna, and whirlpool, cross-country skiing
Rates: $150 to $190 double

The Middle Atlantic States

Delaware   /   131
District of Columbia   /   132
Maryland   /   133
New Jersey   /   135
North Carolina   /   137
Pennsylvania   /   142
South Carolina   /   151
Virginia   /   158
West Virginia   /   164

DELAWARE

B&B Reservation Services

BED & BREAKFAST OF DELAWARE
3650 SILVERSIDE RD. (P.O. BOX 177), WILMINGTON, DE 19810

Offers B&B Homes In: City and suburbs of Wilmington, Newark, Odessa, Lewes, in Delaware; Chadds Ford and other towns in nearby Pennsylvania and Maryland

Reservations Phone: 302/479-9500
Phone Hours: 9 a.m. to 9 p.m. daily (any hour on answering service)
Price Range of Homes: $30 to $35 single, $45 to $65 double (beach homes to $65 in summer)
Breakfast Included in Price: Full American (juice, eggs, bacon, toast, coffee)
Brochure Available: Free
Reservations Should Be Made: 2 weeks in advance (last-minute reservations accepted if possible)

Scenic Attractions Near the B&B Homes: Winterthur, Longwood Gardens, Brandywine River Museum, Hagley Museum, Nemours, Old New Castle, beach resorts, Philadelphia attractions
Major Schools, Universities Near the B&B Homes: U. of Delaware, Delaware Law School, West Chester U.

B&B Bonuses

"Beautiful restored 18th- and 19th-century homes furnished with authentic antiques" are the specialty of this B&B organization. Some hosts have served as docents at major museums.

Some homes have swimming pools open to guests during the summer. Ask for one of these homes when you call.

Occasional extras are sightseeing tours, tennis and golf club privileges, and gourmet dinners.

DISTRICT OF COLUMBIA

B&B Reservation Service

SWEET DREAMS & TOAST, INC.
P.O. BOX 4835-0035, WASHINGTON, DC 20008

Offers B&B Homes In: Annapolis, Chevy Chase, and Bethesda in Maryland; McLean, Arlington, Alexandria in Virginia; and the District of Columbia
Reservations Phone: 202/483-9191
Phone Hours: 11 a.m. to 5 p.m. Monday to Friday, except holidays
Price Range of Homes: $35 to $55 single, $48 to $70 double
Breakfast Included in Price: Continental (juice, roll or toast, coffee)
Brochure Available: Free
Reservations Should Be Made: 2 or 3 weeks in advance (last-minute reservations accepted if possible); two-night minimum

Scenic Attractions Near the B&B Homes: National Zoo, the Smithsonian, John F. Kennedy Center for the Performing Arts, U.S. Capitol and all national buildings open to the public (National Archives, Bureau of Printing and Engraving, etc.), Arlington National Cemetery, Mount Vernon, Children's Museum
Major Schools, Universities Near the B&B Homes: Howard, George Washington, Georgetown U., U. of District of Columbia, Catholic University (Washington); U.S. Naval Academy, St. John's (Annapolis)

B&B Bonuses
A quiet antique-filled suburban Maryland home can accommodate two couples. The host speaks Spanish and French. If you prefer to be in the heart of Washington, a restored Victorian home is within a mile of the Capitol-Smithsonian area. They offer a total of 110 host homes. Numerous restaurants and excellent transportation characterize the area.

MARYLAND

B&B Reservation Services

THE TRAVELLER IN MARYLAND, INC.
33 WEST ST., ANNAPOLIS, MD 21401

Offers B&B Homes In: Annapolis, Baltimore, and 45 other cities and towns throughout Maryland
Reservations Phone: 301/269-6232 or 301/261-2233
Phone Hours: 9 a.m. to 5 p.m. Monday to Thursdays to noon on Friday
Price Range of Homes: $40 to $55 single, $40 to $65 double (yachts, $60 and up)
Breakfast Included in Price: Continental
Brochure Available: No; please reserve by phone only
Reservations Should Be Made: As far in advance as possible; not less than 24 hours

Scenic Attractions Near the B&B Homes: Baltimore Inner Harbor, Chesapeake Bay, U.S. Naval Academy, hiking and biking, major-league sports, horse racing, historic homes
Major Schools, Universities Near the B&B Homes: Johns Hopkins, Goucher, U.S. Naval Academy, St. John's, Washington College, U. of Maryland

B&B Bonuses
For $10 (a one-time fee) this reservation service offers a membership in the "Traveller in Maryland Bed & Breakfast Society." Members receive an information packet which includes Maryland guidebooks and a roadmap, and subsequent notes about special vacations available through the reservation service in Maryland. Write for details.

AMANDA'S BED & BREAKFAST RESERVATION SERVICE

1428 PARK AVE., BALTIMORE, MD 21217

Offers B&B Homes In: Baltimore area, Annapolis, eastern shore of Maryland, Gettysburgh, Pennsylvania, and Washington, D.C.
Reservations Phone: 301/225-0001
Phone Hours: 8:30 a.m. to 5 p.m. Monday to Friday (weekend calls accepted)
Price Range of Homes: $30 to $100 single, $35 to $120 double
Breakfast Included in Price: Continental or full American . . . regional specialties sometimes served include shoo-fly pie and sausage bread
Brochure Available: Free if you send a stamped, self-addressed no. 10 envelope; $5 for a printout of all listings
Reservations Should Be Made: 2 weeks in advance (last-minute reservations accepted when possible)

Scenic Attractions Near the B&B Homes: Baltimore Inner Harbor, the Aquarium, Science Center, Baltimore Museum of Art, Zoo, historic neighborhoods
Major Schools, Universities Near the B&B Homes: Johns Hopkins, Peabody, Loyola

B&B Bonuses

Ask about the B&B in a completely redecorated mansion in a country setting. You can stay in a two-room suite with a fireplace, perfect for a honeymoon or anniversary celebrations. You also can stay on a sailboat in the harbor. Some hosts even offer spa services—a sauna, Jacuzzi, hot tub, plus swimming pools and tennis. Tours can be arranged by hosts.

B&B Inns

WASHINGTON HOTEL INN

SOMERSET AVENUE, PRINCESS ANNE, MD 21853

Reservations Phone: 301/651-2525
Description: Located in historic Princess Anne, Maryland, the inn was built in 1744 and has been in operation ever since. The interior is decorated with antiques, with pictures of all the presidents lining the walls. The front hall has a lovely double staircase.

Nearby Attractions: Walking tour of old houses, day trips to several islands, cycling
Rates: $34 single, $38 to $40 double

THE ROSEBUD INN
4 N. MAIN ST., WOODSBORO, MD 21798

Reservations Phone: 301/845-2221
Description: Opened as an inn in 1981, it was once the home of the founder of the Rosebud Perfume Co., which is still in operation next door to the inn. A rose motif is carried throughout the interior, reflected in the rosebud designs in the leaded-glass doors. There are five large air-conditioned rooms, two with private bath. Marble mantels decorate the parlor and living room fireplaces.
Amenities: Continental breakfast

Nearby Attractions: Tennis, ice skating, bicycling
Rates: $35 single, $60 double

NEW JERSEY

B&B Reservation Services

NORTHERN NEW JERSEY BED & BREAKFAST
11 SUNSET TRAIL, DENVILLE, NJ 07854

Offers B&B Homes In: Northern New Jersey
Reservations Phone: 201/625-5129
Phone Hours: 9 a.m. to 4 p.m. Monday to Saturday
Price Range of Homes: $30 to $66 single, $40 to $66 double
Breakfast Included in Price: Continental or full American (depending on the host)
Brochure Available: Free
Reservations Should Be Made: 2 weeks in advance

Scenic Attractions Near the B&B Homes: Washington's Headquarters, Waterloo Village, Meadowlands Sports Complex
Major Schools, Universities Near the B&B Homes: Drew, Fairleigh Dickinson, Montclair State

B&B Bonuses

This B&B service can book you in a completely restored inn in Stanhope, where the bathroom fixtures were recovered from the old Essex & Sussex Hotel in Spring Lake.

Many host homes accommodate corporate transferees and consultants for stays of one to three months. Weekly and monthly rates are available at about half the usual B&B rates.

B&B Inns

HOLLY HOUSE
20 JACKSON ST., CAPE MAY, NJ 08204

Reservations Phone: 609/884-7365
Description: The house (c. 1890) is one of seven Victorian cottages that are famous as Cape May's Seven Sisters. Renaissance Revival in style, it's the work of Stephen Decatur Button. It has six guest rooms with two shared baths, plus an ocean-view front porch with swing and rockers. The inn has achieved National Historic Landmark status.

Nearby Attractions: Physick House Victorian Museum, the Cold Spring Village restoration, a bird sanctuary and wildlife preserve
Special Services: Parking permits and beach tags are supplied.
Rates: $50 double in summer, $45 double in winter

THE 7TH SISTER GUEST HOUSE
10 JACKSON ST., CAPE MAY, NJ 08204

Reservations Phone: 609/884-2280
Description: The guesthouse with its ocean-view rooms is on the National Register. The artist/owner has amassed a large wicker collection and manages to have an art gallery on the premises.

Nearby Attractions: Beach, horseback riding
Rates: $56 double in summer, $48 double in winter

B&B Reservation Services

BED AND BREAKFAST IN THE ALBEMARLE
P.O. BOX 248, EVERETTS, NC 27825

Offers B&B Homes In: Northeastern North Carolina
Reservations Phone: 919/792-4584
Phone Hours: 9 a.m. to 5 p.m. Monday to Friday, and weekends
Price Range of Homes: $30 to $50 single, $35 to $50 double
Breakfast Included in Price: Continental (juice, roll or toast, coffee); some hosts also serve Carolina country ham, and most homes serve country biscuits.
Brochure Available: Free; a host listing is also available for $5
Reservations Should Be Made: 2 weeks in advance (can accept last-minute reservations for some locations)

Scenic Attractions Near the B&B Homes: Hope Plantation, Historic Edenton, Historic Bath, Museum of the Albemarle, Elizabeth City Historic District
Major Schools, Universities Near the B&B Homes: East Carolina U., Chowan, Roanoke Bible College, College of the Albemarle

B&B Bonuses _____
   Some hosts will provide weekend guests with tours of nearby historic areas.

B&B Inns

WOMBLE INN
301 W. MAIN ST. (P.O. BOX 1441), BREVARD, NC 28712

Reservations Phone: 704/884-4770
Description: Furnished with 18th- and 19th-century antiques, all rooms have private baths. The seven guest rooms are air-conditioned.

Amenities: Breakfast is served on a silver tray in your room, in the dining room, or on the porch

Nearby Attractions: Pisgah National Forest, Biltmore House, North Carolina State Theater, the Brevard Music Center
Special Services: Swimming pool, tennis, shuttle to the Music Center
Rates: $32 single, $38 double, in summer; $28 single, $32 double, in winter

NANTAHALA VILLAGE
P.O. DRAWER J, BRYSON CITY, NC 28713

Reservations Phone: Toll free 800/438-1507
Description: Built of stone and wormy chestnut, the inn dates back to 1949. The cottages and log cabins are earlier. They offer simple but comfortable rustic accommodations.
Amenities: Continental breakfast

Nearby Attractions: Great Smoky Mountain National Park, Cherokee Indian Reservation, white-water rafting, swimming, horseback riding, tennis, shuffleboard
Rates: $70 double in summer, $50 double the rest of the year

HEMLOCK INN
GALBREATH CREEK ROAD, BRYSON CITY, NC 28713

Reservations Phone: 704/488-2885
Description: In a high, cool, quiet, restful country inn atmosphere, the rooms are furnished in antiques and furniture made by local craftsman. Rooms have porches or balconies. Cottages and a log cabin are also available.
Amenities: Country breakfast (coarse-ground grits, country meats, homemade biscuits, honey butter)

Nearby Attractions: Great Smoky Mountain National Park, Nantahala River, creeks for tubing
Special Services: Dinner is included in the price—real honest-to-goodness "home cookin' " served on round lazy Susan tables.
Rates: $52 single, $77 to $99 double

THE COLONIAL INN

153 W. KING ST., HILLSBOROUGH, NC 27278

Reservations Phone: 919/732-2461
Description: One of the ten oldest inns in the country, the Colonial has been in continuous operation since 1759. Lord Cornwallis and Aaron Burr stayed here. The ten bedrooms all have private baths and are air-conditioned.
Amenities: Country breakfast

Nearby Attractions: Historic museum, 100 historic buildings within walking distance
Rates: $48 to $65 double

HIGHLANDS INN

P.O. BOX 1030, HIGHLANDS, NC 28741

Reservations Phone: 704/526-9380
Description: Built in 1879 in the highest incorporated Town (4,100 feet) east of the Mississippi, the inn has undergone extensive renovations in the last three years. There are 46 well-furnished rooms with private baths. The public rooms include a tea room, stock exchange, private club, a card room, a TV room, and dining rooms. There's a large porch for "sitting out front," a favorite pastime since the inn opened.
Amenities: Breakfast buffet

Nearby Attractions: Highlands is "the land of Waterfalls"; Satulah, Yellow, Whiteside, and Sunset Rock are just a few of the mountains around; Great Smoky Mountain National Park, Appalachian Trail, Highlands Playhouse
Rates: $39 single, $59 to $69 double

THE GREYSTONE INN

P.O. BOX 6, LAKE TOXAWAY, NC 28747

Reservations Phone: 704/966-4700, or toll free 800/824-5766 from out of state
Description: Built in 1915, the Greystone offers complete resort facilities: heated pool, four soft-surface and two all-weather tennis courts, fishing, waterskiing (boat, skis, and driver provided), canoe,

sailboat, hiking, and sunset cruises on a party boat, *Mountain Lily II*
Amenities: Breakfast of juice, fruit, cereal, bread and pastries, eggs, waffles, corned-beef hash, grits, coffee, tea, hot chocolate, and milk

Nearby Attractions: Blue Ridge Mountains; Biltmore House; waterfalls; Brevard Music Festival; 18-hole par-72 championship golf course on North Carolina's largest lake
Special Services: White wicker sun porch, afternoon tea, library
Rates: $75 to $150 per person

OSCAR'S HOUSE
RTE. 12 (P.O. BOX 206), OCRACOKE ISLAND, NC 27960

Reservations Phone: 919/928-1311
Description: This island, to which Europeans first came in the 1500s, was later the home of Blackbeard the Pirate and retains the feeling of its historical beginnings. Oscar's House, built in 1940 by the lighthouse keeper, now provides accommodations for island visitors. Single or double rooms are available with shared baths.
Amenities: Breakfast is liable to include fresh fruit, garden tomatoes, omelets, grits, cooked apples, French toast, muffins or breads

Nearby Attractions: The Lighthouse, British Cemetery, Pamlico Sound, Silver Lake Harbor, Coast Guard Station
Rates: $38 single, $45 double, in summer; $35 single, $40 double, in spring and fall

THE PINES COUNTRY INN
719 HART RD., PISGAH FOREST, NC 28768

Reservations Phone: 704/877-3131
Description: Accommodations in this 1883 inn include two double rooms with private bath, three double rooms with shared bath, and four cabins and cottages. A family room with an open fireplace is available to all guests.
Amenities: A full breakfast with eggs any way you'd like them

Nearby Attractions: Pisgah National Forest, Holmes State Park, Brevard Music Center, Biltmore House, Carl Sandburg's House, Flatrock Playhouse

Special Services: Airport pickup upon request; rates include breakfast and dinner, which are served family style.
Rates: $55 single, $68 double

BLUE BOAR LODGE
200 SANTEELAH RD., ROBBINSVILLE, NC 28771

Reservations Phone: 704/479-8126
Description: The lodge is a mountain hideaway in the Nantahala
Forest. The accommodations are rustic but comfortable. The wood-
paneled rooms sit on the edge of a lake.
Amenities: Breakfast with country sausage and ham, grits, gravy,
and homemade biscuits

Nearby Attractions: Nantahala National Forest, Great Smokies,
white-water rafting, fishing, Joyce Kilmer Memorial Forest
Special Services: Breakfast and supper are included in the room
rate. Picnic lunches can be arranged.
Rates: $45 single, $80 double

PINE CREST INN
200 PINE CREST LANE, TRYON, NC 28782

Reservations Phone: 704/859-9135
Description: The inn's ten buildings on a wooded knoll containing
a variety of accommodations—rooms, suites, and cottages.

Nearby Attractions: Blue Ridge Parkway, waterfalls
Special Services: Fox hunting in season, tennis, golf, swimming
pool
Rates: $53 to $90 double in spring and fall, $48 to $85 double in
summer and winter

STONE HEDGE INN
P.O. BOX 366, TRYON, NC 28782

Reservations Phone: 704/859-9114
Description: Set at the base of Mount Tyron, the inn offers a cottage
complete with fireplace next to the pool and three quaint but
spacious rooms in the main house. All rooms have private bath,
color TV, air conditioning, and mountain views.

Amenities: Full house breakfast

Nearby Attractions: Swimming pool, tennis, golf
Rates: $50 to $68 double

THE GREYSTONE GUEST HOUSE
100 S. 3RD ST., WILMINGTON, NC 28401

Reservations Phone: 919/762-0358
Description: A European-style establishment in the Bridges Mansion in the heart of Wilmington's Historic District. Furnishings appropriate to the house are found in the public rooms and in the guest rooms.
Amenities: Continental breakfast served in your room on silver and fine china

Nearby Attractions: Historic homes and gardens
Rates: $65 to $85 single, $75 to $95 double

PENNSYLVANIA

B&B Reservation Services

BED & BREAKFAST OF SOUTHEAST PENNSYLVANIA
RD #1, BOX 278, BARTO, PA 19504

Offers B&B Homes In: Easton, west through Bethlehem, Allentown, Kutztown, Reading, to East Greenville, and Sumneytown
Reservations Phone: 215/845-3526
Phone Hours: 24 hours daily
Price Range of Homes: $15 to $35 single, $35 to $90 double
Breakfast included in Price: Continental or full American (one hostess serves a vegetarian, or macrobiotic breakfast)
Brochure Available: For $2
Reservations Should Be Made: 2 weeks in advance (last-minute reservations accepted if possible)

Scenic Attractions Near the B&B Homes: Canal Museum, historic Bethlehem, Dorney Park Velodrome and Art Museum, French Creek

State Park, Hopewell Village, Antique Car Museum, Kutztown Folk Festival, Reading shopping outlets
Major Schools, Universities Near the B&B Homes: Lehigh, Lafayette, Moravian, Allentown, Cedar Crest, Muhlenberg, Albright, and Alvernia colleges; Kutztown U., Perkiomen School

B&B Bonuses _____

You can stay in a hide-away furnished with handmade country furniture. Or ask about the B&B inn with a sunken copper bathtub.

BED & BREAKFAST OF PHILADELPHIA
P.O. BOX 680, DEVON, PA 19333

Offers B&B Homes In: Center City Philadelphia, all four surrounding counties of Bucks, Chester, Montgomery, and Delaware, including Main Line, New Hope, Doylestown Valley Forge, West Chester, Chadds Ford, and Chestnut Hill, Wilmington (Delaware); Moorestown and Riverton (New Jersey)
Reservations Phone: 215/688-1633
Phone Hours: 9 a.m. to 9 p.m. Monday through Friday, plus some weekend hours
Price Range of Homes: $25 to $35 single, $35 to $125 double (family rates in some specific homes)
Breakfast Included in Price: "Gourmet" continental or full breakfasts, which may include quiches, Philadelphia sticky buns, scrapple, other host specialties and regional fare
Brochure Available: Free with stamped, self-addressed no. 10 envelope (detailed listings directory is $5.30)
Reservations Should Be Made: 1 week in advance or sooner; last-minute reservations accepted, according to availability.

Scenic Attractions Near the B&B Homes: Valley Forge National Park, Independence Hall and National Park, Philadelphia Museum of Art, Franklin Institute, Rodin Museum, Longwood Gardens, Winterthur Museum and Gardens, Hagley Museum, Brandywine River Museum (Wyeth paintings), Skippack Village, Mennonite and Amish country, Sesame Place, New Hope
Major Schools, Universities Near the B&B Homes: U. of Pennsylvania, Drexel, Temple, Haverford, Bryn Mawr, Villanova, Swarthmore, Eastern, Beaver, Cabrini, St. Josephs, La Salle, Rosemont, Philadelphia Textile College, Jefferson Medical School, Wills Eye Hospital, American College of Physicians, Presbyterian Hospital, Dufreye Medical Center.

B&B Bonuses

Accommodations for every taste include a turreted Victorian row home, a 300-acre working dairy farm, a 200-year-old farmhouse, a renovated grist mill, and a Mennonite farm. Some homes have been shown on ABC–TV, Hal Linden's show, "For Your Information," and others featured in national magazines and local papers.

HERSHEY BED & BREAKFAST RESERVATION SERVICE

P.O. BOX 208, HERSHEY, PA 17033

Offers B&B Homes In: Lancaster County (Lancaster, Strasburg); Dauphin County (Hershey, Harrisburg); Lebanon County (Annville, Palmyra); southeastern Pennsylvania
Reservations Phone: 717/367-9408
Phone Hours: 7 a.m. to 10 p.m. daily
Price Range of Homes: $30 to $50 single, $35 to $60 double
Breakfast Included in Price: Continental or full American . . . many Lancaster area farm homes provide Pennsylvania Dutch country breakfasts, with their own cured hams and sausages, and breads and rolls baked early in the same morning; special gourmet breakfasts are served at a historic home in Annville.
Brochure Available: Free if you send a stamped, self-addressed no. 10 envelope
Reservations Should be Made: 2 weeks in advance preferred, 1 week accepted (no last-minute reservations accepted)

Scenic Attractions Near the B&B Homes: Pennsylvania Farm Museum, Amish Homestead, Strasburg Railroad, Dutch Wonderland, Hershey Park, Hershey Museum of American Life, Hershey Rose Gardens, William Penn Museum, Antique Automobile Club of America, Zoo America, Chocolate World, many shopping outlets
Major Schools, Universities Near the B&B Homes: Franklin and Marshall, Millersville, Elizabethtown College, Lebanon Valley College, Capitol Campus of Penn State, M.S. Hershey Medical Center of Penn State, Harrisburg Area Community College

B&B Bonuses

A historic home in Hershey offers the luxury of a bedroom with private powder room and porch decorated in "Laura Ashley" style. Or tour the dairy and herb and craft shop in a farm home in Mount Joy. Besides country breakfast, a herbal luncheon is available here, with advance reservation.

Many Lancaster farm hosts will custom-tailor sightseeing tours to meet the guest's particular interests. Another hostess provides round-trip transportation to and from her farm house and Harrisburg International Airport for only $10.

BED AND BREAKFAST OF CHESTER COUNTY
P.O. BOX 825, KENNETT SQUARE, PA 19348

Offers B&B Homes In: Brandywine Valley, from the Philadelphia suburbs and Wilmington, Delaware to Pennsylvania Dutch country.
Reservations Phone: 215/444-1367
Phone Hours: Anytime daily
Price Range of Homes: $30 to $50 single, $40 to $85 double
Breakfast Included in Price: Continental or full American, depending on individual home . . . a specialty is Pennsylvania Dutch scrapple mushroom quiche; "Kennett Square is the mushroom capital of the world."
Brochure Available: For $3
Reservations Should Be Made: At least 1 week in advance preferred—"We try to accommodate immediately, or as soon as possible."

Scenic Attractions Near the B&B Homes: Longwood Gardens, Winterthur, Brandywine River Museum (Wyeth paintings), Delaware Natural History Museum, Valley Forge, Brandywine Battlefield, Phillips Mushroom Museum, Pennsylvania Dutch Country
Major Schools, Universities Near the B&B Homes: West Chester U., Lincoln, Widener, U. of Delaware, Penn State at Lima

B&B Bonuses
An antique-laden 1836 farmhouse situated in the middle of 275 acres of pastoral beauty also offers such modern amenities as a swimming pool, hot tub in a greenhouse, and TVs in the rooms— "The delightful hostess loves to meet and entertain new people, offering a full country breakfast with homemade goodies." If you appreciate a view of horses grazing in pastures, you can feast your eyes from a Victorian mansion, circa 1840, and then take a dip in the pool.

Hosts are glad to direct guests to local restaurants and sights.

CENTER CITY BED & BREAKFAST

1804 PINE ST., PHILADELPHIA, PA 19103

Offers B&B Homes In: Center City Philadelphia, plus some outside the city
Reservations Phone: 215/735-1137
Phone Hours: 9 a.m. to 5 p.m. six days a week, except holidays
Price Range of Homes: $20 to $45 single, $35 to $65 double
Breakfast Included in Price: Continental or full American (juice, eggs, bacon, toast, coffee); full breakfast served at certain homes
Brochure Available: Free
Reservations Should Be Made: 2 weeks in advance (last-minute reservations accepted if possible)

Scenic Attractions Near the B&B Homes: Independence Hall, Betsy Ross House, Liberty Bell, Fairmount Park, Carpenters' Hall, Rodin Museum, Franklin Museum, Amish Country, Philadelphia Art Museum, Philadelphia Zoo
Major Schools, Universities Near the B&B Homes: U. of Pennsylvania, Temple, Drexel Institute, Moore College of Art, largest number of medical schools in mid-Atlantic area

B&B Bonuses

A restored town house furnished with antiques and canopied beds was mentioned in a recent issue of *National Geographic.* An elegantly furnished high-rise apartment affords a spectacular view, and a house "right out of Charles Dickens" is situated in a cobblestone courtyard with gaslight-type lanterns. Hosts will help locate a parking space, and make club membership privileges available.

REST & REPAST BED & BREAKFAST SERVICE

P.O. BOX 126, PINE GROVE MILLS, PA 16868

Offers B&B Homes In: Central Pennsylvania
Reservations Phone: 814/238-1484
Phone Hours: 7 to 11 p.m. Monday to Friday, 9 a.m. to noon on Saturday; other hours, answering machine
Price Range of Homes: $25 to $29 single, $30 to $40 double (on football weekends, $38 to $55 double, and a $7 surcharge for one-night stays; two-night minimum on Homecoming Weekend)
Breakfast Included in Price: Continental or full American . . . almost half the hosts serve full breakfasts, including Pennsylvania

Dutch specialties, home-grown eggs and homemade sausage
Brochure Available: Free
Reservations Should Be Made: 2 weeks in advance (last-minute
reservations accepted if possible); 3 to 6 months in advance for
football weekends, and especially Homecoming Weekend

Scenic Attractions Near the B&B Homes: Penns Cave, Indian Cav-
erns, Woodward Cave, 28th Division Military Shrine and Museum,
Governor Curtin Mansion Village, four wineries, Belleville Amish
Market, Baalsburg (home of Memorial Day)
Major Schools, Universities Near the B&B Homes: Penn State,
Bucknell

B&B Bonuses

One host has a herb farm, shop, and trading post behind her
home. Three other homes are on the National Historic Register,
"beautifully furnished and lovingly restored." The hosts are glad to
share their extensive knowledge with their guests. Several are
within walking distance of the Penn State campus.

"Each host home has been inspected for comfort, cleanliness and
individual charm."

PITTSBURGH BED AND BREAKFAST

2190 BEN FRANKLIN DR., PITTSBURGH, PA 15237

Offers B&B Homes In: Pittsburgh, Greensburgh, Mercer, Cranberry,
Washington, Shellsburg, and the Northeast
Reservations Phone: 412/367-8080
Phone Hours: 9 a.m. to 5 p.m. Monday to Friday, to noon on week-
ends
Price Range of Homes: $25 to $45 single, $34 to $65 double
Breakfast Included in Price: Continental . . . some hosts prepare
special muffins or rolls and herb teas (you can pick your own
home-grown herbs)
Brochure Available: Free if you send a stamped, self-addressed no.
10 envelope
Reservations Should Be Made: 2 weeks in advance (last-minute
reservations accepted when possible)

Scenic Attractions Near the B&B Homes: Amish antique shopping,
Lake Erie
Major Schools, Universities Near the B&B Homes: U. of Pittsburgh,
Carnegie-Mellon, Duquesne

B&B Bonuses _____

Ask for the Millstone House, located in historic Bedford County in Schellsburg. The rooms are decorated with antiques. There is an ornate mantel in the living room, a player piano, and a fireplace on the side porch for roasting chestnuts. Good antique shopping is nearby.

BED & BREAKFAST OF VALLEY FORGE
P.O. BOX 562, VALLEY FORGE, PA 19481

Offers B&B Homes In: Valley Forge, Downingtown, Phoenixville, Chestnut Hill, Berwyn, Strafford, Newtown Square, Malvern, Horsham (all in Pennsylvania)
Reservations Phone: 215/783-7838
Phone Hours: 9 a.m. to 9 p.m. daily
Price Range of Homes: $35 to $45 single, $45 to $60 double
Breakfast Included in Price: Continental or full American (depending on the hostess)
Brochure Available: Free
Reservations Should Be Made: 2 weeks in advance (last-minute reservations accepted)

Scenic Attractions Near the B&B Homes: Valley Forge National Park, many historic homes, hiking and horse trails in the park; Pennsylvania Dutch Country; Reading factory discount shopping; Longwood Gardens; Andrew Wyeth Art Museum; King of Prussia (largest shopping center in the U.S.); Devon Horse Show
Major Schools, Universities Near the B&B Homes: West Chester U., Villanova, Rosemont, Immaculate College, Ursinus, Eastern College, Valley Forge Military Academy, Bryn Mawr, Harcum, Penn State Graduate School

B&B Bonuses _____

Hostesses can provide sightseeing tours.

B&B Inns

THE OVERLOOK INN
DUTCH HILL ROAD, CANADENSIS, PA 18325

Reservations Phone: 717/595-7519
Description: The inn has 20 rooms furnished with individually chosen antiques and decorated with a mixture of prints, plants, and country crafts. There are also accommodations in the carriage house and in the lodge. Six rooms have fireplaces.
Amenities: Fresh-squeezed orange juice, farm-fresh eggs, popovers, muffins, fruit pancakes, homemade sausage, scrapple, coffee and tea are served; dinner is included in the price.

Nearby Attractions: Pennsylvania Dutch Country
Special Services: Library stocked with books, games, and color TV; shuffleboard, bocci, badminton; pool; high tea at 4 p.m., iced tea by the pool
Rates: $73 single, $126 double

CEDAR RUN INN
CEDAR RUN, CEDAR RUN, PA 17727

Reservations Phone: 717/353-6241
Description: Situated in Pennsylvania's Grand Canyon, the inn is 100 years old and furnished with the original furniture. The chef/owner is from the Culinary Institute of America.
Amenities: Full breakfast (choice of blueberry pancakes, French toast, eggs, or fruit and yogurt plate)

Nearby Attractions: Trout trophy streams, Black Forest hiking and skiing trails, Pine Creek directly in front of inn for swimming, fishing, or canoeing
Rates: $34 double, MAP; $16 double for room only

CENTER BRIDGE INN
BOX 74, STAR ROUTE, NEW HOPE, PA 18938

Reservations Phone: 215/862-9139

Description: This Williamsburg colonial overlooking the Delaware River has a private house guest deck and fireplace.
Amenities: Continental breakfast

Nearby Attractions: Canoeing, tubing, fishing, horseback riding, swimming, summer theater
Rates: $70 to $115 double on weekends; $60 to $90 double on weekdays

THE INN AT PHILLIPS MILL

NORTH RIVER ROAD, NEW HOPE, PA 18938

Reservations Phone: 215/862-2984
Description: Aaron Phillips built a grist mill here in 1756. Over the years an art colony formed around the mill and organized art exhibitions, concerts, dances, and theatrical productions, and it's still a cultural center. There are now five comfortable bedrooms with private bath and three dining rooms. Each bedroom is furnished with antiques, quilts on four-poster beds, and embroidered cloths.

Nearby Attractions: Swimming pool, craft shows, an annual play production
Rates: $60 to $70 double

LOGAN INN

10 W. FERRY ST., NEW HOPE, PA 18938

Reservations Phone: 215/862-5134
Description: Established in 1727, this inn has hosted travelers ever since. George Washington visited the tavern and made final plans for the Battle of Trenton here. Later visitors have included Richard Rodgers and Lorenz Hart, Helen Hayes, Tallulah Bankhead, Dorothy Parker, and Liza Minnelli. There are ten rooms, eight with private bath, furnished with such antiques as marble-topped tables and armoires.

Special Services: Sizable collection of clocks
Rates: $75 double

UPPER BLACK EDDY INN
RIVER ROAD, RTE. 32, UPPER BLACK EDDY, PA 18972

Reservations Phone: 215/982-5554
Description: The inn dates back to 1830 when it served canal travelers. There are six bedrooms (sharing two baths), with early American decor—sconces with etched-glass covers and paintings of country scenes adorning the walls.

Nearby Attractions: Ringing rocks geological attraction; fishing, boating, canoeing, tubing on the Delaware River; historic sites; arts, crafts, and antiques
Rates: $90 double

SOUTH CAROLINA

B&B Reservation Services

CHARLESTON SOCIETY BED & BREAKFAST
84 MURRAY BLVD., CHARLESTON, SC 29401

Offers B&B Homes In: The historic area of Charleston
Reservations Phone: 803/723-4948
Phone Hours: 9 a.m. to 5 p.m. daily
Price Range of Homes: $45 to $70 single, $60 to $100 double
Breakfast Included in Price: Continental (juice, roll or toast, coffee)
Brochure Available: Free
Reservations Should Be Made: 2 or 3 weeks in advance (last-minute reservations accepted if possible)

Scenic Attractions Near the B&B Homes: All the Historic District homes and other historic points of interest are within easy walking distance
Major Schools, Universities Near the B&B Homes: The Citadel, the College at Charleston, Baptist College

B&B Bonuses
"Enjoy the gracious hospitality of a stay in America's most historic city. The 18th-century homes, handsome interiors, period

furniture, and charming Charleston gardens characterize the lifestyle of the aristocrats who lived in these great houses during the pre-Revolutionary, post-Revolutionary, and antebellum days, all within easy walking distance of shops, restaurants, and historic points of interest." A licensed tour guide is available.

HISTORIC CHARLESTON BED AND BREAKFAST

43 LEGARE ST., CHARLESTON, SC 29401

Offers B&B Homes In: The Historic District of Charleston
Reservations Phone: 803/722-6606
Phone Hours: 24 hours daily
Price Range of Homes: $40 to $100 single, $45 to $100 double
Breakfast Included in Price: Continental (juice, roll or toast, coffee)
Brochure Available: Free
Reservations Should Be Made: 2 weeks in advance; for the period March to June, 2 to 3 months in advance (last-minute reservations accepted if possible)

Scenic Attractions Near the B&B Homes: Historic homes, museums, harbor tours, famous gardens, beaches
Major Schools, Universities Near the B&B Homes. The Citadel, College of Charleston, Medical University of South Carolina

B&B Bonuses

For something really unusual, ask for the gazebo garden house, from circa 1838; this was the original bath and card house for the Kerrison mansion. Another home has been created from the stables and kitchen building of a circa 1720 Georgian mansion, and a 1797 house is owned by the seventh generation of the same family. Guests are treated like "nonpaying friends" and have been invited for cocktails or elaborate brunches, and given gift mementos.

B&B Inns

PINE KNOLL INN AT HIGHLAND PARK

305 LANCASTER ST. SW, AIKEN, SC 29801

Reservations Phone: 803/649-5939

Description: Pine Knoll was built as a winter residence in 1930. Situated on the 17th green of the Highland Park Country Club, it is included in the National Register of Historical Places. The seven guest rooms have preserved the past with all the comforts of today—central air and heat, and some rooms have private bath.
Amenities: Fresh juices and fruits, home-baked muffins, pastries, coffee, and cereal served at breakfast

Nearby Attractions: Hopeland Gardens, National Horse Racing Hall of Fame, Sunday polo games, Aiken Triple Crown Horse Races each March, Masters Golf Tournament in April
Special Services: Complimentary round of golf, swimming pool, bicycles, recreation room
Rates: $40 to $55 single, $45 to 65 double

THE CHANCELLOR CARROL HOUSE
112 GREGG AVE., AIKEN, SC 29801

Reservations Phone: not available at press time
Description: This 150-year-old home is on the National Register. The guest rooms are the old maid's quarters.
Amenities: Continental breakfast

Nearby Attractions: Historic homes, polo, horse races, golf
Special Services: Swimming pool, tennis court, use of kitchen
Rates: $50 double

EVERGREEN INN
1103 S. MAIN ST., ANDERSON, SC 29621

Reservations Phone: 803/225-1109
Description: The inn located in Anderson's Historic District is one of the oldest mansions. The accommodations consist of seven rooms, six baths, and eight fireplaces. The house is on the National Register.
Amenities: Continental breakfast with fresh fruit, yogurt, and cheeses

Nearby Attractions: Jane Hartwell Park, Anderson Historic District
Rates: $52 single, $65 double

BAY STREET INN

601 BAY ST., BEAUFORT, SC 29902

Reservations Phone: 803/524-7720
Description: A Greek Revival building used in South Carolina's advertisements, this inn is on the water within the Beaufort Historic District. Furnishings include a large collection of American art and antiques.
Amenities: Juice, melon or fruit, homemade regional breads and jellies, coffee and tea

Nearby Attractions: Verdier and Elliot House Museums, Hunting Island State Park
Special Services: Croquet, golf, tennis, bicycling, beach equipment, ocean swimming, historic tours
Rates: $45 to $60 single, $50 to $65 double

OLD POINT INN

212 NEW ST., BEAUFORT, SC 29902

Reservations Phone: 803/524-3177 or 803/525-6104
Description: This 1898 Victorian in the "Beaufort Style," with double porches, front and side, is located in the Historic District with views of the Beaufort River.
Amenities: Full breakfast, sometimes including spoonbread, homemade sourdough bread, or muffins

Nearby Attractions: Hunting Island State Park, Hilton Head Island
Special Services: Mints and flowers in the rooms, bicycles
Rates: $50 to $55 double

THE CHURCH STREET INN

177 CHURCH ST., CHARLESTON, SC 29401

Reservations Phone: Toll free 800/845-7638, 800/922-7638, in South Carolina
Description: Located in the heart of the market area of Charleston, the Church Street has 31 two-story town houses with luxury living rooms, 1 1/2 baths, and full kitchens.
Amenities: Breakfast is served in the lobby and consists of juice, coffee, danish, and croissants

Nearby Attractions: Fort Sumter, the Battery, Old Slave Market, Confederate Museum, and historical houses
Special Services: A glass of champagne or sherry on arrival, a bottle of imported wine for each room
Rates: $115 double in a one-bedroom suite in summer, $150 double in a two-bedroom suite in fall and winter

THE HAYNE HOUSE
30 KING ST., CHARLESTON, SC 29401

Reservations Phone: 803/577-2633
Description: This graceful private home in the Historic District dates back to the 1770s. It has three rooms with bath for guests.
Amenities: Continental breakfast with fresh fruit

Nearby Attractions: The Battery, Fort Sumter, Historic Charleston, tennis
Rates: $50 to $65 double

INDIGO INN
ONE MAIDEN LANE, CHARLESTON, SC 29401

Reservations Phone: Toll free 800/845-7639, 800/922-1340 in South Carolina
Description: Located in historic downtown Charleston, the Indigo Inn has 18th-century decor, a courtyard, down pillows and comforters, two queen-size beds in each room, and facilities for the handicapped. Pets are allowed.
Amenities: "Hunt breakfast" (ham biscuits, homemade breads, fresh fruits, coffee, and juice)

Nearby Attractions: Within walking distance of the open-air market, historic churches and mansions, and fine restaurants
Rates: $75 to $95 double in summer, $65 to $85 double in winter

THE JASMINE HOUSE
64 HASELL ST., CHARLESTON, SC 29401

Reservations Phone: Toll free 800/845-7639, 800/922-1340 in South Carolina

Description: The inn has pre-civil War Greek Revival architecture, 14-foot ceilings, fireplaces, and Oriental rugs.
Amenities: "Hunt breakfast" (ham biscuits, homemade breads, fresh fruit, coffee, and juice)

Nearby Attractions: Within walking distance of open-air markets, historic churches, and fine restaurants
Special Services: Jacuzzi and daily periodicals
Rates: $75 to $100 double

MEETING STREET INN
113 MEETING ST., CHARLESTON, SC 29401

Reservations Phone: Toll free 800/945-7638, 800/845-7638 in South Carolina
Description: Located in the center of the historic district, the inn has 55 rooms plus a conference suite. Some parts of the building date back to 1871.
Amenities: Orange juice, freshly baked pastries (including cheesecake, from a family recipe), coffee and tea

Nearby Attractions: Fort Sumter, Patriot's Point Museum, White Point Gardens, the Battery
Special Services: Heated Jacuzzi in courtyard, a bottle of wine in each guest room, afternoon chamber music concert
Rates: $88 to $108 double

THE JOHN LAWTON HOUSE
159 3RD ST. EAST, ESTIL, SC 29918

Reservations Phone: 803/625-2586, or toll free 800/625-3240
Description: Built around the turn of the century from lumber and materials brought by mule and wagon from nearby Jericho Plantation, and extensively renovated in 1985, the inn is decorated with antiques, rich woods, Oriental rugs, and painted porcelains. Original family oil portraits are softly lit by crystal chandeliers. The draperies, wall coverings, and fabrics are period reproductions.
Amenities: Specialties include pear pie and homemade sausage served on silver, crystal, and fine china

Nearby Attractions: Charleston, Columbia, Hilton Head Island, and the South Carolina coast all less than two hours away

Special Services: A small kitchen and private entrance are available to guests, and there's parking on the premises for cars and campers
Rates: $40 double

CASSENA INN
P.O. BOX 5, PAWLEY'S ISLAND, SC 29585

Reservations Phone: 803/787-4556
Description: Rooms are located in three beachfront cottages. All cottages have rocking chairs and tables on the large porches. Some rooms have air conditioning and private bath.
Amenities: Full country breakfast

Nearby Attractions: Bellefield Nature Center, Rice Museum, Huntington Beach
Special Services: Airport pickup, golf, tennis
Rates: $67 to $86.50 double

LIBERTY HALL INN
621 S. MECHANIC ST., PENDLETON, SC 29630

Reservations Phone: 803/646-7500
Description: The inn is a restored Piedmont farmhouse with private baths, air conditioning and TVs in rooms furnished with period antiques.
Amenities: Continental breakfast

Nearby Attractions: Woodburn Plantation, Clemson University, John Calhoun's Home, lakes for boating and fishing, golf
Rates: $45 double

CHAUGA RIVER HOUSE
COBB'S BRIDGE ROAD, WESTMINSTER, SC 29691

Reservations Phone: 803/647-9587
Description: Located directly on the rapids of the Chauga River in the center of the Sumter National Forest, the inn has five guest rooms decorated with French country antiques.
Amenities: Continental breakfast plus cereal and fruit

Nearby Attractions: Whitewater Falls, Clemson University
Special Services: Barbecue area, swimming, TV lounge, white-water rafting packages
Rates: $36 to $52 double

VIRGINIA

B&B Reservation Services

PRINCELY BED & BREAKFAST LTD.

819 PRINCE ST., ALEXANDRIA, VA 22314

Offers B&B Homes In: Alexandria
Reservations Phone: 703/683-2159
Phone Hours: 9 a.m. to 6 p.m. Monday to Friday
Price Range of Homes: $48 single, $65 to $75 double
Breakfast Included in Price: Continental (juice, roll or toast, coffee)
Reservations Should Be Made: 2 weeks in advance (no last-minute reservations accepted)

Scenic Attractions Near the B&B Homes: Washington, D.C.; Mount Vernon

B&B Bonuses

   "Our houses in Alexandria's famous 'Old Town' date from 1750 to 1830. Most are filled with museum-quality antiques."
   Some hosts drive guests to Mount Vernon (George Washington's home and estate), the Capitol, the White House, and all of the many places of interest in the District of Columbia. There are at least seven major universities in the area.

SHENANDOAH VALLEY BED & BREAKFAST RESERVATIONS

P.O. BOX 305, BROADWAY, VA 22815

Offers B&B Homes In: Many areas of Virginia, including Staunton, northern Shenandoah Valley, Mount Jackson, Amissville, Front Royal, and Rawley Springs

Reservations Phone: 703/896-9702
Phone Hours: 4 to 11 p.m. Monday to Friday; answering machine available at other times
Price Range of Homes: $20 to $50 single, $39 to $95 double (MasterCard and VISA accepted for reservation deposit)
Breakfast Included in Price: Continental (juice, toast or roll, coffee)
Brochure Available: Description of homes, $1

Scenic Attractions Near the B&B Homes: Wayside Theater, Belle Grove Plantation, Shenandoah Summer Music Theater, Stonewall Jackson's Headquarters, Endless Taverns, Orkney Springs Open Air Concerts, Woodrow Wilson birthplace, American Frontier Museum
Major Schools, Universities Near the B&B Homes: Shenandoah College, James Madison U., Eastern Mennonite, Bridgewater, Mary Baldwin, Shenandoah Valley Academy, Massanutten Military Academy

B&B Bonuses _____

Says the reservation service, "We can plan a B&B sampler for travelers making a loop from metropolitan areas through the valley eastward to Charlottesville or Richmond."

ROCKRIDGE RESERVATIONS
SLEEPY HOLLOW, P.O. BOX 76, BROWNSBURG, VA 24415

Offers B&B Homes In: Lexington and Rockbridge County
Reservations Phone: 703/348-5698
Phone Hours: 10 a.m. to 4 p.m. Monday to Friday (on weekends)
Price Range of Homes: $45 to $55 single, $45 to $55 double
Breakfast Included in Price: Continental
Brochure Available: Yes
Reservations Should Be Made: 2 weeks in advance

Scenic Attractions Near the B&B Homes: Blue Ridge Parkway, Natural Bridge Virginia, Stonewall Jackson House, George C. Marshall Museum and Library
Major Schools, Universities Near the B&B Homes: Washington and Lee, Virginia Military Institute, Southern Seminary

B&B Bonuses _____

An 1840 Tuscan villa is a typical brick antebellum mansion furnished with antiques, mostly family pieces.

GUESTHOUSES RESERVATION SERVICES, INC.

P.O. BOX 5737, CHARLOTTESVILLE, VA 22905

Offers B&B Homes In: City of Charlottesville and others in Albemarle County, Shenandoah National Park (Luray, Virginia)
Reservations Phone: 804/979-7264
Phone Hours: noon to 5 p.m. Monday to Friday
Price Range of Homes: $30 and up single, $36 to $160 double
Breakfast Included in Price: Continental or full American (small additional price for full breakfast—hostess specialties range from a "breakfast soufflé" to homemade breads and muffins)
Brochure Available: For $1
Reservations Should Be Made: 2 to 6 weeks in advance (last-minute reservations accepted if possible)

Scenic Attractions Near the B&B Homes: Monticello, Ash Lawn (James Madison's Home), Skyline Drive, Shenandoah National Park, Blue Ridge Parkway, Appalachian Trail, April Historic Garden Week
Major Schools, Universities Near the B&B Homes: U. of Virginia (founded by Thomas Jefferson)

B&B Bonuses

Some of the interesting homes are a 150-year-old log cabin for guests with its own driveway, a private wing in a newly built Georgian home in horse country, a picturesque country cottage from a design by a renowned architect of the past, and an upstairs suite in old slave quarters, adjacent to the University of Virginia.

SOJOURNERS BED & BREAKFAST

3609 TANGLEWOOD LANE, LYNCHBURG, VA 24503

Offers B&B Homes In: Lynchburg, and Bedford and Amherst Counties
Reservations Phone: 804/384-1655
Phone Hours: Before 10 a.m.; an answering service is available for calls after 6 p.m.
Price Range of Homes: $32 to $40 single, $36 to $50 double
Breakfast Included in Price: Some homes serve a continental, but most serve full American breakfasts, with homemade breads.
Brochure Available: Free if you send a stamped, self-addressed no. 10 envelope

Reservations Should Be Made: 3 weeks in advance (last-minute reservations accepted if possible)

Scenic Attractions Near the B&B Homes: Blue Ridge Parkway, Appomattox National Park, Jones Memorial Library, Virginia Ten Miler Road Race, Virginia House & Garden Tour, Patrick Henry home, Thomas Jefferson's summer home, Booker T. Washington birthplace

Major Schools, Universities Near the B&B Homes: Lynchburg College, Randolph Macon Woman's College, Sweet Briar, Virginia Episcopal School, Liberty U.

B&B Bonuses

Guests can request a wide selection of brochures on central Virginia, books and magazines of particular interest to history buffs, copies of menus from the best restaurants, and guides to shopping, sightseeing, and nature trails. Airport pickups can be arranged, with sufficient notice.

BED & BREAKFAST OF TIDEWATER VIRGINIA

P.O. BOX 3343, NORFOLK, VA 23514

Offers B&B Homes In: Norfolk, Virginia Beach, Portsmouth, Chesapeake, the Eastern Shore and Northern Neck of Virginia

Reservations Phone: 804/627-1983 or 804/627-9409

Phone Hours: 8 a.m. to 8 p.m. daily (answering service 24 hours a day)

Price Range of Homes: $30 to $60 single, $35 to $75 double

Breakfast Included in Price: "We leave it up to the hosts. Some serve elaborate breakfasts, and the rate is consequently higher than for continental. A minimum of fruit, beverage, and rolls or muffins, is required."

Brochure Available: Free

Reservations Should Be Made: At least 2 weeks in advance, but the earlier the better (last-minute reservations accepted if possible)

Scenic Attractions Near the B&B Homes: Norfolk Naval Base and Air Station, Chrysler Museum, MacArthur Memorial, Waterside Festival Marketplace, Chesapeake Bay fishing and water sports, Virginia Beach

Major Schools, Universities Near the B&B Homes: Old Dominion, Eastern Virginia Medical School, Virginia Wesleyan

B&B Bonuses _____

Ask about the house with its own private beach on the bay. The house is a traditional Eastern Shore design—big house, little house, colonnades and kitchen—attractively furnished with antiques. Or enjoy the working fireplace in an elegant guest room a few minutes from downtown Norfolk and its most popular restaurants.

"We have a most genial and enthusiastic group of hosts who roll out the red carpet for their B&B guests."

BENSONHOUSE OF RICHMOND

P.O. BOX 15131, RICHMOND, VA 23227

Offers B&B Homes In: Richmond
Reservations Phone: 804/648-7560
Phone Hours: 10:30 a.m. to 4 p.m. Monday to Friday (24-hour answering service)
Price Range of Homes: $38 to $72 single, $48 to $84 double
Breakfast Included in Price: Continental or full American, depending on individual home; many homes serve home-baked breads and muffins.
Brochure Available: $1 with a stamped, self-addressed no. 10 envelope
Reservations Should Be Made: 3 or more weeks in advance (last-minute reservations accepted if accommodations available)

Scenic Attractions Near the B&B Homes: St. John's Church, Edgar Allan Poe Museum, Museum of the Confederacy, John Marshall House, State Archives, Virginia Historical Society, Science Museum of Virginia, Virginia Museum, and Virginia Theater for the Performing Arts; within a short drive of Colonial Williamsburg, Busch Gardens, Kings Dominion, and James River Plantations
Major Schools, Universities Near the B&B Homes: U. of Richmond, Medical College of Virginia, Virginia Commonwealth U., Randolph Macon, Union Theological Seminary, St. Catherine's School, St. Christopher's School

THE TRAVEL TREE

P.O. BOX 838, WILLIAMSBURG, VA 23187

Offers B&B Homes In: Williamsburg
Reservations Phone: 804/253-1571

Phone Hours: 6 to 9 p.m. Monday to Friday
Price Range of Homes: $28 to $60 single, $35 to $75 double
Breakfast Included in Price: Continental (juice, roll or toast, coffee)
Brochure Available: Free
Reservations Should Be Made: Several weeks in advance

Scenic Attractions Near the B&B Homes: Colonial Williamsburg, Busch Gardens, Yorktown, Jamestown
Major Schools, Universities Near the B&B Homes: College of William and Mary

B&B Bonuses _____

Among their comfortable homes are a colonial-style house, a newly furnished and decorated ranch house with private entrance, a cozy Cape Cod with a four-poster bed and a twin-bedded room with a private entrance.

B&B Inns

CONSTANT SPRING INN

413 S. ROYAL AVE., FORT ROYAL, VA 22630
Reservations Phone: 703/635-7010
Description: The inn sits above the town on landscaped grounds.
Amenities: Full breakfast from the menu; on Sunday a breakfast buffet is served. Dinner is also included in the room charge.

Nearby Attractions: Shenandoah National Park, Skyline Drive
Special Services: Pool, tennis, and horseback riding all found nearby
Rates: $82 double

FREDERICK HOUSE

18 E. FREDERICK ST., STAUNTON, VA 24401
Reservations Phone: 703/885-4220
Description: The inn consists of three restored town houses in historic downtown Staunton, across from Mary Baldwin College. The two- and three-room suites and large single rooms have private bath, TV, and individual heat and air conditioning.

Nearby Attractions: Woodrow Wilson's birthplace, Museum of American Frontier Culture, Blue Ridge Parkway, Skyline Drive

Special Services: Golf, tennis, horseback riding, canoeing, skiing, swimming
Rates: $35 single, $45 double

THE CEDARS
616 JAMESTOWN RD., WILLIAMSBURG, VA 23185
Reservations Phone: 804/229-3591
Description: This stately three-story brick colonial is within a ten-minute walk to the restored area. It has a lovely sitting room and porch, plus six rooms and a cottage.
Amenities: Sally Lunn toast, juice, coffee or tea

Nearby Attractions: Colonial Williamsburg, Busch Gardens, Yorktown, Jamestown, Colonial Parkway
Rates: $40 to $55 double

WEST VIRGINIA

B&B Inns

HILLSBROOK INN ON BULL SKIN RUN
RTE. 2 (P.O. BOX 152), CHARLES TOWN, WV 25414
Reservations Phone: 304/725-4223
Description: This English half-timbered manor house set on 17 country acres with trees, ponds, and streams is decorated with antiques and fine art.
Amenities: Breakfast may include French toast Tatiana served with warm cranberry-orange syrup and a dollop of sour cream; hot cereal thick with nuts and dried fruits, drenched in heavy cream and topped with sweet butter and brown sugar; country ham or sausage

Nearby Attractions: Harper's Ferry National Park, Charles Town Races, white-water rafting, Summit Point Raceway
Special Services: Swimming, cross-country skiing
Rates: $100 to $130 double

MOUNTAIN VILLAGE INN

RTE. 219, HORSE SHOE, WV 26769
Reservations Phone: 304/735-3563
Description: A spruce-log lodge surrounded by a forest set beside a
mountain stream, the inn has three bedrooms tucked up under the
eaves with a shared bath. The building is board and batten, and the
guest rooms share a sitting room and a large enclosed porch.
Amenities: A full country breakfast including flapjacks, buckwheats,
and Mexican specialties; dinner is included in the tariff

Nearby Attractions: Canaan State Park, Cathedral State Park,
Blackwater Falls State Park, tennis, skiing, swimming
Special Services: A menagerie of farm animals on the grounds
Rates: $90 double

WELLS INN

316 CHARLES ST., SISTERSVILLE, WV 26175
Reservations Phone: 304/652-3111
Description: Following the drilling of the "Pole Cat," some 2,500 oil
wells were opened. To accommodate the "boomtown," this Victorian
inn was opened. Now modernized, it offers its 36 bedrooms for your
accommodation. Victorian and new furniture combine to join the past
with the present. The inn is on the National and State Historic
Registers.

Nearby Attractions: Glass factories, historic oil town
Special Services: Pool, tennis courts, and golf available
Rates: $42.50 to $45.50 double

The Great Lakes Area

Illinois / 169
Michigan / 170
Ohio / 173
Wisconsin / 175

ILLINOIS

B&B Reservation Services

BED & BREAKFAST CHICAGO, INC.
P.O. BOX 14088, CHICAGO, IL 60614

Offers B&B Homes In: Chicago and nearby areas of Wisconsin, Michigan, and Indiana
Reservations Phone: 312/951-0085
Phone Hours: 9 a.m. to 5 p.m. Monday to Friday
Price Range of Homes: $40 to $55 single, $50 to $65 double
Breakfast Included in Price: Continental
Brochure Available: Free
Reservations Should Be Made: 2 weeks in advance (last-minute reservations accepted if possible)

Scenic Attractions Near the B&B Homes: Lake Michigan, McCormick Place, Glencoe Botanic Garden, Bahai Temple, Ravinia Festival, Old Town (Chicago)
Major Schools, Universities Near the B&B Homes: Northwestern, Lake Forest, Loyola, U. of Chicago, U. of Illinois at Chicago, Wheaton, De Paul

B&B Bonuses

In Glencoe, a home overlooking a lake is filled with antiques, needlepoint, and quilts, and has charming hosts. The hostess of a remodeled, air-conditioned Victorian home is a caterer and will prepare meals.

Frequently offered are airport pickups. Small unhosted apartments are also available.

B&B Reservation Services

BETSY ROSS BED & BREAKFAST
P.O. BOX 1731, DEARBORN, MI 48121

Offers B&B Homes In: All over the state of Michigan, including the lower peninsula
Reservations Phone: 313/561-6041
Phone Hours: After 6 p.m. weekdays, or weekends
Price Range of Homes: $25 to $55 single, $30 to $60 double
Breakfast Included in Price: Some homes serve continental, but many offer a full breakfast, featuring special dishes. There is also a "Howell Festival" celebrating the Howell melons and hand-blended coffee in one of the homes.
Brochure Available: Free if you send a stamped, self-addressed no. 10 envelope
Reservations Should Be Made: 2 weeks in advance (last-minute reservations accepted if possible)

Scenic Attractions Near the B&B Homes: Henry Ford Museum, Greenfield Village, Fisher Theater, Cranbook Art Museum, Sleeping Bear Dunes National Park, Marshall Homes Tour, Meadow Brook Hall, Michigan Space Center, Ethnic Festivals Downtown Detroit, Grand Prix racing, Convention Center, Detroit Zoo, Irish Hills, resort areas.
Major Schools, Universities Near the B&B Homes: U. of Michigan, Michigan State, Wayne State, Albion, Cranbrook Schools, Oakland

B&B Bonuses

Want to play some golf? Ask for the condo right on the Wabeek golf course. Want to fish? There's a country home with a pond full of trout.

Some hosts offer discount tickets to Greenfield Village and will arrange to pick you up at the airport.

BED & BREAKFAST OF GRAND RAPIDS
334 COLLEGE ST., GRAND RAPIDS, MI 49503

Offers B&B Homes In: Heritage Hill Historic District in downtown Grand Rapids
Reservations Phone: 616/456-7125 or 616/451-4849
Phone Hours: 9 a.m. to 9 p.m. daily
Price Range of Homes: $45 single, $55 double
Breakfast Included in Price: Deluxe continental
Brochure Available: Free
Reservations Should Be Made: 2 weeks in advance (last-minute reservations accepted if possible)

Scenic Attractions Near the B&B Homes: Gerald R. Ford Museum, Holland Tulip Festival, Lake Michigan, Heritage Hill District
Major Schools, Universities Near the B&B Homes: Grand Rapids Junior College, Davenport Business College, Grand Valley State, Kendall School of Design, Calvin College

B&B Bonuses
All accommodations are in private, turn-of-the-century homes in the Heritage Hill Historic District.
"We provide tourist packets, and can make arrangements for theater, ballet, opera, etc."

B&B Inns

THE TERRACE INN
216 FAIRVIEW, BAY VIEW, MI 49770

Reservations Phone: 616/347-2410
Description: A four-story Victorian structure built in 1910, the inn has changed little over the years. Each of the 35 bedrooms contains original oak furnishings. Solid pine paneling lines the spacious lobby and the dining room.
Amenities: Continental breakfast

Nearby Attractions: Private bay-view beach, state park, Harbor Springs, fishing, tennis, sailing, nature trails, drama and musical

theater productions, weekly chamber music concerts, horseback riding
Special Services: An old-fashioned ice cream parlor is open in summer, and there are facilities for meetings and receptions.
Rates: $38 to $78 double

Wickwood Inn
510 BUTLER ST., SAUGATUCK, MI 49453

Reservations Phone: 616/857-1097
Description: An English country manor with several common rooms with Laura Ashley papers and fabrics and antiques, the inn has 11 air-conditioned rooms with private bath.
Amenities: Homemade coffee cake, fruit in season, coffee. Brunch is served on Sunday, and hot and cold hors d'oeuvres are served each night in the library bar.

Nearby Attractions: Cross-country ski area with 200 miles of mapped trails, charter fishing boats, two blocks from quaint Victorian Village
Special Services: "Our London taxi is at our door to drive guests to dinner or town." Crabtree & Evelyn soaps and shampoo are in each bath.
Rates: $75 to $110 double in summer, $60 to $95 double in winter

CLIFFORD LAKE HOTEL
561 CLIFFORD LAKE DR., STANTON, MI 48888

Reservations Phone: 517/831-5151
Description: A Michigan historic site overlooking Clifford Lake, the inn contains rooms in the hotel and cottages with two, three, and four bedrooms. The rooms are furnished with antiques, and have corner sinks and country furniture.
Amenities: Continental breakfast

Nearby Attractions: Crystal Speedway, Morelands Moto-Cross, swimming, paddleboats, snowmobiles, fishing-boat rentals
Rates: $55 single, $65 double, in summer; $45 single, $55 double, in fall and winter

OHIO

B&B Reservation Services

PRIVATE LODGINGS INC.
P.O. BOX 18590, CLEVELAND, OH 44118

Offers B&B Homes In: Greater Cleveland area, including outlying suburbs
Reservations Phone: 216/321-3213
Phone Hours: 9 a.m. to 5 p.m. Monday to Friday (on Saturday and Sunday, 10 a.m. to 6 p.m. answering service)
Price Range of Homes: $30 to $50 single, $35 to $65 double
Breakfast Included in Price: Continental (juice, roll or toast, coffee) or full American in some host homes
Brochure Available: Free if you send a stamped, self-addressed no. 10 envelope
Reservations Should Be Made: 1 to 2 weeks in advance (last-minute reservations accepted if possible)

Scenic Attractions Near the B&B Homes: Cleveland Museum of Art, Severance Hall, Cleveland Natural History Museum, Crawford Auto Museum, Cleveland Zoo, metropolitan parks
Major Schools, Universities Near the B&B Homes: Case Western Reserve, Cleveland State, John Carroll U., Cuyahoga Community College

B&B Bonuses
   Ask for the beautifully decorated duplex with cathedral ceiling and balcony overlooking the living room, within walking distance of transportation, shopping, and restaurants.

COLUMBUS BED & BREAKFAST
769 S. 3RD ST., COLUMBUS, OH 43206

Offers B&B Homes In: Columbus, Ohio, area
Reservations Phone: 614/443-3680
Phone Hours: 8 a.m. to 11 p.m. daily (closed in January)
Price Range of Homes: $30 single, $50 double

Breakfast Included in Price: Continental (juice, roll or toast, coffee)
Brochure Available: Free
Reservations Should Be Made: 2 weeks in advance (last-minute reservations accepted if possible)

Scenic Attractions Near the B&B Homes: German Village, restored residential area listed in the National Register
Major Schools, Universities Near the B&B Homes: Ohio State, Franklin, Dennison, Otterbein, Kenyon, Capital

B&B Bonuses

A host home in German Village is close to downtown Columbus, but "a century away in character and ambience. "Small brick houses, brick-paved streets and sidewalks, and wrought-iron fences combine to create an old-world atmosphere, with shops and restaurants within walking distance.

BUCKEYE BED & BREAKFAST

P.O. BOX 130, POWELL, OH 43065

Offers B&B Homes In: Columbus, Cincinnati, Delaware, Cambridge, Germantown, Spring Valley, Waynesville, Dublin, Muirfield, Westerville, Worthington, Marietta, Dayton, Logan, North Olmstead, and Seville, all in Ohio
Reservations Phone: 614/548-4555
Phone Hours: 24 hours daily
Price Range of Homes: $22 to $25 single, $30 to $50 double
Breakfast Included in Price: Some homes serve continental, others full American. Many hosts who are gardeners and "nutrition-oriented" serve organically grown specialties.
Brochure Available: Free
Reservations Should Be Made: 10 days in advance (last-minute reservations accepted if possible)

Scenic Attractions Near the B&B Homes: Kings Island, Cincinnati Opera/Zoo, Ohio Historical Center, Muirfield Golf Course, Mound Builders' Sites, Little Brown Jug Harness Classic, Vandalia Trap Shoot, Marietta River Festival
Major Schools, Universities Near the B&B Homes: Ohio State, Ohio U., Ohio Wesleyan, Otterbien, Capital, Kenyon, Muckingum, Marietta, Wilmington, Wright State, U. of Cincinnati, Wittenberg, Concordia College, Antioch, U. of Dayton, Columbus Tech, Ohio Dominican

B&B Bonuses

The Buell House in Marietta is a 150-year-old home which is listed on the National Historic Register. It is authentically furnished and has many special exhibits to delight the collector's heart, such as dolls and china, and boasts no fewer than seven porches.

"Aspen in Ohio" comes to mind at a cabin-style house nestled on Rockies-like slopes in Worthington. Your host is a well-traveled educator who likes to meet new people.

WISCONSIN

B&B Reservation Services

BED & BREAKFAST GUEST HOMES

RT. 2, ALGOMA, WI 54201

Offers B&B Homes In: Wisconsin
Reservations Phone: 414/743-9742
Phone Hours: 7 a.m. to 9 p.m. daily
Price Range of Homes: $30 to $55 single, $35 to $65 double
Breakfast Included in Price: "Practically all hosts serve a generous full breakfast."
Brochure Available: Free if you send a stamped, self-addressed no. 10 envelope
Reservations Should Be Made: Preferably 1 or more weeks in advance (last-minute reservations filled if possible)

Scenic Attractions Near the B&B Homes: State parks, fishing, villages, cherry orchards, farms, urban and rural settings

B&B Bonuses

On seven acres of meadow overlooking Kangaroo Lake, a re-modeled home boasts three guest bedrooms, each with a country motif. And how about a room in a home perched on the edge of Lake Michigan? This one's a rural setting too, with thousands of feet of shoreline available for exploring. Many locations are in popular Door County. Many of their knowledgeable hosts are glad to accompany guests on sightseeing trips. Some homes are on Historic Registers.

BED & BREAKFAST OF MILWAUKEE, INC.
P.O. BOX 182, WAUKESHA, WI 53187

Offers B&B Homes In: Milwaukee, Wisconsin (Lakeshore area)
Reservations Phone: 414/342-5030
Phone Hours: 9 a.m. to 7 p.m. six days a week
Price Range of Homes: $40 to $65 single, $35 to $80 double
Breakfast Included in Price: Continental (juice, roll or toast, coffee);
may include fresh fruit, croissant, cheese, yogurt, tea
Brochure Available: Free
Reservations Should Be Made: 2 weeks in advance (last-minute
reservations accepted if possible)

Scenic Attractions Near the B&B Homes: Botanical Gardens, Zoo,
Grand Avenue Mall, Audubon Center, Lake Michigan, museums,
city parks, ethnic restaurants, major-league baseball, symphony,
ballet, repertory theater, summerfest, ethnic festivals
Major Schools, Universities Near the B&B Homes: U. of Wisconsin,
Marquette, Medical College of Wisconsin

B&B Bonuses
   Ask for the lovely 50-year-old English Tudor home located in a
sophisticated urban setting within walking distance of the park on
Lake Michigan and the University area. Or you want a unique spot
in Milwaukee while visiting the city? Try the ninth-floor loft apartment with a good view of the skyline: the king-size bed converts to
twins, and the unit has a kitchen, full bath, and living room.

B&B Inns

LOUE HOUSE
1111 S. MAIN ST., ALMA, WI 54610

Reservations Phone: 608/685-4923
Description: This Italianate house was designed by Charles May-
bury in 1853 and is on the National Register of Historic Places.
There are sinks in most rooms, and baths down the hall.
Amenities: Continental breakfast: "Help yourself—toast your own
muffin."

Nearby Attractions: Beautiful swamp, canoeing, excellent fishing, tennis, and golf
Special Services: Coffee in rooms, fish-cleaning facilities, gas grill and picnic table
Rates: $16 single, $30 double

The Northwest & Great Plains

Idaho / 181
Iowa / 182
Minnesota / 184
Montana / 185
North Dakota / 186
Oregon / 187
South Dakota / 191
Washington / 192

IDAHO

B&B Inns

DEEP CREEK INN
SCENIC RTE. 95, BANNERS FERRY, ID 83805

Reservations Phone: 208/267-2373
Description: This inn is set in a lovely little valley with a creek running through it, hence the name. It has a relaxed atmosphere.
Amenities: Cinnamon rolls and coffee and tea

Nearby Attractions: Fishing, rafting on the Moyie River, cross-country skiing, biking trails, golf, Ski Schweitzer, paddleboat
Special Services: Sundeck, lounge, restaurant, heated pool
Rates: $34 double

INDIAN CREEK GUEST RANCH
RTE. 2 (P.O. BOX 105), NORTH FORK, ID 83466

Reservations Phone: Ask the Salmon operator for 24F-211.
Description: The rustic main lodge with three cabins is hidden in a mountain valley. A fishing stream runs through the front yard.
Amenities: Juice, eggs, hotcakes, sausage, hash-browns, coffee or tea

Nearby Attractions: Ride on horseback to the old ghost town of Ulysses, the scenic Salmon River
Special Services: Pickups from the airport or from Salmon
Rates: $25 single, $50 double

SAWTOOTH HOTEL
P.O. BOX 52, STANLEY, ID 83278

Reservations Phone: 208/774-9947
Description: Each room is decorated with a lodgepole double bed and old-fashioned furnishings.

Amenities: Breakfast highlights include sourdough pancakes, cinnamon rolls, and country sausage.

Nearby Attractions: Sawtooth Recreation Area, Salmon River, Sawtooth National Fish Hatchery, rafting, field trips, horseback riding
Special Services: Will serve predawn breakfast and pack a lunch for day-trippers.
Rates: $15 to $22 single, $26 to $35 double

IOWA

B&B Reservation Services

BED & BREAKFAST IN IOWA, LTD.

P.O. BOX 430, PRESTON, IA 52069

Offers B&B In: Iowa
Reservations Phone: 319/689-4222
Phone Hours: Anytime in person or via an answering machine
Price Range of Homes: $20 to $35 single, $35 to $55 double
Breakfast Included in Price: Full, with Iowa breakfast specialties
Brochure Available: Free; send $1 for a directory of homes
Reservations Should Be Made: 2 weeks in advance; short notice also accepted by most homes when space is available

Scenic Attractions Near the B&B Homes: Iowa Great Lakes, historic homes, Iowa farms
Major Schools, Universities Near the B&B Homes: Drake, U. of Northern Iowa, Iowa State, U. of Iowa, Grandview, Simpson, Grinnell, Morningside, Wm. Penn

B&B Bonuses

You can stay on a working farm and join hosts on community celebrations. Missouri River tours and Mississippi River cruises are available.

B&B Inns

THE REDSTONE INN
504 BLUFF, DUBUQUE, IA 52001

Reservations Phone: 319/582-1894
Description: This restored Victorian mansion is in the heart of the city and has undergone extensive renovations in the last few years. It is furnished in antiques, and has a plaster crown molding with gold-leaf cherubs in the parlor. The four double suites have whirlpool baths.
Amenities: Continental breakfast

Nearby Attractions: River rides, Woodward Riverboat Museum, the Fenelon Rivers Hall of Fame, arboretum, cross-country and downhill skiing
Special Services: Turn-down service and morning coffee
Rates: $58 to $120 double in summer, $55 to $120 in winter

STOUT HOUSE
1105 LOCUST, DUBUQUE, IA 52001

Reservations Phone: 319/582-1894
Description: Purchased in 1985 from the archdiocese of Dubuque, the house was built in the Richardsonian Romanesque style by lumber baron F. D. Stout. It is a massive red sandstone home with a hexagonal tower and stone archways, now an elegant accommodation for guests.
Amenities: Continental breakfast

Nearby Attractions: Dubuque Greyhound Park, National Rivers Hall of Fame, Fenelon Place Elevator, skiing
Special Services: Complimentary beverages
Rates: $45 to $55 double

MINNESOTA

B&B Inns

GUNFLINT LODGE
GT100, GRAND MARAIS, MN 55604

Reservations Phone: Toll free 800/328-3325, 800/328-3362 in Minnesota
Description: This rustic lodge and cottages are set in Minnesota's North Woods on a glacial lake surrounded by towering bluffs.
Amenities: Full breakfast

Nearby Attractions: Gunflint Trail, Boundary Waters Canoe Wilderness Area
Rates: $45 single, $90 double

LOWELL INN
102 N. 2ND ST., STILLWATER, MN 55082

Reservation Phone: 612/439-1100
Description: The Lowell Inn is a three-story colonial manor house with a quiet dining room and 31 overnight rooms, located two blocks from the St. Croix River

Nearby Attractions: Boating, fishing, and canoeing on the St. Croix River; the town and river valley are considered the birthplace of the state.
Special Services: Each room has a complimentary bottle of wine and an embroidered Swiss handkerchief.
Rates: $69 to $119 double

MONTANA

B&B Inns

IZAAK WALTON INN
P.O. BOX 653, ESSEX, MT. 59916

Reservations Phone: 406/888-5569
Description: Built in 1939 by the Great Northern Railway, the inn is now listed on the National Register of Historic Places. The inns wall's are lined with railroad pictures and memorabilia, and some rooms have private bath.

Nearby Attractions: Cross-country skiing, fishing, annual eagle migration, railfanning, glacier park with the Bob Marshall and Great Bear Wilderness
Special Services: Sauna
Rates: $40 single, $30 to $45 double

FAIRWEATHER INN
P.O. BOX 338, VIRGINIA CITY, MT 59755

Reservations Phone: 406/843-5377
Description: Located in a preserved mining camp, the inn has an authentic 19th-century decorated lobby and accommodations for overnight guests.
Amenities: Complete breakfast menu with fresh cinnamon rolls and pie

Nearby Attractions: Nevada City Museum, Yellowstone National Park (1 1/2 hours away)
Special Services: Special midweek rates, live entertainment
Rates: $34 double

FOXWOOD INN

P.O. BOX 404, WHITE SULPHUR SPRINGS, MT 59645

Reservations Phone: 406/547-3918
Description: The Foxwood Inn is a renovated 1890 Montana poor farm. Situated in the Smith River Valley between the Crazy Castle, Big Belt, and Little Belt Mountains, the inn has 28 rooms.
Amenities: Breakfast is farm style, and consists of six to ten different foods each morning

Nearby Attractions: Castle Museum, two ghost towns (Diamond City and Castle Town) the inn is located halfway between Glacier and Yellowstone National Parks.
Special Services: Fishing and floating guide service
Rates: $24 to $34 double

NORTH DAKOTA

B&B Reservation Services

OH WEST B&B

P.O. BOX 211, REGENT, ND 58650

Offers B&B Homes In: North Dakota
Reservations Phone: No phone listed
Price Range of Homes: $20 to $45 single, $25 to $50 double
Breakfast Included in Price: Full American breakfast, with specialties including Swedish and Ukrainian breads, and home-processed maple syrup
Brochure Available: Free; also a directory for $3
Reservations Should Be Made: 2 weeks in advance

Scenic Attractions Near the B&B Homes: State and national parks, Badlands, State Capitol
Major Schools, Universities Near the B&B Homes: Minot State College, U. of North Dakota

B&B Bonuses _____

"Most of our hosts are more interested in meeting people than primarily earning extra income. They are very hospitable and willing to accommodate guests."

OREGON

B&B Reservation Services

GALLUCCI HOSTS HOSTEL, BED & BREAKFAST
P.O. BOX 1303, LAKE OSWEGO, OR 97034

Offers B&B Homes In: Oregon, parts of Washington, and in Vancouver, British Columbia
Reservations Phone: 503/636-6933
Phone Hours: 10 a.m. to 6 p.m. daily
Price Range of Homes: $12 to $35 single, $15 to $50 double
Breakfast Included in Price: Continental (juice, roll or toast, coffee)
Brochure Available: For a $1 fee, plus a stamped, self-addressed no. 10 envelope
Reservations Should Be Made: 3 days in advance (last-minute reservations accepted if possible)

Scenic Attractions Near the B&B Homes: Mount St. Helens, Fort Vancouver, state parks, zoos, historic homes

B&B Bonuses _____

Hosts have a wide variety of special interests which may match yours, such as Oriental art, psychology, classical and country music and jazz, antiques, real estate, finance, travel, law, history, sports, cooking, drama, fishing, horseback riding, vegetarianism, sci-fi, puppeteering, painting—you name it. Homes are on the ocean, in the countryside, and in major cities. Hosts often make airport pickups and arrange sightseeing tours.

P.T. INTERNATIONAL
1318 S.W. TROY ST., PORTLAND, OR 97219

Offers B&B Homes In: 48 states throughout the U.S.
Reservations Phone: 503/245-0440, or toll free 800/547-1463 outside Oregon (Telex: 277311)
Phone Hours: 8 a.m. to 5 p.m. Monday to Friday
Price Range of Homes: $20 to $129 single, $30 to $200 double
Breakfast Included in Price: Continental or full American, according to the individual host
Brochure Available: Free
Reservations Should Be Made: Any time; last-minute reservations accepted

B&B Bonuses

"We benefit the [B&B] traveler by offering information and reservations through any travel agency, or by calling our office toll free from anywhere in the nation, excluding Oregon . . . brochures on request . . . assistance in trip planning . . . car-rental information and reservations for most destinations."

This organization represents, besides B&B homes, nearly 300 inns across the country.

B&B Inns

THE AUBURN STREET COTTAGE
549 AUBURN ST., ASHLAND, OR 97520
Reservations Phone: 503/482-3004
Description: The inn is newly built in 1900s style, with separate cottages in a quiet garden setting. Each cottage contains a kitchenette (with microwave oven), skylight, and large windows, and sleeps four.

Nearby Attractions: Shakespeare Festival Theater, Britt Garden Music Festival, mountain lakes, many rafting rivers, Crater Lake Park, Oregon Caves
Rates: $56 double in summer, $46 double in winter

SPINDRIFT BED & BREAKFAST

2990 BEACH LOOP RD., BANDON, OR 97411
Reservations Phone: 503/347-2275
Description: Spindrift is a comfortable home furnished with antiques, about two miles from the center of Bandon with the ocean at the foot of its deck. A common room juts from the house providing a 180° view of the Pacific Ocean.
Amenities: Full breakfast, including fresh fruits, hot breads, eggs, breakfast meats, coffee, and a selection of teas, served on china, with sterling silver, linen cloths, and napkins

Nearby Attractions: National Bird Sanctuary with museum, local cheese factory, cranberry bogs (Bandon is the cranberry capital of Oregon); a Sternwheeler boat offers dinner trips up the Coquille River in season
Special Services: Pickup at North Bend Airport ($25 round trip); piano, games, crab rings, fishing gear available
Rates: $48 to $58 single, $53 to $63 double

OREGON CAVES CHÂTEAU

20,000 CAVES HWY., CAVE JUNCTION, OR 97523

Reservations Phone: 503/592-3400
Description: This six-story structure (no elevator) was built in 1934 in rustic style. The rooms are comfortable, and the lobby is framed with fir timber, with two large marble fireplaces. There's also a campground.

Nearby Attractions: Redwood National Park, Crater Lake National Park, Illinois and Rogue Rivers
Special Services: Cave tours, hiking trails
Rates: $42 to $47 double

THE TU TU TUN LODGE

96550 NORTH BANK ROGUE, GOLD BEACH, OR 97444

Reservations Phone: 503/247-6664
Description: The lodge is between the forest and the river on the banks of the Rogue River. Each room has its own patio or balcony overlooking the river.

Nearby Attractions: The Rogue is one of the first rivers to be declared a wild river. It is world famous for Chinook salmon and steelhead fishing, and for white-water excursions.
Special Services: Heated lap pool, nine-hole pitch and putt, horseshoe court
Rates: $70 single, $79 double

PARADISE RANCH INN

7000 MONUMENT DR., GRANTS PASS, OR 97526

Reservations Phone: 503/479-4333
Description: Set in the Rogue River Valley, the inn has comfortably furnished rooms and an indoor recreation center.

Nearby Attractions: Crater Lake, Oregon Cave, Ashland Shakespeare Theater, Peter Britt Music Festival, salmon and steelhead fishing, rafting on the Rogue River, volleyball
Special Services: Heated pool and spa, tennis courts, chip and putt green, hot tub, recreation barn
Rates: $69 to $84 single, $74 to $89 double, in summer; $44 to $54 single, $49 to $59 double, in winter

WOLF CREEK TAVERN

P.O. BOX 97, WOLF CREEK, OR 97497

Reservations Phone: 503/866-2474
Description: This original stagecoach inn was built in 1870 and is listed on the National Register of Historic Places. Furnishings in the guest rooms are representative of the period.

Nearby Attractions: Shakespeare Theater, Rogue River for fishing and rafting
Special Services: Ladies parlor, men's sitting rooms, banquet and meeting rooms, horsehoe pit
Rates: $28 single, $30 double

THE OREGON HOUSE

94288 HWY. 101, YACHATS, OR 97498

Reservations Phone: 505/547-3329 days, 505/547-3962 evenings
Description: The secluded cottages and studios at the Oregon

House are located on high cliffs of the Pacific Ocean.
Amenities: Yogurt, fresh berries, croissants, muffins, coffee, herb teas, espresso, and juices

Nearby Attractions: Suislaw Forest, swimming, fishing, beach-combing, national and state parks, deep-sea fishing, caves
Special Services: Glass tower for beach viewing
Rates: $46 to $66 double

FLYING M RANCH
23029 N.W. YAMHILL, OR 97148

Reservations Phone: 503/662-3222
Description: The ranch, built of fir logs, is located in the Oregon Coast Range near the base of 3,500-foot Trask Mountain. The bar in the lounge is made from a six-ton log. The Bunk House Motel contains 24 units, each with two queen-size beds and bath.

Nearby Attractions: Champoeg Park, the Minithorn House
Special Services: Swimming pool, fishing in river, horseback riding, 2,200-foot airstrip
Rates: $38 to $48 double

SOUTH DAKOTA

B&B Reservation Services

SOUTH DAKOTA BED & BREAKFAST
P.O. BOX 80137, SIOUX FALLS, SD 57116

Offers B&B Homes In: All of South Dakota, including the cities of Sioux Falls, Salem, Buffalo, Volga, Rapid City, Deadwood, Vivian, Canton, and Beresford
Reservations Phone: 605/339-0759 or 528-6571
Phone Hours: Any time before 10 p.m. daily
Price Range of Homes: $20 to $30 single, $30 to $50 double
Breakfast Included in Price: Full American (juice, eggs, bacon, toast, coffee) and continental

Brochure Available: Free
Reservations Should Be Made: 2 weeks in advance (last-minute reservations accepted if possible)

Scenic Attractions Near the B&B Homes: Mount Rushmore, the Black Hills, Laura Ingalls Wilder Pageant, Missouri River fishing and hunting
Major Schools, Universities Near the B&B Homes: South Dakota State, U. of South Dakota, South Dakota School of Mines, Augustana, Sioux Falls College, Black Hills State

B&B Bonuses

"Accommodations for hunters, and tips for touring the Black Hills" are offered; also farm vacations, National Register historic homes on the road to Boot Hill, double parlors with 10½-foot ceilings, Eastlake woodwork, and antiques.

WASHINGTON

B&B Reservation Services

TRAVELLER'S BED & BREAKFAST (SEATTLE)

P.O. BOX 492, MERCER ISLAND, WA 98040

Offers B&B Homes In: Seattle, Tacoma, Olympia, Port Angeles, Port Townsend, Spokane, San Juan Islands, Mount Rainier; also in Oregon and Canada
Reservations Phone: 206/232-2345
Phone Hours: 8:30 a.m. to 4:30 p.m. Monday to Friday
Price Range of Homes: $25 to $75 single or double
Breakfast Included in Price: Continental or full American, plus such regional specialties as danish rolls and blueberry muffins
Brochure Available: $5 for a descriptive directory with maps and photos
Reservations Should Be Made: As early as possible (last-minute reservations accepted)

Scenic Attractions Near the B&B Homes: Mount Ranier National Park, Glencove Historic Hotel, Woodland Zoo, Seattle Center (World's Fair 1961), Salmon Locks, ferries to Washington islands,

Mount St. Helena tours, Stanley Park, provincial museum, Empress Hotel, and Butchart Gardens in Victoria
Major Schools, Universities Near the B&B Homes: U. of Washington, Seattle College, Seattle Pacific U., U. of British Columbia, U. of Puget Sound

B&B Bonuses

Want something different? Ask about the B&B on a 60-foot sailboat in the San Juan Islands, or a turn-of-the-century railroad hotel in eastern Washington.

PACIFIC BED & BREAKFAST

701 N.W. 60TH ST., SEATTLE, WA 98107

Offers B&B Homes In: Greater Metropolitan Seattle area and throughout the state of Washington, including Mount Rainier and the San Juan Islands; also British Columbia, Canada
Reservations Phone: 206/784-0539
Phone Hours: 9 a.m. to 5 p.m. Monday to Friday
Price Range of Homes: $30 to $49 single, $35 to $60 double
Breakfast Included in Price: "Gourmet" continental or full American (homemade breads, muffins, and croissants a specialty)
Brochure Available: Free if you send a stamped, self-addressed no. 10 envelope (or $2 for the listing directory)
Reservations Should Be Made: 3 weeks in advance (last-minute reservations accepted if possible)

Scenic Attractions Near the B&B Homes: City and national parks, museums, theaters, opera house, ferry rides
Major Schools, Universities Near the B&B Homes: U. of Washington and more than eight other universities and colleges (inquire when you call for reservations about a specific school).

B&B Bonuses

Want to live in a mansion with priceless stained-glass windows, an oak staircase, and a magnificent fireplace? Then ask for this home, which even has its own gazebo. Or choose a Queen Anne home built in the early 1900s, with a view of Puget Sound.

"We offer lakefront home and island rentals for long-term vacations, in the most undiscovered area of the Pacific Northwest. Languages spoken: German, French, Spanish, Scandinavian, Italian, and Dutch."

B&B Inns

GUEST HOUSE ON WHIDBEY ISLAND
835 CHRISTENSON RD., GREENBANK, WA 98253

Reservations Phone: 206/678-3115
Description: A guest room in the house has a private entrance, bedroom sitting room, and bathroom. The three rustic log-cabin cottages have kitchens, fireplaces, and private baths.
Amenities: For those staying in the lodge, at 9 a.m. breakfast baskets arrive at the door steaming with homemade delicacies.

Nearby Attractions: The town of Langley, a quaint seaside village with antique stores, art galleries, and arts and crafts shops; Fort Casey State Park
Special Services: Hot tub, swimming pool, dressing room, exercise bike, a rowing machine, and a suntan lamp available to guests
Rates: $60 to $120 double

HAUS ROHRBACH PENSION
12882 RANGER RD., LEAVENWORTH, WA 98826

Reservations Phone: 509/548-7024
Description: In the foothills of the Washington Cascades, the inn has 13 comfortable rooms and a separate chalet with kitchen and accommodations for six.
Amenities: In fine weather, breakfast is served on the deck.

Nearby Attractions: The Bavarian village of Leavenworth, skiing, tobogganing, sleigh rides
Special Services: Heated pool, hot tub
Rates: $45 to $55 single, $55 yo $65 double

UNICORN'S REST
316 E. 10TH ST., OLYMPIA, WA 98501

Reservations Phone: 206/754-9613
Description: This 1937 Cape Cod house has two dormer rooms for guests, with shared bath.

Amenities: Full breakfast

Nearby Attractions: The State Capitol, Washington Center for the Performing Arts, Evergreen State College, Olympia Brewery
Rates: $39 to $45 double

PALACE HOTEL
1004 WATER ST., PORT TOWNSEND, WA 98368

Reservations Phone: 206/385-0773
Description: In this three-story restored Victorian building overlooking the harbor in historic downtown Port Townsend are 11 units, 8 with private bath. Children are welcome. The house is listed on the National Historic Register.

Nearby Attractions: Fort Worden State Park, biking, fishing, beachcombing
Special Services: Coffee and tea in each room
Rates: $32 to $62 double in spring and summer, $27 to $57 double in fall and winter

THE SWALLOW'S NEST
RTE. 3 (P.O. BOX 221), VASHON ISLAND, WA 98070

Reservations Phone: 206/463-2646
Description: The inn includes individual cottages on a bluff overlooking a spectacular view of Puget Sound and Mount Rainier a 20-minute ferryboat ride from the mainland. In addition to the cottages, there are double rooms with shared bath in the main house.

Nearby Attractions: Point Robinson Lighthouse, Beall Greenhouses, Wax Orchard fruit juice factory
Special Services: Pool, tennis courts, riding stables, dock, golf
Rates: $35 to $45 double daily, $250 double weekly

The Southeastern States

Alabama / 199
Florida / 202
Georgia / 206
Kentucky / 211
Mississippi / 213
Tennessee / 214

ALABAMA

B&B Reservation Services

BED & BREAKFAST MONTGOMERY
P.O. BOX 886, MILLBROOK, AL 36054

Offers B&B Homes In: Montgomery
Reservations Phone: 205/285-5421
Phone Hours: 7 a.m. to 9 p.m. daily
Price Range of Homes: $32 to $40 single, $36 to $45 double
Breakfast Included in Price: Continental (juice, roll or toast, coffee); some hosts serve full breakfasts if guests desire, and at least two will serve dinner (for a fee) if requested
Brochure Available: Free
Reservations Should Be Made: 2 weeks in advance (last-minute reservations accepted if possible)

Scenic Attractions Near the B&B Homes: Montgomery, the capital and a pre–Civil War city on the Alabama River; many beautiful antebellum homes in nearby Lowndesboro; home of nationally famous Alabama Shakespeare Theater
Major Schools, Universities Near the B&B Homes: Auburn, U. of Montgomery, Huntingdon College

B&B Bonuses

Here you can stay in an older home with a walled "hidden" garden surrounding the pool area and a second-story guest home overlooking a breathtaking view. It's located in historic "Garden Area" in the center of the city.

BED & BREAKFAST MOBILE
P.O. BOX 66261, MOBILE, AL 36606

Offers B&B Homes In: Mobile, Spanish Fort, Daphne
Reservations Phone: 205/473-2939
Phone Hours: 8 a.m. to midnight daily
Price Range of Homes: $30 to $80 single, $35 to $80 double
Breakfast Included in Price: Continental (juice, roll or toast, coffee)

Brochure Available: Free
Reservations Should Be Made: 2 weeks in advance (last-minute reservations accepted if possible)

Scenic Attractions Near the B&B Homes: Mardi Gras (February), Mobile Bay, Dauphin Islands, Gulf Shores, U.S.S. *Alabama,* U.S.S. *Drum,* Fort Conde, Oakleigh and other antebellum homes, Junior Miss Pageant, Bellingrath Gardens, Mobile Greyhound Park, Village of Fairhope
Major Schools, Universities Near the B&B Homes: U. of South Alabama, Springhill College, Mobile College

B&B Bonuses

Located in Old Springhill, a guesthouse offers complete privacy "among the azaleas." Or step back in time to 1867 in a barn-red Gothic home. Or hit the beaches in Gulf Shores, in accommodations perfect for several couples vacationing together.

Some of the special amenities provided are a package of brochures in each guest room, restaurant and sightseeing suggestions, and directions. "Each host will bend over backward to make visits as enjoyable as possible."

B&B Inns

MALAGA INN
359 CHURCH ST., MOBILE, AL 36602

Reservations Phone: 205/438-4701
Description: The rooms are decorated with a flair for southern living. Rooms have balconies facing out on a courtyard landscaped with flower beds and a fountain.
Amenities: Continental breakfast

Nearby Attractions: Oakleigh, U.S.S. *Alabama* Memorial Park, Richards Oar House, Fort Conde, Bellingrath Gardens
Special Services: Conference room, elevators, enclosed swimming pool
Rates: $38 to $44 single, $44 to $52 double

THE MENTONE INN

P.O. BOX 284, MENTONE, AL 35984

Reservations Phone: 205/634-4836
Description: This rustic inn on top of Lookout Mountain offers 12 guest rooms. Rooms are furnished simply but comfortably. One of the popular activities is watching the sunset from the big front porch (there's a beautiful view of the valleys).
Amenities: Full breakfasts are served. The fare is varied and can include eggs, country ham, waffles (if there aren't too many guests), pancakes and french toast.

Nearby Attractions: An old log church, St. Joseph's on the Mountain, DeSoto State Park and Falls, many antique shops
Rates: $30 single, $49 double (plus 7% room tax)

B&B Reservation Services

TROPICAL ISLES BED & BREAKFAST

P.O. BOX 49000382, KEY BISCAYNE, FL 33149

Offers B&B Homes In: Miami, Key Biscayne, Florida Keys, Fort Myers, Vermount
Reservations Phone: 305/361-2937
Phone Hours: After 7 p.m. daily
Price Range of Homes: $35 and up single, $55 to $65 double, $75 and up for deluxe rooms
Breakfast Included in Price: Continental or full American . . . most homes serve a full breakfast, which might include imported German ham served by a German hostess or gourmet delights whipped up by another hostess who is a professional cook
Brochure Available: Free if you send a stamped, self-addressed no. 10 envelope
Reservations Should Be Made: 3 weeks in advance (last-minute reservations accepted if possible)

Scenic Attractions Near the B&B Homes: Plant Ocean, Miami Seaquarium, homes of Ernest Hemingway and Tennessee Williams, Vizcaya, Parrot Jungle, Metro Zoo, Sunrise Theater, Serpentarium, Monkey Jungle, Shark Valley, Coral Castle, jai-alai
Major Schools, Universities Near the B&B Homes: Barry College, Biscayne College, Florida International U., Florida Memorial, Miami-Dade Community College, U. of Miami (Marine Laboratory), Rosenstile U. (Nova)

B&B Bonuses _____

   Ask about the lovely waterfront home which has a private beach, pool, and a great view of Miami's skyline.

BED & BREAKFAST OF THE FLORIDA KEYS, INC.

5 MAN-O-WAR DR., MARATHON, FL 33050

Offers B&B Homes In: The Florida Keys and along the east coast of Florida

Reservations Phone: 303/743-4118
Phone Hours: 8 a.m. to 8 p.m. Monday to Friday, on Saturday to noon
Price Range of Homes: $35 to $45 single, $38 to $60 double
Breakfast Included in Price: Continental (juice, roll or toast, coffee) or full American . . . banana bread is one of the specials served
Brochure Available: Free
Reservations Should Be Made: 2 weeks in advance (last-minute reservations accepted if possible)

Scenic Attractions Near the B&B Homes: John Pennekamp State Park, Bahia Honda State Park, Theater of the Sea, Seven Mile Bridge
Major Schools, Universities Near the B&B Homes: Florida Atlantic U.

B&B Bonuses _____
Want a tropical retreat? Ask for the oceanfront home with bamboo furnishings, tropical plants, and banana and palm trees.
Hosts will pick up guests at nearby airports.

BED & BREAKFAST CO. TROPICAL FLORIDA
P.O. BOX 262, MIAMI, FL 33242

Offers B&B Homes In: Boca Raton, Naples, Fort Myers, Miami, Fort Lauderdale, Pompano Beach, Jupiter, Lake Worth, Palm Beach, and other Florida areas
Reservations Phone: 305/661-3270
Phone Hours: 8:30 a.m. to 5 p.m. (answering service 24 hours a day)
Price Range of Homes: $25 to $54 single, $30 to $65 double (depending on season)
Breakfast Included in Price: Continental (juice, roll or toast, coffee)
Brochure Available: Free if you send a stamped, self-addressed no. 10 envelope
Reservations Should Be Made: 2 weeks in advance (last-minute reservations accepted if possible)

Scenic Attractions Near the B&B Homes: Everglades National Park, Coconut Grove Village, Hialeah Racetrack, Monkey Jungle, Seaquarium, Planet Ocean, Parrot Jungle, Serpentarium, Vizcaya, homes of Ernest Hemingway and Tennessee Williams, Burt Reynolds Dinner Theater, Dania Jai-Alai, Flagler Museum, Pennekamp Coral Reef, Ringling Museums, Miccosukee Indian Village

Major Schools, Universities Near the B&B Homes: U. of Miami (including medical and law schools), Florida International U., Miami-Dade Community College, U. of South Florida.

B&B Bonuses

Stay on a private residential island in Biscayne Bay in an original art deco home, the former Hoover estate, with three guest rooms and private baths. Breakfast is served on the loggia next to the rose garden courtyard. Discount admission tickets are provided to many of the major attractions in each area.

FLORIDA SUNCOAST BED & BREAKFAST

119 ROSEWOOD DR., PALM HARBOR, FL 33563

Offers B&B Homes In: Clearwater, St. Petersburg, Tampa, Sarasota, Bradenton, Venice, Fort Myers, Palm Harbor, Orlando, Tarpon Springs, and other Florida areas
Reservations Phone: 813/784-5118
Phone Hours: 8 a.m. to 8 p.m. daily
Price Range of Homes: $22 to $35 single, $28 to $60 double
Breakfast Included in Price: Continental (juice, roll or toast, coffee), plus such regional specialties available in some homes as home-grown grapefruit and orange juice, and homemade bread and muffins
Brochure Available: Free if you send a stamped, self-addressed no. 10 envelope
Reservations Should be Made: 3 weeks in advance (last-minute reservations accepted if possible)

Scenic Attractions Near the B&B Homes: Walt Disney World, EPCOT, Sea World, Cypress Gardens, Silver Springs, gulf beaches, Busch Gardens, Tampa, Tampa Bay Football Stadium
Major Schools, Universities Near the B&B Homes: South Florida U., U. of Tampa, St. Petersburg Jr. College

B&B Bonuses

You can select the lovely Bayboro House, the oldest house in the city, which has been beautifully restored and furnished with fine antiques. You can look out on the bay from a large veranda.

Some hosts offer mini-tours of the area, with maps and brochures. They will all pick up guests at the airport. They're excellent sources of information about special places and really good restaurants known only to the locals.

SUNCOAST ACCOMMODATIONS

8690 GULF BLVD., ST. PETERSBURG, FL 33706

Offers B&B Homes In: Florida, specializing in the Gulf Coast
Reservations Phone: 813/360-1753
Phone Hours: 8 a.m. to noon and 5 to 10 p.m. daily
Price Range of Homes: $30 to $60 single, $45 to $65 double, for
the winter 1986–1987 season
Breakfast Included in Price: Continental (juice, roll or toast, coffee)
. . . "But a few hosts are gourmet cooks and enjoy whipping up a
full, delicious breakfast"; many breakfasts are "Help yourself."
Brochure Available: Free for Florida ($3 for listings throughout the
U.S. and foreign countries)
Reservations Should Be Made: 2 weeks to 1 month in advance
(last-minute reservations accepted in the St. Petersburg area)

Scenic Attractions Near the B&B Homes: Walt Disney World, Sea
World, Sunken Gardens, Dali Museum
Major Schools, Universities Near the B&B Homes: St. Petersburg Jr.
College, Eckard College, U. of Florida, Tampa College, Stetson Law
School, Bay Pines VA Hospital

B&B Bonuses

From pool to hot tub homes or private efficiencies in waterfront
homes to traditional Victorian homes, there is a B&B here for everyone. Some hosts will pick up from the airport, take guests on tours
and boat rides, and take care of laundry (a small extra charge
may be made for these services). Many allow kitchen privileges
and most B&B rooms have private baths.

B&B Inns

CABBAGE KEY, INC.

P.O. BOX 489, BOKEELIA, FL 33922

Reservations Phone: 813/283-2278
Description: On a unique hideaway island, the main house was
constructed in 1983 by novelist Mary Roberts Reinhart. There are
rooms with private or shared bath, a suite for four, a houseboat,
and a cottage.

Neary Attractions: Intracoastal Waterway, the islands of Sanibel
and Captiva, Fort Myers, fishing, sailing, water sports
Rates: $35 to $90 double

SEMINOLE COUNTRY INN

15885 WARFIELD BLVD. (P.O. BOX 625), INDIANTOWN, FL 33456

Reservations Phone: 305/597-3777
Description: The inn was built by the uncle of the Duchess of Windsor, and the lobby has an open fireplace, twin white staircases, pecky cypress ceilings, and brass chandeliers molded with the crest of royalty.

Nearby Attractions: Indiantown with is $1-million marina, the largest citrus grove in Florida four miles away, Lake Okeechobee less than ten miles from the inn.
Special Services: Grass airfield, tennis courts, racquetball courts, 18-hole golf course
Rates: $34 single, $39 to $50 double, in winter; $29 single, $34 double, in summer

---

GEORGIA

B&B Reservation Services

ATLANTA HOSPITALITY

2472 LAUDERDALE DR. NE, ATLANTA, GA 30345

Offers B&B Homes In: Atlanta (Georgia), Brooklyn (New York), Massachusetts, Barbados (West Indies)
Reservations Phone: 404/493-1930
Phone Hours: 9 a.m. to 10 p.m. daily
Price Range of Homes: $20 to $30 single, $35 to $55 double
Breakfast Included in Price: Mostly continental, but may include grits and country ham, pecan rolls, red-eye gravy
Brochure Available: Free
Reservations Should Be Made: 2 weeks in advance (last-minute reservations accepted if possible)

Scenic Attractions Near the B&B Homes: Martin Luther King Memorial Site, High Museum, Stone Mountain Park, largest shopping mall in the Southeast
Major Schools, Universities Near the B&B Homes: Emory, Atlanta U., Mercer

B&B Bonuses _____

A hostess who knows all about Atlanta can entertain you in a beautiful five-bedroom home near the downtown area with swimming pool and other recreational facilities nearby.

"Several host homes invite guests to special dinners, take them to church, pick them up at airports, train and bus stations, and take them on sightseeing tours."

BED & BREAKFAST ATLANTA

1801 PIEDMONT AVE. NE, ATLANTA, GA 30324

Offers B&B Homes In: Metropolitan Atlanta, Stone Mountain, Marietta, Decatur, Roswell, McDonough, Smyrna, and other retreat areas around the state
Reservations Phone: 404/875-0525
Phone Hours: 9 a.m. to noon and 2 to 5 p.m. Monday to Friday
Price Range of Homes: $24 to $60 double; $48 to $100 double for guesthouses, suites, condominiums, and B&B inns; monthly rates starting at $750
Breakfast Included in Price: Continental or full American; southern breakfasts sometimes served at the discretion of the individual hosts
Brochure Available: Free if you send a stamped, self-addressed no. 10 envelope
Reservations Should Be Made: 2 weeks or more in advance (last-minute reservations accepted on a space-available basis)

Scenic Attractions Near the B&B Homes: Stone Mountain, Cyclorama, Civil War monuments, World Congress Center, the High Museum of Art, Six Flags, Atlanta Historical Society
Major Schools, Universities Near the B&B Homes: Emory, Georgia Institute of Technology, Atlanta U., Oglethorpe, Georgia State, Agnes Scott

B&B Bonuses _____

Have sons or daughters going to Emory University? Ask about the spacious older home with the beautifully landscaped, tree-shaded yard nearby.

"Hosts are a repository of information on shopping, eating, sightseeing, and recreation. Special services are often available when needed—a garden for a small reception, a microwave oven, an antiquing jaunt, and suggestions for employment, housing, and education for our many relocating guests."

BED & BREAKFAST HIDEAWAY HOMES

P.O. BOX 300, BLUE RIDGE, GA 30513

Offers B&B Homes In: North Georgia mountains, tri-state Copper
Basin area of North Carolina, Georgia, and Tennessee
Reservations Phone: 404/632-2411
Phone Hours: 9 a.m. to 9 p.m. daily
Price Range of Homes: $30 single, $35 to $45 double
Breakfast Included in Price: Continental, which may include such
extras as sourdough bread, country butter, sausage and biscuits,
apple cider, and home-canned juices, jams, jellies, and local honey
Brochure Available: Free
Reservations Should Be Made: 2 weeks in advance (last-minute
reservations accepted if possible)

Scenic Attractions Near the B&B Homes: Appalachian Trail, Cohutta Wilderness, Chattahoochie National Forest, Ocoee river
rafting, the T.V.A., Lake Blue Ridge with life management areas for
hunting and fishing, tubing on the wild Toccoa River
Major Schools, Universities Near the B&B Homes: Young Harris
College, Picken Tech., Chattanooga and Atlanta area

B&B Bonuses

   Three contemporary homes along the Toccoa River are furnished
with antiques and local crafts, with fireplaces and fully equipped
kitchens.
   "We offer southern mountain hospitality, can accommodate
family reunions and small groups, and can arrange hiking, horseback riding, visits to local craft studios, antique shops, and fine
country restaurants."

QUAIL COUNTRY BED & BREAKFAST, LTD.

1104 OLD MONTICELLO RD., THOMASVILLE, GA 31792

Offers B&B Homes In: Thomasville, Georgia (city and country)
Reservations Phone: 912/226-7218 or 912/226-6882
Phone Hours: 8 a.m. to 10 p.m. daily
Price Range of Homes: $30 to $40 single, $35 to $50 double
Breakfast Included in Price: Continental (juice, roll or toast, coffee)
Brochure Available: Free if you send a stamped, self-addressed no.
10 envelope
Reservations Should Be Made: 1 week in advance (last-minute
reservations accepted if possible)

Scenic Attractions Near the B&B Homes: Pebble Hill Plantation Museum, April Rose Festival, plantation tours, historic restorations, hunting preserves, 30 miles from Tallahassee attractions
Major Schools, Universities Near the B&B Homes: Florida State, Valdosta State

B&B Bonuses

"A lovely neoclassical house, circa 1903, is located in the Thomasville Historic District. Your hospitable hostess will fascinate you with stories of her extensive world travels. The guest wing with a private entrance includes bedroom, full bath, and screened porch where guests may enjoy breakfast."

"Any of our hosts will be happy to share their knowledge of Thomasville history and points of interest in the surrounding area."

B&B Inns

FORREST HILLS MOUNTAIN RESORT
RTE. 3, WESLEY CHAPEL ROAD (P.O. BOX 510), DAHLONEGA, GA 30533

Reservations Phone: 404/864-6456
Description: The resort is in a very private setting—140 acres—with a national forest on three sides. Accommodations range from individual rooms to cottages with in-bedroom spas.
Amenities: Full breakfast ("all you care to eat") . . . juice, melon, scrambled eggs, grits, pancakes, French toast, sausage or bacon, coffee or tea

Nearby Attractions: Amicalola Falls, site of the first major gold rush, Alpine Village
Special Services: Swimming pool, tennis, fitness center, horseback riding, panning for gold
Rates: $60 to $138 double in October and November, $40 to $138 double from December through September

THE SMITH HOUSE, INC.
202 S. CHESTATEE ST., DAHLONEGA, GA 30533

Reservations Phone: 404/864-3566

Description: This 100-year-old home has rooms with color-coordinated furnishings, tile baths, and wide porches with rockers.

Nearby Attractions: Amicalola DeSoto Falls, Vogel State Park, Dockery Lake, the Gold Museum, rafting, canoeing, tennis, panning for gold
Special Services: Air conditioning, cable TV
Rates: $43 to $53 single, $50 to $59 double, in summer; $31 single, $38 double, in winter

B&B Inns

LAKE RABUN HOTEL
LAKE RABUN ROAD (RTE. 1, BOX 2090), LAKEMONT, GA 30552

Reservations Phone: 404/782-4946
Description: This rustic hotel is built of wood and stone, the lobby furnished in handmade rhododendron and mountain laurel furniture. It's across the street from one of Georgia's most beautiful lakes.
Amenities: Self-serve continental breakfast

Nearby Attractions: Chattahoochee State Park, Dahlonega Gold Museum, Anna Ruby Falls
Rates: $25 single, $32 double

SUSINA PLANTATION INN
RTE. 3 (P. O. BOX 1010), THOMASVILLE, GA 31792

Reservations Phone: 912/377-9644
Description: This antebellum mansion built in the Greek Revival style was the plantation house for a cotton farmer who employed 100 slaves. This gracious inn still has 115 acres of lawns and woodlands as an attractive setting. There are eight bedroom suites for guests.
Amenities: Full breakfast and dinner included

Nearby Attractions: Pebble Hill Historic Plantation House, Annual Arts and Crafts Fair, Rose Test Gardens
Special Services: Swimming pool, tennis court, stocked fish pond, jogging trails, conference rooms, screened veranda
Rates: $90 single, $130 double

KENTUCKY

B&B Reservation Services

OHIO VALLEY BED & BREAKFAST
6876 TAYLOR MILL RD., INDEPENDENCE, KY 41015

Offers B&B Homes In: Southwestern Ohio, southeastern Indiana, and northern Kentucky
Reservations Phone: 606/356-7865
Phone Hours: Anytime
Price Range of Homes: $25 to $35 single, $35 to $60 double
Breakfast Included in Price: Continental (juice, roll or toast, coffee), full American (juice, eggs, bacon, toast, coffee), and homemade breads, biscuits, yogurt
Brochure Available: Free
Reservations Should Be Made: 2 weeks in advance (last-minute reservations accepted if possible)

Scenic Attractions Near the B&B Homes: Major-league sports, zoo, Kings Island Park, College Football Hall of Fame, symphony, opera, ballet, repertory theater, state parks, recreational lakes
Major Schools, Universities Near the B&B Homes: U. of Cincinnati, Northern Kentucky, Xavier, Mount St. Joseph, Thomas More

B&B Bonuses _____
   Ask for the decorated Victorian mansion, or a restored log cabin (has swimming, horses, canoes), or homes in the country, where deer are seen routinely. Hosts will often pick up at the airport, give sightseeing tours, reccomend local festivities.

KENTUCKY HOMES BED & BREAKFAST
1431 ST. JAMES COURT, LOUISVILLE, KY 40208

Offers B&B Homes In: Kentucky
Reservations Phone: 502/635-7341
Phone Hours: 8 to 11 a.m. and 4 to 7 p.m. weekdays (answering machine on holidays and off-hours)

Price Range of Homes: $33 to $71 single, $38 to $75 double
Breakfast Included in Price: Full American
Brochure Available: Free if you send a stamped, self-addressed no. 10 envelope
Reservations Should Be Made: As far in advance as possible (preferably by mail)

Scenic Attractions Near the B&B Homes: National Historic Preservation of Old Louisville, Churchill Downs, Dale Hollow Lake, Mammoth Cave, Lexington, bluegrass, Old Kentucky Home, Bardstown, Cumberland Falls, Cumberland Gap
Major Schools, Universities Near the B&B Homes: Bellarmine, U. of Louisville, Spalding, Western Kentucky, Morehead, Eastern Kentucky

B&B Bonuses

Be sure to mention if you're on your honeymoon or celebrating an anniversary. Honeymooners will enjoy a complimentary champagne breakfast. Anniversary couples receive very special treatment. For a B&B in a Georgian mansion, ask for Barnard Hall in Louisville (regularly toured by students of architecture). You may even want to try the king-size waterbed or play a game in the billard room, just as the millionaires used to do.

BLUEGRASS BED & BREAKFAST
RTE. 1, BOX 263, VERSAILLES, KY 40383

Offers B&B Homes In: Central Kentucky (Lexington)
Reservations Phone: 606/873-3208
Phone Hours: 8 a.m. to 8 p.m. daily
Price Range of Homes: $36 to $60 double
Breakfast Included in Price: Full American (juice, eggs, bacon, toast, coffee)
Brochure Available: Free
Reservations Should Be Made: 2 weeks in advance (no last-minute reservations accepted)

Scenic Attractions Near the B&B Homes: Kentucky Horse Park, Mary Todd Lincoln House, Mammoth Cave, Lake Cumberland, Henry Clay's home, Shakertown
Major Schools, Universities Near the B&B Homes: U. of Kentucky

B&B Bonuses _____
This is a good area for exploring and staying in homes built in the 18th century.

MISSISSIPPI

B&B Reservation Services

LINCOLN LTD. BED & BREAKFAST; MISSISSIPPI RESERVATION SERVICE
P.O. BOX 3479, MERIDIAN, MS 39303

Offers B&B Homes In: The whole state of Mississippi, from Holly Springs in the north to Pass Christian in the south
Reservations Phone: 601/482-5483
Phone Hours: 8:30 a.m. to 4:30 p.m. Monday to Friday, and also Saturday mornings (answering machine on weekends)
Price Range of Homes: $45 to $95 single, $45 to $107 double
Breakfast Included in Price: Full American (juice, eggs, bacon, toast, coffee), served simply or elegantly according to guest's preference
Brochure Available: Free; host list available for $3
Reservations Should Be Made: 1 or 2 weeks in advance (no last-minute reservations accepted)

Scenic Attractions Near the B&B Homes: National Civil War Park and historic homes in Vicksburg, Natchez, Jackson State Capitol, Columbus Pilgrimage, Holly Springs Pilgrimage, William Faulkner home in Oxford, Jimmy Rodgers Festival, Meridian
Major Schools, Universities Near the B&B Homes: U. of Mississippi at Oxford, Mississippi State, Starkville, Millsaps, Mississippi College, Mississippi U. for Women, Columbus, Belhaven, Jackson

B&B Bonuses _____
Step back in time in the oldest house in Columbus, built in 1828, or on a working plantation of 100 acres surrounding a home built in 1857, where you breakfast in formal elegance in the family dining room. In William Faulkner's hometown there is a National

Register antebellum home made entirely of native timber, in 1838. In this "perfect example of planter-type architecture" you can meet and talk with the hostess, a retired university professor and world traveler.

NATCHEZ PILGRIMAGE TOURS

CANAL AT STATE STREET (P.O. BOX 347), NATCHEZ, MS 39120

Offers B&B Homes In: Natchez, Adams County, Mississippi
Reservations Phone: 601/446-6631, or toll free 800/647-6742
Phone Hours: 9 a.m. to 5 p.m. daily (except Christmas)
Price Range of Homes: $60 to $85 single, $70 to $105 double
Breakfast Included in Price: Continental or full southern
Brochure Available: Free
Reservations Should Be Made: 2 weeks in advance (last-minute reservations accepted if possible)

Scenic Attractions Near the B&B Homes: Natchez State Park, Natchez Bluffs (overlooking the Mississippi River), Natchez Under the Hill (on the river), 500 historic structures and 30 historic antebellum tour homes
Major Schools, Universities Near the B&B Homes: Jopiah-Lincoln Jr. College, U. of Southern Mississippi at Natchez

B&B Bonuses

All homes are historic and part of the famous "Natchez Pilgrimage." They are individually owned and are furnished with private collections of antiques and family heirlooms. The "Southern Hospitality" includes southern breakfast, a tour of your host home, airport pickups, and other extras.

TENNESSEE

B&B Reservation Services

BED & BREAKFAST IN MEMPHIS

P.O. BOX 41621, MEMPHIS, TN 38174

Offers B&B Homes In: Memphis, Nashville, New Orleans, and other areas of the mid-South
Reservations Phone: 901/726-5920
Phone Hours: 8 a.m. to 6 p.m. Monday to Friday; on Saturday, 10 a.m. to 3 p.m.; on Sunday, 2 to 6 p.m.
Price Range of Homes: $26 to $45 and up single, $32 to $45 and up double
Breakfast Included in Price: Continental, though a few hosts serve a full American breakfast; specialties include blueberry muffins, homemade jams, and grits
Brochure Available: Free if you send a stamped, self-addressed no. 10 envelope
Reservations Should Be Made: 2 weeks in advance, 3 weeks or more from April through November (last-minute reservations can sometimes be accepted)

Scenic Attractions Near the B&B Homes: Mud Island, famous Beale Street, Victorian Village, Pink Palace Museum of Natural History, Memphis Convention Center, Dixon Gallery and Gardens
Major Schools, Universities Near the B&B Homes: Rhodes College, U. of Tennessee Medical School, Memphis State, U. of Mississippi

B&B Bonuses

If you'd like to live in a country home that's virtually a nature preserve, ask for Host G-3801. That will get you a lovely home in old Germantown, just 20 miles east of downtown. It's on a five-acre pond with resident ducks, geese, gray fox, and wild rabbits. There's a Grecian swimming pool, solarium, library, English herb gardens, and gazebo. Guests can fish—or by special arrangement, play polo or ride horseback at neighboring stables. The guest room has a pond view.

Frequently hosts are available to pick up guests at the airport and to offer "mini-tours" of the city by prior arrangement.

BED AND BREAKFAST HOST HOMES OF TENNESSEE
P.O. BOX 110227, NASHVILLE, TN 37222

Offers B&B Homes In: Throughout Tennessee, including Memphis, Nashville, and Knoxville
Reservations Phone: 615/331-5244
Phone Hours: 9 a.m. to 5 p.m. Monday to Friday (answering machine available other times)

Price Range of Homes: $26 to $50 single, $32 to $80 double
Breakfast Included in Price: Continental plus
Brochure Available: Free
Reservations Should Be Made: 2 weeks in advance (for written confirmation)

Scenic Attractions Near the B&B Homes: All the state parks, lakes, and hunting areas in the state
Major Schools, Universities Near the B&B Homes: Vanderbilt, Austin Peay, Memphis State

B&B Bonuses ───────────────────────────

You have a choice of historic homes, country inns, and lakeside, urban, or suburban homes.

B&B Inns

BUCKHORN INN
RTE. 3 (P.O. BOX 393), GATLINBURG, TN 37738

Reservations Phone: 615/436-4668
Description: This southern colonial inn has a small number of guest rooms made inviting by their spindle beds and antique furniture. Each room has a private bath. Cottages with rustic furnishings, stone fireplaces, and screened-in porches are also available.
Amenities: Full breakfast from the menu

Nearby Attractions: Great Smoky Mountains National Park, Dollywood (Dolly Parton's Park), arts and crafts community
Rates: $48 to $70 single, $65 to $88 double, in October; $38 to $60 single, $55 to $78 double, the rest of the year

MOUNTAIN BREEZE BED & BREAKFAST
501 MOUNTAIN BREEZE RD., KNOXVILLE, TN 37922

Reservations Phone: 615/966-3917
Description: The inn is warmly furnished with antiques, ceiling

fans, and country accents. There are two guest rooms, one with private bath and one with bath down the hall.
Amenities: Full breakfast

Nearby Attractions: Gatlinburg, Cherokee National Forest, Museum of Appalachia, University of Tennessee, 1982 World's Fair Site
Special Services: Fruit and homemade cookies in your room
Rates: $30 to $40 single, $35 to $45 double

NEWBURY HOUSE AT HISTORIC RUGBY
HWY. 52 (P.O. BOX 8), RUGBY, TN 37733

Reservations Phone: 615/628-2441
Description: Single and double rooms with shared or private bath, plus cottages, are available by the night of for longer stays.

Nearby Attractions: Big South Fork National Park
Special Services: Evening tea and cakes
Rates: $32 to $42 single, $37 to $56 double

The Southwest & South Central Area

Arkansas / 221
Colorado / 222
Kansas / 228
Louisiana / 229
Missouri / 234
New Mexico / 236
Oklahoma / 238
Texas / 239

ARKANSAS

B&B Inns

THE GREAT SOUTHERN HOTEL

127 W. CEDAR, BRINKLEY, AR 72021

Reservations Phone: 501/734-4955
Description: The three-story brick hotel has 61 rooms with baths, mosaic-tile floors, and pressed-tin patterned ceilings 15 feet tall. Restored in a turn-of-the-century style, the bedrooms have antique double beds and furnishings. The ground-floor rooms have ceiling fans, air conditioning, and cable TV.
Amenities: Continental breakfast

Nearby Attractions: Louisiana State Park, Mississippi Fly Way
Special Services: Airport pickup
Rates: $37.80 to $42 double

PIAMS HOUSE BED & BREAKFAST INN

420 QUAPAW, HOT SPRINGS NATIONAL PARK, AR 71901

Reservations Phone: 501/624-4275
Description: The inn is on the National Register. Each plant-filled room is furnished with antiques. Rooms with private or shared bath and a parlor suite are available for guests.
Amenities: Full breakfast

Nearby Attractions: Hot Springs, golf, tennis
Rates: $49 to $69 double

B&B Reservation Services

BED & BREAKFAST OF BOULDER, INC.
P.O. BOX 6061 BOULDER, CO 80302

Offers B&B Homes In: Boulder County and nearby mountain area.
Reservations Phone: 303/442-6664
Phone Hours: 8 a.m. to 5 p.m. Monday to Friday (closed Saturday, Sunday, and major holidays)
Price Range of Homes: $23 to $37 single, $32 to $47 double
Breakfast Included in Price: Continental or full American (juice, eggs, bacon, toast, coffee) . . . breakfasts vary with each home: some may offer continental during the week with full breakfast on weekends.
Brochure Available: Free; directory costs $2.
Reservations Should Be Made: 2 weeks in advance (last-minute reservations accepted if possible, but no placements after sundown)

Scenic Attractions Near the B&B Homes: Rocky Mountain National Park, Coors International Bicycle Race, Shakespeare Festival, World Affairs Conference, skiing
Major Schools, Universities Near the B&B Homes: U. of Colorado, Naropa Institute

B&B Bonuses _____

If you need more than one or two B&B rooms, ask about the fully furnished homes available at this agency when their owners go on vacation or sabbaticals. Hosts are friendly and obliging, as one certainly was to a guest with a broken leg. The host drove this guest to and from the university daily during a three-week period.

BED & BREAKFAST ROCKY MOUNTAINS
P.O. BOX 804, COLORADO SPRINGS, CO 80901

Offers B&B Homes In: Colorado, Montana, Wyoming, New Mexico, Utah

Reservations Phone: 303/630-3433
Phone Hours: 9 a.m. to 5 p.m. in summer, or 1 to 5 p.m. in winter, Monday to Friday
Price Range of Homes: $22 to $68 single, $30 to $98 double
Breakfast Included in Price: Over half the hosts serve a full American breakfast, often including homemade delicacies
Brochure Available: Free; descriptive directory updated quarterly listing 100 approved B&B homes and inns costs $3; annual subscription is $8.
Reservations Should Be Made: 2 weeks in advance to avoid special booking fees; MasterCard and VISA accepted on last-minute bookings only

Scenic Attractions Near the B&B Homes: National forests, 30 state parks, skiing, hiking, gold panning, white-water rafting, ballooning, snowmobiling, horseback riding, Jeep tours, sleigh rides, hay rides, fishing, 53 mountain peaks over 24,000 feet high, ghost towns, and mining towns
Major Schools, Universities Near the B&B Homes: Colorado State U., Colorado College, Colorado School of Mines, U. of Colorado, U. of Denver, Colorado Mountain College, U.S. Air Force Academy

B&B Bonuses

Ask for the charming house on a Denver lake with a mountain view (near the Coors Brewery, Buffalo Bill Museum and Heritage Square). Want a ski area? You'll find B&B homes in Aspen, Copper Mountain, Breckenridge, Winter Park in Colorado; Jackson Hole, Wyoming; Alta, Sunbird, Park City, and Brighton in Utah.

Or ask for the "Teton Treetops House" in Wilson, Wyoming (about ten miles from Jackson). The couple who run it are charming, interesting hosts with stories of their travels in many areas.

BED & BREAKFAST COLORADO
P.O. BOX 20596, DENVER, CO 80220

Offers B&B Homes In: Denver, Colorado Springs, Manitou Springs, Aspen, Beulah, Durango, La Veta, Vail, Glenwood Springs, Dillon, Boulder, Gypsum, Englewood
Reservations Phone: 303/333-3340
Phone Hours: 1 to 6 p.m. (Mountain Time) Monday to Friday
Price Range of Homes: $28 to $45 single, $32 to $50 double, (inns: $32.50 to $95)

Breakfast Included in Price: Continental or full American (juice, eggs, bacon, toast, coffee). The type of breakfast is up to the individual host, and many are gourmet cooks. Farm-fresh eggs and whole-wheat cinnamon rolls are a few of the specialties offered.
Brochure Available: $3 for 1987 Directory of Homes
Reservations Should Be Made: 2 weeks in advance, but 1 or 2 months in advance for winter-sports months (last-minute reservations accepted if possible)

Scenic Attractions Near the B&B Homes: Rocky Mountain National Park, Mesa Verde National Park, Winter Park, Buena Vista, Meeker Park, Estes Park, Denver Zoo, Broadmoor Zoo, Air Force Academy, Garden of the Gods, Hot Sulphur Springs, famous mining town, Molly Brown House (Denver), U.S. Mint, Denver Art Museum, Pike's Peak, Red Rocks, major ski areas
Major Schools, Universities Near the B&B Homes: U. of Denver, U. of Southern Colorado, Colorado State (Boulder), Colorado School of Mines (Golden), Metro State, Colorado Mountain College (Glenwood Springs), Colorado College

B&B Bonuses

Host homes in Denver are near all major hospitals. A home in Beulah, Colorado, is an 1870 homestead on 67 acres, run by a 60-year-old lady who restores antique carriages and sleighs, which she uses to take guests riding through the countryside.

Many homes pick up from airports, and there are a few gourmet cooks who furnish menus for guests who wish to have supper with them.

VICTORIAN INN—BED & BREAKFAST OF DURANGO

2117 W. SECOND AVE., DURANGO, CO 81301

Offers B&B Homes In: City limits of Durango
Reservations Phone: 303/247-2223
Phone Hours: 9 a.m. to 9 p.m. daily
Price Range of Homes: $30 to $45 single, $45 to $55 double
Breakfast Included in Price: Continental or full American . . . some homes serve coffee cake with apple butter and local honey
Brochure Available: Free
Reservations Should Be Made: 2 weeks in advance off-season, otherwise 3 weeks in advance (last-minute reservations accepted if possible)

Scenic Attractions Near the B&B Homes: Mesa Verde National Park, Durango Silverton Narrow-Gauge Railroad, Purgatory ski area, Valleoto Lake, Lemon Dam
Major Schools, Universities Near the B&B Homes: Fort Lewis College

B&B Bonuses

Want to go back in time? Stay in a Victorian home built in 1878 filled with antiques. There's a huge lawn—with lawn games available. With notice, guest airport or bus pickups can be arranged. Guests can be treated to complimentary wine at a local restaurant.

BED & BREAKFAST VAIL VALLEY

P.O. 491, VAIL, CO 81658

Offers B&B Homes In: Vail/Beaver Creek ski area and affiliates throughout Colorado for all ski areas
Reservations Phone: 303/949-1212
Phone Hours: 8 a.m. to 6 p.m. Monday to Saturday
Price Range of Homes: $35 to $55 single, $60 to $120 double, in winter; $30 to $35 single, $40 to $75 double, in summer
Breakfast Included in Price: Continental or full American . . . some B&B's serve homemade breads and sourdough pancakes
Brochure Available: Free
Reservations Should Be Made: At least 30 days in advance in winter, 1 week in advance in summer (last-minute reservations accepted when possible)

Scenic Attractions Near the B&B Homes: Vail and Beaver Creek ski areas with annual average snowfall of 300 to 350 inches, 10 square miles of skiing terrain

B&B Bonuses

Hosts can arrange to pick up guests at bus or airline terminals. Some B&B's offer hot tubs, ski storage, wine and cheese, and hot afternoon snacks.

B&B Inns

TIPPLE INN

747 S. GALENA ST., ASPEN, CO 81611

Reservations Phone: Toll free 800/321-7025
Description: This small cozy inn is located in downtown Aspen at the base of Aspen Mountain, near the gondola and between the two chair lifts. The building is built out of heavy timber from an old Aspen silver mine. The studio or bedroom apartments have a fully equipped kitchen and TV, and in most apartments, a fireplace.

Nearby Attractions: Aspen Highlands, Snowmass, and Buttermilk
Special Services: Redwood hot tub, daily maid service, cable color TV
Rates: $145 to $220 double in February and March, $100 to $150 double in December, January, and April

FIRESIDE INN

115 FRENCH ST., (P.O. BOX 2252), BRECKENRIDGE, CO 80424

Reservations Phone: 303/453-6456
Description: The accommodations at this Victorian Inn range from dormitory space to private rooms and even a private suite. All are tastefully decorated and comfortable.

Nearby Attractions: Ski area
Special Services: Hot tub, free shuttle to town and ski areas
Rates: $16.50 in a dorm, $52 double, in fall and winter; $11 in a dorm, $29 double, in spring and summer

THE HOME RANCH

P.O. BOX 822FB, CLARK, CO 80428

Reservations Phone: 303/879-1780
Description: This small guest ranch is located in the mountains of northwestern Colorado. The seven cabins range from a studio to a two-bedroom two-bath with a living room. They are furnished with

antiques and original wall hangings, with down comforters on the beds. Outside on the porch stands your own private spa.
Amenities: The full breakfast is served family style in the lodge dining room. Two meals a day are included in the rates.

Nearby Attractions: Mount Zirkel Wilderness Area, Steamboat and Pearl Lakes State Parks, Continental Divide, horseback riding (the speciality here, and lots of it), fishing, bathing, boating
Special Services: Airport pickup, heated pool, hot tub and sauna, coffee maker and refrigerator stocked with cheeses, crackers, and homemade cookies
Rates: $150 single, $300 double

PURPLE MOUNTAIN LODGE
714 GOTHIC AVE. (P.O. BOX 897), CRESTED BUTTE, CO 81224

Reservations Phone: 303/349-5888
Description: This small lodge with six guest rooms and two shared baths has a view of the ski mountain and surrounding peaks.
Amenities: Full breakfast during the ski season

Nearby Attractions: Crested Butte is a National Historic Town full of interesting buildings, shops, and restaurants.
Special Services: Free shuttle bus, package ski rates available
Rates: $55 double

THE ASPEN LODGE
LONGS PEAK ROAD, ESTES PARK, CO 80517

Reservations Phone: 303/586-8133
Description: This handcrafted log lodge has 36 rooms, individual cabins, and a separate dining facility with three meals a day included in the rate.
Amenities: Breakfast featuring homemade sweet rolls and huevos rancheros

Nearby Attractions: Rocky Mountain National Park, Estes Park, Hidden Valley ski area
Special Services: Racquetball, horseback riding, tennis, skiing, fishing, snowmobiling, heated pool, airport pickup
Rates: $160 double in summer, $120 double in winter

THE ALMA HOUSE

220 E. 10TH ST. (P.O. BOX 787), SILVERTON, CO 81433

Reservations Phone: 303/387-5336
Description: This completely restored inn has ten rooms in the European style furnished with Beautyrest queen-size beds, antique dressers, brass light fixtures, and period wallpapers.

Nearby Attractions: The mountains, a steam-powered railroad, Silverton (once a rip-roaring mining town)
Rates: $28 double

KANSAS

B&B Reservation Services

KANSAS CITY BED & BREAKFAST

P.O. BOX 14781, LENEXA, KS 66215

Offers B&B Homes In: Kansas City, Parkville, Lee's Summit, Grandview, St. Joseph, and Warrensburg (in Missouri); Lenexa, Overland Park, Leawood, and Kansas City (in Kansas)
Reservations Phone: 913/268-4214
Phone Hours: daily (9 a.m. to 5 p.m. in July and August)
Price Range of Homes: $25 to $50 single, $30 to $85 double
Breakfast Included in Price: Some continental, but most homes serve a full breakfast.
Brochure Available: "Homes Directory" for $1 if you send a stamped, self-addressed no. 10 envelope
Reservations Should Be Made: 2 weeks in advance (last-minute reservations usually accepted)

Scenic Attractions Near the B&B Homes: Truman Library, Worlds of Fun, Crown Center Plaza, Kansas City Zoo, Nelson Art Gallery, American Royal
Major Schools, Universities Near the B&B Homes: U. of Missouri, Avila College, U. of Kansas, Central Missouri State

B&B Bonuses

In a farm home resembling a Swiss chalet, the hostess serves a ham-and-egg casserole with homemade cinnamon rolls for breakfast, on a glassed-in patio. Condominiums with swimming and tennis are also available. *Tip:* Ask for the restored Georgian mansion between Crown Center and the Country Club Plaza in Kansas City; or a recently redecorated English Tudor home situated on a former Civil War battleground two blocks from the plaza.

LOUISIANA

B&B Reservation Services

SOUTHERN COMFORT BED & BREAKFAST RESERVATION SERVICE

2856 HUNDRED OAKS, BATON ROUGE, LA 70808

Offers B&B Homes In: 20 cities in Louisiana, Mississippi, New Mexico, and Florida
Reservations Phone: 504/346-1928 or 504/928-9815
Phone Hours: 8 a.m. to 8 p.m. daily (no collect calls)
Price Range of Homes: $25 to $95 single, $32 to $150 double (depending on the number of additional people)
Breakfast Included in Price: Continental or full American . . . some homes serve "plantation breakfasts" which can include various meats, grits and gravy, hot breads, and native preserves
Brochure Available: For a $3 fee
Reservations Should Be Made: 2 weeks in advance (last-minute reservations accepted if possible)

Scenic Attractions Near the B&B Homes: In New Orleans, Audubon Park and Zoo, French Quarter, famous restaurants and museums; in Baton Rouge, old and new State Capitols, historic sites; in Mississippi, antebellum homes, plantations, Civil War battle sites, museums, Gulf Coast; in New Mexico, desert, mountains, and art colonies; the beach in Florida
Major Schools, Universities Near the B&B Homes: Louisiana State, Southern U., Tulane, Loyola, Xavier, Dillard, U. of Mississippi, Mississippi Southern, U. of New Mexico

B&B Bonuses _____

   Stay on a 100-acre working plantation near Vicksburg, in a 125-year-old classic Greek Revival mansion which is on the National Historic Register. Save time to tour this fascinating house and grounds. There's even a friendly ghost who reportedly shows up from time to time.

BED & BREAKFAST, INC.
1360 MOSS ST. (P.O. BOX 52257), NEW ORLEANS, LA 70152

Offers B&B Homes In: New Orleans and surrounding areas
Reservations Phone: 504/525-4640; or toll free 800/228-9711, ext. 184
Phone Hours: 24 hours daily
Price Range of Homes: $25 to $110 single, $35 to $110 double (some rates may go up seasonally)
Breakfast Included in Price: Continental (juice, roll or toast, coffee or tea)
Brochure Available: Free
Reservations Should Be Made: Anytime (last-minute reservations accepted if possible)

Scenic Attractions Near the B&B Homes: French Quarter, Mississippi River, Superdome, Audubon Zoo, New Orleans Museum of Art, Jazz Halls, world-famous restaurants, antique stores, historic St. Charles Avenue streetcar, Jackson Square artists
Major Schools, Universities Near the B&B Homes: Tulane, Loyola, U. of New Orleans, Dominican College, Tulane Medical School, LSU Dental School, French Quarter

B&B Bonuses _____

   Homes include a historic house and another luxury 19th century mansion with antiques amid landscapes surroundings. Some hosts offer babysitting, assistance to the blind and handicapped, and accommodations for pets. Hosted apartments are also available. All are personally inspected by B&B.

PEGGY LINDSAY ENTERPRISES
3307 PRYTANIA ST., NEW ORLEANS, LA 70115

Offers B&B Homes In: New Orleans area

Reservations Phone: 504/897-3867
Phone Hours: 7 a.m. to 11 p.m. Monday to Friday (accept calls on weekends)
Price Range of Homes: $40 single, $50 to $75 double, (rates 20% more during Mardi Gras and Super Bowl periods, and about 20% less during the summer)
Breakfast Included in Price: Continental (juice, roll or toast, coffee)
Brochure Available: Free
Reservations Should Be Made: 2 weeks in advance (last-minute reservations accepted when possible)

Scenic Attractions Near the B&B Homes: Historic areas (French Quarter, Garden District), St. Charles Ave. streetcar, Audubon Zoo, battlefields, many five-star restaurants
Major Schools, Universities Near the B&B Homes: Tulane, Loyola

B&B Bonuses

Ask for the Victorian home in the Garden District, with a private suite (bedroom, sitting room, bath) with separate entance. It's decorated with antiques and contemporary paintings by the owner/artist. Some hosts have special knowledge of local art shows and "jam sessions" with local musicians.

NEW ORLEANS BED & BREAKFAST

3658 GENTILLY BLVD. (P.O. BOX 8163), NEW ORLEANS, LA 70182

Offers B&B Homes In: New Orleans, Baton Rouge, Shreveport, Ruston, Lake Charles, Sulphur, Natchitoches, Opelousas, and Wakefield (all in Louisiana)
Reservations Phone: 504/949-6705 or 504/822-5038 or 504/822-5046
Phone Hours: 8 a.m. to 8 p.m. daily.
Price Range of Homes: $20 to $50 single, $25 to $150 double
Breakfast Included in Price: Continental (juice, roll or toast, coffee)
Brochure Available: Free if you send a stamped, self-addressed no. 10 envelope
Reservations Should Be Made: As early as possible for special events and best selection (last-minute reservations accepted if available)

Scenic Attractions Near the B&B Homes: Historic homes, Audubon Park Zoo, plantation tours and river cruises, Cajun bayou tours, Gulf Coast, Acadian Country, French Quarter, New Orleans nightlife, Longvue Gardens, Magazine Street antique shops, West

End Yacht Club and restaurants on Lake Pontchartrain
Major Schools, Universities Near the B&B Homes: Tulane, Loyola,
U. of New Orleans, Dillard, New Orleans Baptist Seminary

B&B Bonuses

Listings include an "artsy-eclectic" home in the French Quarter, a
large 1920s home in an area of great live oak trees, homes in a
lovely garden district, and many more, from hostel-type to deluxe
rooms and apartments. Special needs of guests are usually met,
such as tourist information and occasional transportation. Past
extra services have included nursing a guest who was ill and
providing clothes for special occasions and emergencies.

B&B Inns

TEZCUCO
3138 HWY. 44, DARROW, LA 70725

Reservations Phone: 504/562-3929
Description: This 1855 Greek Revival Plantation is set beneath
majestic live oaks. It has individual cottages with bedroom, sitting
room, and bath, plus formal gardens, a chapel, dollhouse, black-
smith shop, carriage house, and a commissary.
Amenities: Country Créole breakfast served in your cottage on a
silver tray consists of juice, eggs, grits, sausage or bacon, biscuits,
jellies, coffee or tea

Nearby Attractions: Center of plantation country on a historic
Mississippi road
Special Services: Hot tub, complimentary wine, tour of the planta-
tion
Rates: $50 to $95 double

M. A. PATOUT & SON LTD.
RTE. 1 (P.O. BOX 288), JEANERETTE, LA 70544

Reservations Phone: 318/276-4592
Description: The company guest house has two bedrooms, a
kitchen, living room, bathroom, and large screened-in porch.

Nearby Attractions: Jungle Garden on Avery Island, Jefferson Island home of Joe Jefferson (Rip Van Winkle), New Iberia
Special Services: Tour of factory and sugarcane fields
Rates: $40 double

NINE-O-FIVE ROYAL HOTEL
905 ROYAL ST., NEW ORLEANS, LA 70116

Reservations Phone: 504/523-0219
Description: This quaint European-style hotel built in the 1980s is located in the heart of the French Quarter. The rooms are furnished with kitchenettes and balconies.

Nearby Attractions: The French Market, Jackson Square, riverboat rides, famous restaurants
Special Services: Color TV, daily maid service
Rates: $35 to $65 double

MARQUETTE HOUSE HOSTEL
2253 CARONDELET ST., NEW ORLEANS, LA 70130

Reservations Phone: 504/523-3014
Description: You'll find clean, simple, basic accommodation for the budget traveler in this 100-year-old antebellum home located a block off the historic St. Charles streetcar line next to the Garden District, 22 blocks from the French Quarter. All rooms are with hall bath.

Nearby Attractions: Chalmette National Historic site commemorating the Battle of New Orleans, the Mississippi River with its steamboats, Jean Lafitte National Park
Special Services: Guest kitchen, garden patio, picnic tables, arrangements for tours
Rates: $19 single, $26 double

B&B Reservation Services

OZARK MOUNTAIN COUNTRY BED & BREAKFAST

P.O. BOX 295, BRANSON, MO 65726
Phone Hours: Anytime, daily
Price Range of Homes: $20 to $40 single, $25 to $50 double
Breakfast Included in Price: Continental (juice, roll or toast, coffee) . . .
some homes serve a regional specialty called "funnel cakes."
Brochure Available: Free if you send a stamped, self-addressed no. 10
envelope
Reservations Should Be Made: 2 weeks in advance (last-minute
reservations accepted if possible)

Scenic Attractions Near the B&B Homes: Mountain Music Shows,
Silver Dollar City, White Water Fun Park, trout fishing in Taneycomo
and Table Rock Lakes

B&B Bonuses

Several host homes are located on beautiful Table Rock Lake. All
homes are located near the great trout fishing for which the area is
famous, and other outstanding tourist attractions.

"The traveler is treated more like a guest than a source of income."

TRUMAN COUNTRY B&B

P.O. BOX 14, INDEPENDENCE, MO 64051

Offers B&B Homes In: Independence, Missouri
Reservations Phone: 816/254-6657
Phone Hours: 10 a.m. to 5 p.m. daily
Price Range of Homes: $20 to $37.50 single, $25 to $40 double
Breakfast Included in Price: Full American (juice, eggs, bacon,
toast, coffee)
Brochure Available: Free
Reservations Should Be Made: 2 weeks in advance (last-minute
reservations accepted if possible)

Scenic Attractions Near the B&B Homes: Kansas City Zoo, Harry S. Truman home, many historical homes and sites, antique and handcraft shops
Major Schools, Universities Near the B&B Homes: U. of Missouri/ Kansas City Extension Center

B&B Bonuses

In an 1850s Victorian home near the Harry Truman house, the hostess will give you a tour of the furnishings of the period. Another home, in the suburbs, features Early American decor, including a featherbed. There is a patio and picnic area, and this gracious hostess also gives tours.

One hostess picks up guests at the local train stop, known as the Harry Truman Whistle Stop.

ST. LOUIS BED & BREAKFAST
4418 W. PINE, ST. LOUIS, MO 63108

Offers B&B Homes In: City and suburbs of St. Louis
Reservations Phone: 314/868-2335 or 314/533-9299
Phone Hours: 7 a.m. to 10 p.m. daily
Price Range of Homes: $30 to $40 single, $35 to $55 double
Breakfast Included in Price: Continental or full American (often including home-baked rolls, coffee cakes, buttermilk waffles, and regional specialties like sausage strata and huevos rancheros)
Brochures Available: Free if you send a stamped, self-addressed no. 10 envelope
Reservations Should Be Made: 2 weeks in advance (last-minute reservations accepted if possible)

Scenic Attractions Near the B&B Homes: Riverfront, Gateway Arch, Busch Stadium, Forest Park Zoo, Muny Outdoor Opera Theater, restored Fox Theater, brewery and winery tours, steamboat excursions, Laclede's Landing
Major Schools, Universities Near the B&B Homes: St. Louis U., Washington U., U. of Missouri at St. Louis, Fontbonne, Kenrick Seminary, Covenant Presbyterian Seminary, Logan Chiropractic College, Concordia

B&B Bonuses

An energetic teacher who "loves having the world come to her door through her guests" welcomes travelers to a refurbished turn-of-the-century Gothic-style residence, centrally located. If you prefer rustic pleasures, there is a barn-style home "nestled in a three-acre hideaway in rolling wooded hills" with a park nearby that offers horseback riding, trails, and swimming.

Many hosts are glad to provide local and airport transportation, and interesting historical information about the area.

NEW MEXICO

B&B Reservation Services

BED & BREAKFAST OF SANTA FE

436 SUNSET, SANTA FE, NM 87501

Offers B&B Homes In: Santa Fe only
Reservations Phone: 505/982-3332
Phone Hours: 9 a.m. to 5 p.m. weekdays September to April, daily May to August
Price Range of Homes: $25 to $30 single, $45 to $65 double
Breakfast Included in Price: Continental; in some homes food is left for guests to prepare and enjoy at their leisure
Reservations Should Be Made: 2 weeks in advance (last-minute reservations accepted if possible)

Scenic Attractions Near the B&B Homes: Annual Indian Market (third week of August), cliff dwellings, pueblo and Spanish church ruins, colorful adobe architecture, major art center, ski basin, opera, Chamber Music Festival, Arts Festival

B&B Bonuses

Several accommodations are in typical Santa Fe style, with adobe walls, walled yards, shady patios, ceiling "vigas," and tiled baths with Mexican decor. Host families have driven guests to local festivities, served cool drinks, and made restaurant reservations. Many close friendships have been formed, with continuing correspondence.

B&B Inns

PRESTON HOUSE
106 FAITHWAY ST., SANTA FE, NM 87501

Reservations Phone: 505/982-3465
Description: This Queen Anne–style building was built in 1886 and is listed on the National Historic Register. It provides the comfort of the present in a turn-of-the-century setting. Some rooms have private baths and fireplaces.
Amenities: Continental breakfast

Nearby Attractions: Skiing, museums, art galleries, hiking, fishing, opera, Indian pueblos
Special Services: Afternoon refreshments, help with trip planning
Rates: $45 to $98 double

HOTEL EDELWEISS
TAOS SKI VALLEY, TAOS, NM 87571
Reservations Phone: 505/776-2301
Description: In the winter season this is a high-mountain resort hotel. The comfortable accommodations afford spectacular views.
Amenities: Breakfast specialties include a variety of egg dishes and special sauces

Nearby Attractions: Indian ruins, pueblos, art galleries, craft fairs, music and theater
Special Services: Jacuzzi, sauna, tennis, ski packages, week-long cooking schools
Rates: $95 single, $120 double

OKLAHOMA

B&B Reservation Services

REDBUD RESERVATIONS/BED & BREAKFAST FOR OKLAHOMA

P.O. BOX 23954, OKLAHOMA CITY, OK 73123

Offers B&B Homes In: Oklahoma City, Tulsa, other areas of Oklahoma
Reservations Phone: 405/720-0212
Phone Hours: 5 to 9 p.m. Monday to Friday; also accepts calls on weekends (answering machine 24 hours a day)
Price Range of Homes: $20 to $50 single, $30 to $60 double
Breakfast Included in Price: Continental (juice, roll or toast, coffee)
Brochure Available: Free if you send a stamped, self-addressed no. 10 envelope
Reservations Should Be Made: 2 weeks in advance (last-minute reservations accepted when possible)

Scenic Attractions Near the B&B Homes: National Cowboy Hall of Fame, Lincoln Park Zoo, Philbrook Art Museum, Blue Ribbon Downs
Major Schools, Universities Near the B&B Homes: U. of Oklahoma, Oklahoma Christian, Oklahoma City U., Central State, Oklahoma State

B&B Bonuses

One home in Edmond offers two rooms with private bath (one room has a waterbed). There's a large pool and hot tub in the yard, available to guests. Horseback riding can be arranged.

The reservation service says, "One of our homes, while not specifically equipped for handicapped persons, does have excellent access for people with limited mobility."

Some hosts provide discount coupons for area attractions and will help arrange local transportation.

B&B Reservation Services

SAND DOLLAR HOSPITALITY/BED & BREAKFAST
3605 MENDENHALL, CORPUS CHRISTI, TX 78415

Offers B&B Homes In: Texas Coastal Bend, primarily Corpus Christi
Reservations Phone: 512/853-1222 or 512/992-4497
Phone Hours: 8 a.m. to 8 p.m. daily
Price Range of Homes: $27 to $48 single, $30 to $51 double
Breakfast Included in Price: Continental or full American, depending on individual home . . . plus some Mexican specialties, such as breakfast taquitos and Mexican sweet breads
Brochure Available: Free
Reservations Should Be Made: 5 days in advance preferred (last-minute reservations accepted if possible)

Scenic Attractions Near the B&B Homes: Padre Island, King Ranch, Aransas Wildlife Refuge (home of the whooping crane), Rockport Art Colony, Japanese Art Museum, Corpus Christi Art Museum
Major Schools, Universities Near the B&B Homes: Corpus Christi State, Del Mar Jr. College

B&B Bonuses

Corpus Christi is sometimes called the "Texas Riviera." Dine on freshly caught fish and shrimp at fine restaurants overlooking the ocean, dress up for an evening at the symphony or down for country and western dancing, or experience a different facet of southwestern living, at the famous King Ranch.

Want to float yourself to sleep? Ask for the 41-foot sailboat *Lord Nelson*. The nightly rate of $75 includes refreshments, breakfast, and a two-hour sail.

Several homes have three or four bedrooms available, making them ideal for groups traveling together.

BED & BREAKFAST TEXAS STYLE

4224 W. RED BIRD LANE, DALLAS, TX 75237

Offers B&B Homes In: Dallas, Houston, Austin, San Antonio, Fort Worth, Arlington, Jefferson, Garland, University Park, Waco, and other Texas areas
Reservations Phone: 214/298-8586 or 298-5433
Phone Hours: 8 a.m. to 6 p.m. Monday to Saturday
Price Range of Homes: $20 to $40 single, $35 to $60 double
Breakfast Included in Price: Continental or full American, which may include such regional specialties as jalapeña muffins, JR pancakes, sourdough biscuits and gravy, grits, crêpes, omelets
Brochure Available: Free; for a full directory, send $3 plus a stamped, self-addressed no. 10 envelope
Reservations Should Be Made: 2 weeks in advance (last-minute reservations accepted if possible)

Scenic Attractions Near the B&B Homes: Texas Stadium, Texas Hill Country, Japanese Botanical Gardens, Carthage Home, Azalea Trails, Gulf of Mexico, Galveston Bay, Texas Safari Wild Game Park, lakes
Major Schools, Universities Near the B&B Homes: Southern Methodist, Rice, U. of Houston, Texas U., Texas Christian U. at Fort Worth, Trinity, Our Lady of the Lake in San Antonio

B&B Bonuses

You could select a comfortable home in North Dallas. Three upstairs bedrooms are decorated with country charm and boast two heirloom spool beds; it overlooks a pool. Or a family might pick the Sam Rayburn Lake Guesthouse; it has a lake for waterskiing or fishing. Hosts are nearby and will stock the new refrigerator with breakfast food for weekend visitors.

This B&B service now accepts VISA and MasterCard.

THE BED & BREAKFAST SOCIETY OF TEXAS

921 HEIGHTS BLVD., HOUSTON, TX 77008

Offers B&B Homes In: Houston and throughout Texas
Reservations Phone: 713/868-4654
Phone Hours: 8 a.m. to 5 p.m. daily
Price Range of Homes: $25 to $50 single, $35 to $85 double
Breakfast Included in Price: Hearty continental or full American (juice, eggs, bacon, toast, coffee). Some hosts offer a full breakfast

plus regional specialties such as huevos rancheros, jalapeña corn-bread, taquitos, etc., and some will accommodate special diets.
Brochure Available: Free catalog of listings
Reservations Should Be Made: 2 weeks in advance (last-minute resevations accepted if possible)

Scenic Attractions Near the B&B Homes: NASA Space Center, Astrodome, San Jacinto Monument, Miller Outdoor Theater, Galveston Bay, San Antonio Riverwalk
Major Schools, Universities Near the B&B Homes: U. of Houston, U. of St. Thomas, Rice, Baylor College of Medicine

B&B Bonuses

Ask about two beautiful suburban homes near Houston's major attractions. Each offers three guest bedrooms with private bath for only $35 (double occupancy). There are also waterfront and country cabins throughout Texas, apartments along the San Antonio Riverwalk, and other locations in most major Texas cities.

B&B Inns

GAST HAUS LODGE

952 HIGH ST., COMFORT, TX 78013
Reservations Phone: 512/995-2304
Description: Opened in 1862 as an original stagecoach stop, German Rock Haus was built in 1869, the boarding house in 1887 and the hotel in 1920. There's a swimming pool on the property.

Nearby Attractions: Biking, boating, canoeing, and walking in the hill country area, and shopping in nearby San Antonio
Special Services: Swimming pool, creek fishing
Rates: $26 single, $40 double

THE FARRIS 1912

201 N. MCCARTY, EAGLE LAKE, TX 77434

Reservations Phone: 409/234-2546
Description: This 1912 building has a courtyard enclosed with an iron fence. The rooms, with private or shared bath, are furnished with antiques.

Amenities: The full country breakfast includes local Bohemian sausage and grits. Rates include three meals a day.

Nearby Attractions: National Wildlife Refuge, Prairie Edge Museum, Northington Plantation, golf, tennis
Special Services: Airport pickup, private bird sanctuary
Rates: $85 to $95 double November to January, $40 to $48 double February to October

LA BORDE HOUSE

601 E. MAIN ST., RIO GRANDE, TX 78582

Reservations Phone: 512/487-5101
Description: The inn was built in 1877 by Francis La Borde. The nine rooms are furnished with original Victorian furniture, as is the large parlor. A rear building contains 13 efficiency apartments. The house is on the National Register of Historic Places.
Amenities: Continental breakfast

Nearby Attractions: Falcon State Park, golf, historic homes, excellent hunting and fishing
Special Services: Tropical courtyard and patio, much historical reference material available to guests
Rates: $40 to $59 double

BULLIS HOUSE INN

621 PIERCE ST. (P.O. BOX 8059), SAN ANTONIO, TX 78208

Reservations Phone: 512/223-9426
Description: This historic white mansion is only minutes from the Alamo, Riverwalk, and downtown. The interior is decorated with chandeliers, fireplaces, 14-foot ceilings, and geometrically patterned floors of fine woods. Built in 1906 for Gen. John Bullis, a noted cavalry officer famous for his efforts in taming the Texas frontier, it's a registered Texas Historic Landmark.
Amenities: Continental breakfast with a variety of muffins

Nearby Attractions: Fort Sam Houston and Old Army Museum, Botanical Gardens and Brackenridge Park and Zoo, Institute of Texas Culture, San Antonio Art Museum, Spanish Missions National Park, LBJ Ranch
Rates: $22 to $39 single, $28 to $45 double

California & the West

Arizona / 245
California / 248
Utah / 265

B&B Reservation Services

BED & BREAKFAST IN ARIZONA, INC.
8433 N. BLACK CANYON HWY., SUITE 150, PHOENIX, AZ 80521

Offers B&B Homes In: Arizona (240 homes, ranches, guesthouses, and inns)
Reservations Phone: 602/995-2831
Phone Hours: 8 a.m. to 5 p.m. Monday to Friday (no holidays)
Price Range of Homes: $25 to $60 single, $35 to $110 double
Breakfast Included in Price: Full American . . . many hosts are gourmet cooks, serving quiches, homemade breads, and an "Arizona" breakfast featuring a Spanish omelet or Indian bread.
Brochure Available: Free if you send a stamped, self-addressed no. 10 envelope
Reservations Should Be Made: 2 weeks in advance (last-minute reservations accepted if possible)—two night minimum stay

Scenic Attractions Near the B&B Homes: Grand Canyon, Indian monuments, Phoenix and Tucson Zoos, Zane Grey home, national forests, 19 state parks, Lake Havasu, Lake Powell, Lowell Observatory, Kitt Peak Observatory, botanical gardens and art museums
Major Schools, Universities Near the B&B Homes: American Graduate School of Business, U. of Arizona at Tucson, Northern Arizona U. at Flagstaff, Arizona State U. at Tempe, Orme and Judson private schools

B&B Bonuses
You can ride on a host's houseboat on Lake Powell, or relax in a movie star's guest suite while she fixes you an omelet or enjoy ranch, Spanish contemporary, or restored older homes. Hosts often meet guests at the airport, make reservations, plan sightseeing, reserve tickets to sports events or concerts. They also, on request, can take guests shopping, backpacking, birdwatching, etc., and even plan menus for special diets.

BED & BREAKFAST SCOTTSDALE

P.O. BOX 624, SCOTTSDALE, AZ 85252

Offers B&B Homes In: Scottsdale and Paradise Valley, Fountain
Hills and Cave Creek
Reservations Phone: 602/998-7044
Phone Hours: 7 a.m. to 10 p.m. daily
Price Range of Homes: $40 to $75 single, $65 to $125 double
Breakfast Included in Price: Continental (juice, roll or toast, coffee),
and full American with specialties (pecan rolls, chili and eggs) . . .
pick your own breakfast fruit from some hosts' orchards.
Brochure Available: Free
Reservations Should Be Made: 2 to 3 weeks in advance, 1 month
in advance for February reservations (last-minute reservations
accepted when possible)

Scenic Attractions Near the B&B Homes: Desert Botanical Gardens,
zoo, art galleries, Rawhide (the western town), the Frank Lloyd
Wright Foundation (offers architectural tours)
Major Schools, Universities Near the B&B Homes: Scottsdale Artists
School

B&B Bonuses

Some B&B homes have suites with fireplaces and private patios.
Some hosts offer secluded separate guesthouses on their property.
Hosts are very helpful in providing local information.

VALLEY O' THE SUN BED & BREAKFAST

P.O. BOX 2214, SCOTTSDALE, AZ 85281

Offers B&B Homes In: Metropolitan Phoenix area only
Reservations Phone: 602/941-1281
Phone Hours: 8 a.m. to 4 p.m. daily
Price Range of Homes: $25 single, $35 double
Breakfast Included in Price: Some hosts offer only continental;
others serve a full American breakfast
Brochure Available: Free
Reservations Should Be Made: 2 weeks in advance (if possible)

Scenic Attractions Near the B&B Homes: Phoenix Zoo, city parks
and other Phoenix attractions, Grand Canyon, Petrified Forest,
Meteor Crater
Major Schools, Universities Near the B&B Homes: Arizona State

B&B Bonuses

Hosts will pick up guests at airport, and also will make advance reservations for theater and car rentals. On occasion, hosts can provide transportation for guests without cars.

MI CASA–SU CASA BED & BREAKFAST

P.O. BOX 950, TEMPE, AZ 85281

Offers B&B Homes In: Arizona
Reservations Phone: 602/990-0682
Phone Hours: 8 a.m. to 8 p.m. daily
Price Range of Homes: $25 to $50 single, $30 to $100 double
Breakfast Included in Price: Continental or full American . . . many hosts serve homemade breads, crêpes, Belgian waffles, regional specialties.
Brochure Available: Free if you send a stamped, self-addressed no. 10 envelope; directory of homes also available for $3
Reservations Should Be Made: 2 weeks in advance (last-minute reservations accepted if possible)

Scenic Attractions Near the B&B Homes: Grand Canyon, Lake Powell, prehistoric cliff dwellings, Sonora Desert Museum, Botanical Gardens, Colossal Cave, Kitt Peak and Lowell Observatories, Petrified Forest, Phoenix Zoo, Mission San Xavier del Bac, Meteor Crater
Major Schools, Universities Near the B&B Homes: Arizona State, Northern Arizona, U. of Arizona, American Graduate School of International Management, Orme School, Judson School, Verde Valley School

B&B Bonuses

You can choose from luxury houses to historic homes in the National Register—also ranches, guesthouses, and small cozy homes. Most homes are near golf courses and have swimming pools. Guests can sometimes arrange airport pickups, late-afternoon cheese and wine, horseback riding, restaurant and concert reservations, sightseeing tours, and bicycle loans.

BARBARA BED AND BREAKFAST
P.O. BOX 13603, TUCSON, AZ 85732

Offers B&B Homes In: The Tucson area
Reservations Phone: 602/886-5847
Phone Hours: 8 a.m. to 7 p.m. daily
Price Range of Homes: $25 to $40 single, $35 to $55 double
Breakfast Included in Price: Continental or full American (guest's choice)
Brochure Available: Free if you send a stamped, self-addressed no. 10 envelope
Reservations Should Be Made: 2 weeks in advance (last-minute reservations accepted when possible)

Scenic Attractions Near the B&B Homes: Arizona Sonora Desert Museum, Saguaro National Monument, Sabino Canyon, San Xavier Mission, Nogales, Mexico, Old Tucson (movie location and amusement park)
Major Schools, Universities Near the B&B Homes: U. of Arizona

B&B Bonuses

If you like antiques, ask for the home in downtown Tucson that's also an antique shop—you can buy the bed you sleep on that night.

CALIFORNIA

B&B Reservation Services

EYE OPENERS BED & BREAKFAST RESERVATIONS
P.O. BOX 694, ALTADENA, CA 91001

Offers B&B Homes In: California, from San Diego to San Francisco
Reservations Phone: 213/684-4428 or 818/792-2055
Phone Hours: 24 hours daily
Price Range of Homes: $30 to $60 single, $35 to $65 double
Breakfast Included in Price: Continental or full American (juice, eggs, bacon, toast, coffee) and regional specialties

Brochure Available: Free if you send a stamped, self-addressed no. 10 envelope; $1 for home descriptions
Reservations Should Be Made: 2 weeks in advance (last-minute reservations accepted if possible)

Scenic Attractions Near the B&B Homes: Angeles National Forest, Huntington Library and Gardens, San Diego and Los Angeles Zoos, Universal Studios, Rose Bowl, Norton Simon Museum, Asia Pacific Museum, Dodger Stadium, Santa Anita Race Track, NBC-TV Studios, Yosemite, Balboa, Golden Gate Park
Major Schools, Universities Near the B&B Homes: California Institute of Technology, Art Center College of Design, Fuller Theological Seminary, UCLA USC, the Claremont Colleges, San Francisco State, UC San Diego

B&B Bonuses

Adjacent to scenic Angeles National Park is a spacious home with swimming pool and wine cellar, close to hiking equestrian trails. Have breakfast by the garden-fountain in another, old Spanish-style home. Interested in astronomy? Ask for the host with a telescope in an observatory area!

Airport and bus depot pickups are frequently made.

DIGS WEST
8191 CROWLEY CIRCLE, BUENA PARK, CA 90621

Offers B&B Homes In: Approximately 34 cities and towns throughout California
Reservations Phone: 714/739-1669
Phone Hours: 9 a.m. to 5 p.m. (Pacific Time) Monday to Friday (message service on weekends)
Price Range of Homes: $30 to $50 single, $36 to $65 double (luxury accommodations: $65 to $120)
Breakfast Included in Price: Continental or full American, depending on the individual home (homemade muffins and other specialties often served)
Brochure Available: Free if you send a stamped, self-addressed no. 10 envelope; directory available for $3
Reservations Should Be Made: No fixed requirements, but the earlier the better (last-minute reservations are difficult to fill)

Scenic Attractions Near the B&B Homes: The many tourist and natural attractions throughout California

Major Schools, Universities Near the B&B Homes: Cal State at Fullerton and Long Beach, UC Irvine, UC Santa Barbara, UC San Diego, USC, UCLA

B&B Bonuses

"Most of our homes offer a warm family feeling. One with a real country flavor is situated conveniently near Disneyland. Several hosts are artists and offer individualistic atmosphere and decor."

Recently, a couple from England were escorted by their hosts on a tour all over Southern California, and were served dinner on a boat.

CAROLYN'S BED & BREAKFAST HOMES IN SAN DIEGO

416 THIRD AVE., #25 CHULA VISTA, CA 92010

Offers B&B Homes In: San Diego city and county
Reservations Phone: 619/435-5009 or 619/422-7009
Phone Hours: 9 a.m. to 8 p.m. daily
Price Range of Homes: $20 to $60 single, $30 to $85 double (cottages: $55 to $125)
Breakfast Included in Price: Continental or full American, depending on the individual home (fresh-baked muffins often served)
Brochure Available: Free if you send a stamped, self-addressed no. 10 envelope
Reservations Should Be Made: 2 weeks in advance (last-minute reservations accepted if possible, with $5 extra charge)

Scenic Attractions Near the B&B Homes: Pacific Ocean, Torrey Pines Golf Course, Sea World, San Diego Zoo, Scripps Aquarium, Scripps Institute of Oceanography, Del Coronado Hotel, Disneyland, Tijuana, Mexico
Major Schools, Universities Near the B&B Homes: USC, Cal State San Diego

B&B Bonuses

There are modern homes and Victorian homes with beautiful antiques, ranch homes in the mountains with horseback riding available, and homes by the beach and ocean.

Airport, train and bus pickups are frequent, and some hosts offer laundry facilities and sightseeing tours.

BED & BREAKFAST OF SOUTHERN CALIFORNIA

1943 SUNNY CREST DR., #304, FULLERTON, CA 92635

Offers B&B Homes In: Southern California, primarily Orange County
Reservations Phone: 714/738-8361
Phone Hours: 8 a.m. to 9 p.m. daily
Price Range of Homes: $22 to $40 single, $28 to $50 double
Breakfast Included in Price: Continental (juice, roll or toast, coffee)
Brochure Available: Free
Reservations Should Be Made: 3 weeks in advance (last-minute reservations accepted if possible)

Scenic Attractions Near the B&B Homes: Disneyland, Knott's Berry Farm, Movieland Wax Museum, Pageant of the Masters, Irvine Meadows, all Los Angeles attractions a short drive away
Major Schools, Universities Near the B&B Homes: California State U., U. of California, Western State College of Law, Fullerton College, Cypress College, Orange Coast College

B&B Bonuses

A typical host is "Tom," who has traveled through the Orient collecting rugs, furniture, and pieces of art for "The Pink Home." Tom believes that making a guest feel at home and yet free to come and go is part of "the art of being a B&B host." Airport pick-ups, sightseeing tours, and tips on how to get the most for your vacation dollar are frequently provided.

BED & BREAKFAST RENT-A-ROOM

11531 VARNA ST., GARDEN GROVE, CA 92640

Offers B&B Homes In: Los Angeles, Disneyland, San Diego, Newport Beach, Laguna Beach, Lake Arrowhead, and along the coast
Reservations Price: 714/638-1406
Phone Hours: 8 a.m. to 10 p.m. daily
Price Range of Homes: $25 to $35 single, $30 to $60 double
Breakfast Included in Price: Continental (some hosts serve a different continental breakfast every day, with crêpes, French toast, etc.), and some full American
Brochure Available: Free if you send a stamped, self-addressed no. 10 envelope
Reservations Should Be Made: 2 weeks in advance (last-minute reservations accepted if possible)

Scenic Attractions Near the B&B Homes: Hollywood, Universal City, Marineland, Ports O' Call, *Queen Mary*, Disneyland, Knott's Berry Farm, Lion Country Safari, San Diego Zoo, Wild Animal Park, Sea World, Tijuana, Mexico missions in San Diego, San Juan Capistrano

Major Schools, Universities Near the B&B Homes: UCLA, USC, Long Beach State, Fullerton State, UC Irvine, U. San Diego, San Diego State

B&B Bonuses

A large home with four bedrooms and private baths boasts an inside fountain, Jacuzzi, swimming pool, tennis courts, and breakfast served in a gazebo. You will be close to the beaches, Disneyland, and Knott's Berry Farm too. Airport pickups are frequently made, and some hosts offer full- or half-day tours, use of private beach, and local golfing privileges.

WINE COUNTRY RESERVATIONS

P.O. BOX 5059, NAPA, CA 94581

Offers B&B Homes In: The Napa Valley
Reservations Phone: Phone currently not in operation—contact by writing to the address above
Price Range of Homes: $66 to $400 single or double
Breakfast Included in Price: Continental (juice, roll or toast, coffee), which may include muffins, fruit, cheese, coffee, teas, and juices
Brochure Available: For $2
Reservations Should Be Made: 3 to 4 weeks in advance (last-minute reservations accepted if possible)

Scenic Attractions Near the B&B Homes: 150 premium wineries, ballooning, hiking, bike trails, Calistoga mud and mineral baths, walking tours of old homes
Major Schools, Universities Near the B&B Homes: Napa Jr. College, Pacific Union College

B&B Bonuses

A 100-acre ranch in a peaceful valley features a game room, fireplace, pool, Jacuzzi, and "heartwarming hospitality." For Swiss chalet fanciers, this one overlooks acres of vineyards, with French doors opening onto balconies. Pickups and private winery tours can be arranged.

One B&B also operates an inn, "The Ambrose Bierce House," which is the former residence of the celebrated author, humorist, and man of mystery, Ambrose Bierce.

SACRAMENTO INNKEEPERS' ASSOCIATION
2209 CAPITOL AVE., SACRAMENTO, CA 95816

Offers B&B Homes In: Sacramento
Reservations Phone: 916/441-3214
Phone Hours: 8 a.m. to 9 p.m. daily
Price Range of Homes: $50 to $115 double
Breakfast Included in Price: Full American (juice, eggs, bacon, toast, coffee); may include homemade breads and fresh fruit
Brochure Available: Free
Reservations Should Be Made: 2 weeks in advance (last-minute reservations accepted if possible)

Scenic Attractions Near the B&B Homes: State Capitol, Sutter's Fort, Governor's Mansion, Railroad Museum, Oldtown, Crocker Art Museum, Convention Center
Major Schools, Universities Near the B&B Homes: American River College, Sacramento City College, Cal State Sacramento

B&B Bonuses
The famous "Briggs House" is a 1901 colonial revival home furnished with period antiques, elegant and comfortable, with a spa and a sauna in the shaded garden. At the "Amber House" you can partake of wine with the hosts and other guests every afternoon, and the continental breakfast will be served in your room, on Limoges with silver service. The "Morning Glory" house hosts will pick up guests at the airport, with a surprise bubble bath prepared for them! Other hosts will often assist with dinner reservations, babysitting, and guidance on points of interest.

AMERICAN FAMILY INN / BED & BREAKFAST SAN FRANCISCO
P.O. BOX 349, SAN FRANCISCO, CA 94101

Offers B&B Homes In: San Francisco, Marin County, Monterey/ Carmel, and the California Wine Country

Reservations Phone: 415/931-3083
Phone Hours: 9 a.m. to 5 p.m. Monday through Friday (answering machine all other hours)
Price Range of Homes: $45 to $125 single, $55 to $125 double (family accommodations: $70 to $100; boats: $100 and up)
Breakfast Included in Price: Full hearty American
Brochure Available: Free
Reservations Should Be Made: When you know the exact dates (last-minute reservations accepted if space allows)

Scenic Attractions Near the B&B Homes: San Francisco cable cars, Fisherman's Wharf, Chinatown, Moscone Convention Center, Golden Gate Park
Major Schools, Universities Near the B&B Homes: UC Medical Center, San Francisco State, Stanford

B&B Bonuses

A list of over 100 accommodations includes romantic Victorian homes as well as modern houses with decks and hot tubs. For real luxury, you can live on a yacht in San Francisco Bay.

All hosts are experts on San Francisco and offer the real hospitality of San Franciscans.

MEGAN'S FRIENDS BED & BREAKFAST RESERVATION SERVICE
1776 ROYAL WAY, SAN LUIS OBISPO, CA 93401

Offers B&B Homes In: The West Coast of the U.S. (a private membership group with an exclusive listing of hosts—Megan's Friends' members and referral homes)
Reservations Phone: 805/544-4406
Phone Hours: 11 a.m. to 4 p.m. and 6 to 10 p.m. Monday to Friday, or anytime
Price Range of Homes: $30 to $45 single, $35 to $75 double
Breakfast Included in Price: Full American
Brochure Available: Listing free, if you send a stamped, self-addressed no. 10 envelope
Reservations Should Be Made: 3 weeks in advance (last-minute reservations accepted if possible)

Scenic Attractions Near the B&B Homes: California attractions and sea views

B&B Bonuses _____

To maintain strict standards of cleanliness and comfort, no smoking is permitted in Megan's homes. Host homes are located in Pleasanton, King City, Atascadero, Solvang, Morro Bay, Los Osos, San Luis Obispo, and Sunset Palisades.

Special acts of hospitality have included picnic lunches; invitations to join the host family at a concert, play, or tour; help in getting tickets, restaurant, reservations, flowers—and gifts and cards to celebrate guests' birthdays and anniversaries.

WINE COUNTRY BED & BREAKFAST
P.O. BOX 3211, SANTA ROSA, CA 95403

Offers B&B Homes In: Santa Rosa and approximately 35-mile radius, including Healdsburg, Sebastopol, Sonoma, St. Helena, and Calistoga
Reservations Phone: 707/578-1661
Phone Hours: 10 a.m. to 8 p.m. daily
Price Range of Homes: $40 to $60 single, $45 to $65 double
Breakfast Included in Price: Full American (juice, eggs, bacon, toast, coffee)
Brochure Available: Free if you send a stamped, self-addressed no. 10 envelope
Reservations Should Be Made: 2 weeks in advance (no last-minute reservations, but will accept 1 week ahead if deposit is sent)

Scenic Attractions Near the B&B Homes: Over 24 world-famous wineries and vineyards, Redwood Forest in Armstrong State Park, Bodega Bay, Sonoma Old Spanish Mission, Jack London House and Museum, Russian River resorts, historic Russian settlement at Fort Ross, Luther Burbank Gardens
Major Schools, Universities Near the B&B Homes: Sonoma State, Santa Rosa Jr. College

B&B Bonuses _____

You can breakfast on the terrace of a beautifully restored Victorian Home, or enjoy the pool and sundeck of a house in the Valley of the Moon, or relax in the hot tub at many of the homes. Quite a few of the hosts are originally European, who chose this area of California as the place to live.

CALIFORNIA HOUSEGUESTS INTERNATIONAL, INC.

18533 BURBANK BLVD. (P.O. BOX 190), TARZANA, CA 91356

Offers B&B Homes In: California (statewide), including the Los Angeles area, Carmel, Monterey, Santa Barbara, San Francisco, San Diego, Wine Country
Reservations Phone: 818/344-7878
Phone Hours: 7 a.m. to 5 p.m. daily (answering machine for off-hours with callback)
Price Range of Homes: $40 to $80 single, $45 to $140 double
Breakfast Included in Price: Special continental (croissants, cheese, hot beverage, preserves, fresh fruit, with a flower), or full in selected locations
Brochure Available: Free if you send a stamped self-addressed no. 10 envelope
Reservations Should Be Made: 1 week in advance (last-minute reservations accepted if possible)

B&B Bonuses

Many charming homes close to beaches, or in the cities with pools and other amenities, plus mansions and some large estates, are on this B&B's list in California, including Victorians. Pickups from terminals, babysitting, extra meals, and kitchen privileges are offered at a reasonable extra charge, plus a creative weekend, and seminars on request: art tours, gourmet cooking, stained glass, writing and print-making classes in lovely settings

BED AND BREAKFAST OF LOS ANGELES

32074 WATERSIDE LANE, WESTLAKE VILLAGE, CA 91361

Offers B&B Homes In: Los Angeles, Ventura, and Orange Counties; also along the California coast (San Diego to San Francisco)
Reservations Phone: 818/889-8870 or 818/889-7325
Phone Hours: 9 a.m. to 9 p.m. Monday to Friday
Price Range of Homes: $24 to $50 single, $30 to $65 double
Breakfast Included in Price: Continental or full American (juice, eggs, bacon, toast, coffee), with some homes serving regional specialties
Brochure Available: For $1 with a legal-sized stamped, self-addressed envelope
Reservations Should Be Made: 1 month in advance (last-minute reservations accepted if possible)

Scenic Attractions Near the B&B Homes: All Southern California tourist attractions
Major Schools, Universities Near the B&B Homes: USC, UC Occidental, Pepperdine, Marymount, Loyola, Whittier, Cal College Long Beach, Northridge, Saddleback, Domingas Hills, Los Angeles, Fullerton, Polytech at Pomona, and UC Riverside

B&B Bonuses

Host homes range from exclusive Beverly Hills and Westlake Village to Marina del Rey, Hollywood, Huntington Beach, and many other desirable areas. One host speaks four languages and will prepare gourmet dinners (at an additional cost).

Picnic lunches, babysitting, airport pickups, and use of TV, golf clubs, patio and barbecue, pools, and bicycles are some of the extra services available in certain homes.

BED & BREAKFAST—CALIFORNIA SUNSHINE
22704 VENTURA BLVD., SUITE 1984, WOODLAND HILLS, CA 91364

Offers B&B Homes In: Southern California from Santa Barbara south to San Diego, and from the ocean inland
Reservations Phone: 818/992-1984
Phone Hours: 8 a.m. to 10 p.m. daily
Price Range of Homes: $40 to $60 single, $50 to $80 double
Breakfast Included in Price: Continental, may include fresh fruit; many hosts offer gourmet breakfasts, dinners and picnic lunches for a nominal fee, to be arranged for in advance.
Brochure Available: Free
Reservations Should Be Made: 2 weeks in advance (last-minute reservations accepted if possible)

Scenic Attractions Near the B&B Homes: Hollywood Bowl, Greek Theater, Griffith Park Observatory, Equestrian Center, Zoo, Dodger Stadium, L.A. Art Museum, Disneyland, Knott's Berry Farm, Universal City and Studios, NBC Studios, Santa Anita and Hollywood Park racetracks, Farmers Market, Olvera Street, Coliseum, Forum, Sports Arena
Major Schools, Universities Near the B&B Homes: UCLA, USC, Occidental, Loyola, Marymount, Santa Barbara, the Claremont Colleges, Pasadena City College, Cal State Northridge, Cal Tech, UC San Diego, Pieree, Valley College

B&B Bonuses ───────────────────────

Homes can be quiet and secluded, or right in the heart of the city. "Indescribable ocean views in contractors' ocean homes." One home has extensive facilities for pets, and will only accept guests with a pet! Multilingual homes abound.

Host homes offer all sports facilities, hot tubs and spas, horseback riding and equipment, complimentary use of health clubs and golf privileges. "Most hosts wish to communicate before arrival so that a pleasurable exchange between people of similar background and interests can be experienced."

B&B Inns

SANDPIPER INN AT THE BEACH

2408 BAY VIEW AVE., CARMEL-BY-THE-SEA, CA 93923

Reservations Phone: 408/624-6433
Description: This European-style country inn opened in 1929 in a quiet residential area just 50 yards from the beach. The 15 rooms and cottages all have private baths.
Amenities: Continental breakfast

Nearby Attractions: Point Lobos State Reserve, Old Carmel Mission Basilica, Big Sur, 17-Mile Drive
Special Services: Tennis, golf, swimming
Rates: $70 to $105 double

VAGABOND'S HOUSE INN

FOURTH AND DELORES (P.O. BOX 2747), CARMEL-BY-THE-SEA, CA 93921

Reservations Phone: 408/624-7738
Description: This brick half-timbered Tudor country inn is in the heart of the village. Each of the rooms faces a flagstone courtyard of ferns and flowers.
Amenities: Continental breakfast served each morning in the lobby from 7:30 to 10:30 a.m.

Nearby Attractions: The Carmel Mission, Sunset Center, 17-Mile Drive, Point Lobos Reserve, the Tor

Special Services: Each room is supplied with a coffee pot, fresh-ground coffee, and a decanter of cream sherry
Rates: $65 to $105 double

CARTER HOUSE BED & BREAKFAST INN
1033 3RD ST., EUREKA, CA 95501

Reservations Phone: 707/445-1390
Description: This Victorian mansion has seven rooms for guests, three with private bath. The house has been stylishly restored with antiques and Oriental rugs, yet with modern paintings and ceramics by local artists.
Amenities: Breakfast specialties might include a tart with almond filling, eggs Florentine or Benedict, or kiwi with raspberries
Special Services: Airport pickup with a 1958 Bentley, wine and brie in the afternoon, tea, cookies, and cordials at bedtime, can be arranged.
Rates: $45 to $125 double

THE OLD TOWN BED & BREAKFAST INN
1521 3RD ST., EUREKA, CA 95501

Reservations Phone: 707/445-3951
Description: This 1871 house was moved to its present location in 1915. The five rooms for guests are all individually decorated in soft colors with period furniture; two of the rooms have a shared bath.
Amenities: Full breakfast

Nearby Attractions: State parks, museums, tubing, tennis, golf, racquetball
Special Services: Use of bicycles, complimentary wine and cheese
Rates: $40 to $50 single, $50 to $60 double

CLEONE LODGE
24600 N. HWY. 1, FORT BRAGG, CA 95437

Reservations Phone: 707/964-2788

Description: In a quiet setting on three acres of wooded grounds, each unit in the lodge varies in design and decor and may include antiques, wicker furniture, colorful prints, fireplaces, garden views, and kitchens.
Amenities: Juice, fruit compote, homemade Swedish coffee bread or blueberry muffins, coffee or tea
Nearby Attractions: Mendocino's rugged coast, redwood groves, wineries, MacKerricher State Park, Lake Cleone, canoeing, trout fishing, horseback riding, bicycling
Rates: $45 to $68 double

EAST BROTHER LIGHT HOUSE
117 PARK PL., FORT RICHMOND, CA 94801

Reservations Phone: 415/233-2385
Description: This is an island lighthouse in San Francisco Bay. The bedrooms are furnished with period antiques and have unsurpassed views of San Francisco.
Amenities: Continental breakfast; a five-course dinner with wine and champagne included in the price

Nearby Attractions: San Francisco
Special Services: Boat transportation to and from the island
Rates: $195 single, $225 to $250 double

ST. ORRES
36601 S. HWY. 1, GUALALA, CA 95445

Reservations Phone: 707/884-3303 or 707/884-3335
Description: The inn is situated on the Mendocino coast with eight handcrafted rooms in the hotel and nine cottages on 42 wooded acres, some with ocean views, fireplaces, and skylights.
Amenities: Freshly squeezed orange juice, cheese torta, homemade granola and breads, coffee and tea, served buffet style

Nearby Attractions: Mendocino, Fort Ross
Special Services: Six creekside cottages have exclusive use of a spa with a hot tub and sauna.
Rates: $50 to $125 double

HOTEL LEGER
MAIN AND LAFAYETTE, MOKELUMNE HILL, CA 95245

Reservations Phone: 209/286-1401
Description: Over 100 years ago George Leger came from Europe to this gold rush boomtown and opened a hotel. His spirit of service and hospitality lives on today at the hotel, which combines nostalgia with modern comfort.

Nearby Attractions: Historic and scenic attractions, to golf courses and summer and winter sports areas a short drive away
Special Services: The Court House Theater seating 128 presents popular stage productions in summer and is available for meetings, weddings, and banquets.
Rates: $42 to $60 double on weekends, $53 double weekdays

THE NAPA INN
1137 WARREN ST., NAPA, CA 94559

Reservations Phone: 707/257-1444
Description: This three-story turn-of-the-century home in the quaint preservation area of Napa has four spacious accommodations (rooms, studios, or suites), each with a lovely view and furnished with antiques.
Amenities: Juice, fresh seasonal fruit, hot breakfast breads or muffins, coffee or tea

Nearby Attractions: Napa Valley wineries, balloon rides
Special Services: Refrigerator in the room, breakfast served in your room, fresh flowers, kitchens available
Rates: $50 to $80 double in summer, $35 to $65 double in winter

THE VILLAGE INN
1012 DARMS LANE, NAPA, CA 94558

Reservations Phone: 707/257-2089
Description: The inn's country cottages are sited on two acres. Each separate cottage is decorated in country style (Laura Ashley fabrics), and contains a bedroom, a living room (with trundle bed), a kitchen, and a bath.
Amenities: Continental breakfast, with fresh fruit in season

Nearby Attractions: Wineries, a geyser-fed hot spring with mud baths and massage available, Marine World/Africa
Special Services: The inn accepts well-behaved children and pets.
Rates: $65 to $90 double February to October, prices vary November to January

PORTOFINO BEACH HOTEL

2306 W. OCEAN FRONT, NEWPORT BEACH, CA 92663

Reservations Phone: 714/673-7030
Description: The remodeled rooms are furnished with antiques and have private baths and an ocean view. An antique bar and gourmet Italian restaurant are available to guests.
Amenities: Continental breakfast

Nearby Attractions: McFaddens Wharf, the beach at Newport, Disneyland, Universal Studio Tour
Special Services: Beach chairs, towels, and umbrellas; local airport pickup
Rates: $99 to $155 double in summer, $89 to $125 double in winter

CHRISTY HILL RESTAURANT AND INN

1650 SQUAW VALLEY RD. (P.O. BOX 2449), OLYMPIC VALLEY, CA 195730

Reservations Phone: 916/583-8551
Description: The seven rooms with private bath are attractively decorated in shades of forest green and rosy peach. The comfortable furnishings include queen-size beds with firm mattresses, feather pillows, and goose-down comforters.
Amenities: Continental breakfast in ski season

Nearby Attractions: Squaw Valley Ski Resort, Lake Tahoe
Special Services: Shuttle service to ski area
Rates: $85 to $100 double in fall and winter, $50 to $75 double in spring and summer

THE SHERMAN HOUSE

2160 GREEN ST., SAN FRANCISCO, CA 94123

Reservations Phone: 415/563-3600
Description: An 1876 historic landmark converted from a private mansion into a 15-room accommodation, the house has been meticulously restored to its original beauty with French Second Empire interiors featuring a splendid three-story music room with gallery salon, a carriage house, formal gardens, a Victorian greenhouse, and a gazebo. Rooms have canopied feather beds and fireplaces.

Nearby Attractions: Historic landmarks, cable cars, Fisherman's Wharf
Special Services: Airport limousine service, courtesy membership in one of San Francisco's best athletic clubs
Rates: $170 to $600 double

WHITE SWAN INN

845 BUSH ST., SAN FRANCISCO, CA 94108

Reservations Phone: 415/775-1755
Description: This is an English garden-style inn, with antiques, fresh flowers, a library, and a conference room.
Amenities: Orange and tomato juice, muffins, croissants, brioches, fruit, and coffee, tea, or hot chocolate

Nearby Attractions: Nob Hill, Union Square, cable-car lines, Chinatown, downtown
Special Services: Afternoon tea, sherry, and hors d'oeuvres
Rates: $115 to $135 double

PETITE AUBERGE

863 BUSH ST., SAN FRANCISCO, CA 94108

Reservations Phone: 415/928-6000
Description: This French country inn has antiques, fresh flowers, and fireplaces.
Amenities: Juice, eggs, quiche, or french toast, croissants, muffins, granola, and coffee, tea, or milk

Nearby Attractions: All of San Francisco
Special Services: Afternoon tea or wine and hors d'oeuvres
Rates: $95 to $185 double

THE PARSONAGE

1600 OLIVE ST., SANTA BARBARA, CA 93101

Reservations Phone: 805/962-9336
Description: This two-story, restored Queen Anne Victorian is filled with Oriental rugs and antiques.
Amenities: Fresh-squeezed orange juice, homemade breads and muffins, apple pancakes, chili cheese soufflé featured on the breakfast menu

Nearby Attractions: Santa Barbara Mission, Botanical Gardens, the Pacific Ocean
Special Services: Complimentary wine offered each evening
Rates: $60 to $110 single, $65 to $115 double

CAMPBELL HOT SPRINGS

P.O. BOX 234, SIERRAVILLE, CA 96126

Reservations Phone: 916/994-8984
Description: This historic building lies in the heart of Sierraville.
Amenities: Vegetarian breakfast with hot cereal, toasted home-made bread, hotcakes and waffles on weekends

Nearby Attractions: Lake Tahoe (40 miles away), Reno (60 miles away), fishing, outdoor sports
Rates: $40 double

UTAH

B&B Inns

PETERSON'S BED & BREAKFAST
95 N. 300 WEST (P.O. BOX 142), MONROE, UT 84754

Reservations Phone: 801/527-4830
Description: Parts of the building are 90 to 100 years old, but fit in well with the later additions. The rooms are fitted with king-sized beds, sitting areas, kitchens, private baths, and private entrances.
Amenities: Full breakfast with such specialties as macadamia-nut pancakes, country ham, or Dutch apple pancakes

Nearby Attractions: Five national parks, museum of Indian artifacts, tennis, golf, Monroe Hot Springs
Special Services: Complimentary beverages
Rates: $25 single, $35 double

Alaska & Hawaii

Alaska / 269
Hawaii / 271

B&B Reservation Services

ALASKA PRIVATE LODGINGS

1236 W. TENTH AVE., ANCHORAGE, AK 99501

Offers B&B Homes In: Anchorage, Seward, Homer, Palmer, Willow, Talkeetna
Reservations Phone: 907/258-1717
Phone Hours: 9 a.m. to 7 p.m. Monday to Friday
Price Range of Homes: $30 to $55 single, $38 to $80 double
Breakfast Included in Price: "Breakfasts are as varied as our homes and hosts, ranging from continental to full sourdough Alaska can be found."
Brochure Available: Free if you send a stamped, self-addressed no. 10 envelope
Reservations Should Be Made: 2 weeks in advance (last-minute reservations accepted if possible)

Scenic Attractions Near the B&B Homes: Alaska Oil Pipeline; Alaska Railroad; glaciers, gold mines, salmon-spawning waters, mountain ranges, native wildlife; city, state, and national parks
Major Schools, Universities Near the B&B Homes: U. of Alaska at Anchorage, Alaska Pacific U.

B&B Bonuses ──────────────────────────

Want spectacular views of Mount McKinley and Hunter? Ask for Clouds' Rest B&B. For breakfast you can enjoy sourdough pancakes or scones served with honey-butter. Like to stay in a log cabin with a stone fireplace? Ask for the Talkeetna B&B.

FAIRBANKS BED & BREAKFAST

P.O. BOX 74573, FAIRBANKS, AK 99707

Offers B&B Homes In: Fairbanks
Reservations Phone: 907/452-4967
Phone Hours: 8 a.m. to 8 p.m. daily

Price Range of Homes: $36 and up single, $48 and up double
Breakfast Included in Price: Continental (juice, roll or toast, coffee), cereals
Brochure Available: Free
Reservations Should Be Made: Reservations accepted any time if guaranteed with $25 deposit

Scenic Attractions Near the B&B Homes: Cruises on sternwheeler *Discovery*, Alaska Salmon Bake, mining valley at Alaskaland
Major Schools, Universities Near the B&B Homes: U. of Alaska at Fairbanks

B&B Bonuses

"We are a family-run reservations and referral service. We book travelers into English-style lodgings. Many extras are offered. We meet the express train from Denali Park and Anchorage; all guests receive a free map and Visitors' Guide; we can book your cruise on the *Discovery* and arrange tickets for the Alaska Salmon Bake."

B&B Inns

GUSTAVUS INN

P.O. BOX 31, GUSTAVUS, AK 99826

Reservations Phone: 907/697-2254
Description: The inn combines a traditional homestead atmosphere and magnificent Alaskan setting with modern accommodations and convenient transportation. Bedrooms have double or twin beds; singles may be asked to share. All baths are down the hall.
Amenities: Full breakfast

Nearby Attractions: Glacier Bay National Park, fishing for salmon or halibut
Special Services: Boat tours of Glacier Bay, three meals a day included in the rate
Rates: $59.50 single, $119 double

ALASKAN HOTEL

167 S. FRANKLIN ST., JUNEAU, AK 99801

Reservations Phone: 907/586-1000

Description: Alaska's oldest hotel opened in 1913. It has 10 rooms with private bath and 30 rooms with shared bath. Over 50 pieces of stained glass adorn the hotel. Features of the hotel include steam heat and a radio station of 1½ kilowatts on the roof. The hotel is on the National Register of Historic Places.

Nearby Attractions: The capital city of Juneau
Special Services: Hot tubs and sauna, oak antique phones, kitchenettes, TVs
Rates: $36 to $50 single, $41 to $55 double, in spring and summer; $25 to $36 single, $30 to $41 double, in fall and winter

LOUIE'S PLACE—ELFIN COVE
P.O. BOX 704, JUNEAU, AK 99802

Reservations Phone: 907/586-2032
Description: The inn is located in the isolated, scenic fishing village of Elfin Cove, near Glacier Bay.

Nearby Attractions: Glacier Bay National Monument, streams for fishing or kayaking
Special Services: Pickup at the mailplane or your chartered floatplane, propane cooking, refrigerator, hot showers
Rates: $350 double per week

HAWAII

B&B Reservation Services

PACIFIC-HAWAII BED & BREAKFAST
19 KAI NANI PL., KAIULUA, OAHU, HI 96734

Offers B&B Homes In: Oahu and almost all the other Hawaiian islands
Reservations Phone: 808/262-6026 or 808/263-4848
Phone Hours: 8 a.m. to 10 p.m. Monday to Friday (also on weekends and holidays)
Price Range of Homes: $20 single, $25 to $100 double

Breakfast Included in Price: Continental with Hawaiian fruits
Brochure Available: For $2
Reservations Should Be Made: Anytime; can accept short-notice reservations

Scenic Attractions Near the B&B Homes: Miles of beaches, Pali Lookout, Queen Emma Summer Palace
Major Schools, Universities Near the B&B Homes: U. of Hawaii

B&B Bonuses

Some hosts will adopt guests into the family and take them on picnics or boat rides. Hosts are available who speak German, Spanish, French, Catalan, and Japanese.

BED & BREAKFAST HAWAII

P.O. BOX 449, KAPAA, HI 96746

Offers B&B Homes In: All Hawaiian islands except Lanai
Reservations Phone: 808/822-7771
Phone Hours: 8:30 a.m. to 4:30 p.m. Monday to Saturday
Price Range of Homes: $15 to $45 single, $20 to $75 double
Breakfast Included in Price: Continental (juice, roll or toast, coffee), plus such regional specialties at some homes as banana cakes, papaya and mango breads, Hawaiian French toast with coconut syrup, fresh fruit
Brochure Available: Free
Reservations Should Be Made: 3 weeks in advance (last-minute reservations accepted if possible)

Scenic Attractions Near the B&B Homes: All national and state parks, famous zoos, historic homes, all the beauty and romance of the tropics
Major Schools, Universities Near the B&B Homes: U. of Hawaii and branches on other islands

B&B Bonuses

Many homes feature ocean views, private pools and tennis, lanais, and nearby shopping. Many serve organically grown vegetables. Many hosts will give sightseeing tours, and all will gladly give information as to restaurants, best buys, and discount coupons.

Canada

British Columbia / 275
Nova Scotia / 276
Ontario / 277
Québec / 280

B&B Reservation Services

V.I.P. BED & BREAKFAST LTD.

1786 TEAKWOOD RD., VICTORIA, BC V8N 1E2, CANADA

Offers B&B Homes In: Victoria, Sidney
Reservations Phone: 604/477-5604
Phone Hours: 7 a.m. to 10 p.m. daily
Price Range of Homes: $30 ($22 U.S.) to $35 ($26 U.S.) single, $45 ($33 U.S.) to $50 ($38 U.S.) double
Breakfast Included in Price: Full American (juice, eggs, bacon, toast, coffee)
Brochures Available: Free
Reservations Should Be Made: 2 weeks in advance (last-minute reservations accepted if possible)

Scenic Attractions Near the B&B Homes: Butchart Gardens, Provincial Museum, Craigdarroch Castle, Beacon Hill Park, Parliament Buildings
Major Schools, Universities Near the B&B Homes: U. of Victoria, Camosun College

B&B Bonuses

They are proud of their muffins and waffles and their philosophy that breakfast is "enough to eliminate the need for lunch!" One hostess received a rave letter for her "heartwarming friendship and special touches, like flowers in the room, turning on the light for homecoming   and I can still taste the muffins, fresh fruits, and jam."

NOVA SCOTIA

B&B Reservation Services

CAPE BRETON BED & BREAKFAST

P.O. BOX 1750, SYDNEY, NS BIP 677, CANADA

Offers B&B Homes In: Cape Breton and surrounding areas
Reservations Phone: Each B&B home must be phoned direct; send for a free brochure.
Price Range of Homes: $20 ($15 U.S.) single, $24 ($18 U.S.) double
Breakfast Included in Price: Continental or full American . . . which may include regional specialties of Cape Breton as Bras d'Or trout, Scottish oatcakes, marrigan, oatmeal porridge, and homemade breads and preserves
Brochure Available: Free
Reservations Should Be Made: Advance reservations are welcome but not necessary

Scenic Attractions Near the B&B Homes: Cabot Trail, Miner's Museum, Savoy Theater, Fortress Louisburg, Newfoundland ferry, Seal Island Bridge, Bell Museum, beaches, golf courses, Bras d'Or lakes

B&B Bonuses

One enthusiastic guest wrote: "Following a night of sleeping in a squeaky-clean room with embroidered pillowcases on the bed, and enjoying a breakfast of bacon, eggs, juice, milk, doughnuts, muffins, and two kinds of toast, my colleague and I left really feeling that we had been part of a Nova Scotia family for a day."

Some hosts may prepare picnic lunches and late-night snacks. They also may drive guests to the airport and ferry.

NOVA SCOTIA FARM & COUNTRY VACATION ASSOCIATION

NEWPORT STATION, HANS CO., NS B0N 2B0, CANADA

Offers B&B Homes In: Rural Nova Scotia

Reservations Phone: 902/798-5864
Phone Hours: 24 hours daily
Price Range of Homes: $12 ($9 U.S.) to $15 ($11 U.S.) single, $25 ($18.50 U.S.) to $30 ($22 U.S.) double
Breakfast Included in Price: Continental or full American . . . in some homes, all meals can be provided if the guest so wishes.
Brochure Available: Free
Reservations Should Be Made: Anytime (last-minute reservations accepted)

B&B Bonuses

The homes are located in rural areas; farm vacations are their specialty. "In our program, guests are invited into our homes and they become part of the family. They eat with us, participate in our activities if they so desire, etc. They do not have to stay in their rooms, but have the general use of the house."

ONTARIO

B&B Reservation Services

BED & BREAKFAST PRINCE EDWARD COUNTY
P.O. BOX 160, BLOOMFIELD, ON K0K 1G0, CANADA

Offers B&B Homes In: Prince Edward County on the north shore of Lake Ontario
Reservations Phone: 613/393-3046
Phone Hours: 9 a.m. to 8 p.m. daily
Price Range of Homes: $25 ($18.50 U.S.) to $30 ($22 U.S.) single, $35 ($26 U.S.) to $50 ($37 U.S.) double
Breakfast Included in Price: Full American, including homemade muffins, bread, tea biscuits, jams, jellies, etc.
Brochure Available: For $1
Reservations Should Be Made: 1 month in advance in July and August (last-minute reservations accepted if possible)

Scenic Attractions Near the B&B Homes: Famous sand dunes, beaches, sailing, windsurfing, birdwatching, museums, "Bird City," bicycling, the White Chapel Meeting House, Macaulay House

B&B Bonuses _____

Ask for an 1846 stone house on the Bay of Quinte, 300 yards from a fully equipped marina with docking facilities and near a conservation area. "In the winter the blazing fireplace kitchen beckons cross-country skiers. The hosts are warm and welcoming, and enthusiastic to share their interests in travel, horticulture, genealogy, and crafts."

OTTAWA AREA BED & BREAKFAST

P.O. BOX 4848, STATION E, OTTAWA, ON K1S 5J1, CANADA

Offers B&B Homes In: Ottawa, Nepean, Kanata, Gloucester (in Ontario); Hull, Aylmer, Gatineau (in Québec)
Reservations Phone: 613/563-0161
Phone Hours: 8:30 a.m. to 4:30 p.m. preferred, but available 24 hours daily
Price Range of Homes: $25 ($18.50 U.S.) to $35 ($26 U.S.) single, $35 ($26 U.S.) to $45 ($33 U.S.) double
Breakfast Included in Price: Full American (juice, eggs, bacon, toast, coffee)
Brochure Available: Free
Reservations Should Be Made: 2 weeks in advance (last-minute reservations accepted if possible)

Scenic Attractions Near the B&B Homes: Parliament Buildings of Canada, Rideau Canal, museums, art galleries
Major Schools, Universities Near the B&B Homes: U. of Ottawa, Carleton U., Algonquin College, St. Paul's U.

B&B Bonuses _____

"We can offer you older homes situated right in the heart of the city, suburban homes with such amenities as pools and air conditioning, lovely country properties with farm animals or private beaches."

COUNTRY HOST

R. R. #1, PALGRAVE, ON L0N 1P0, CANADA

Offers B&B Homes In: Ontario, from Toronto, north and almost 300 miles west to Tobermory and also at Point Pelee National Park area on Lake Erie (where thousands of birds migrate in spring and fall)
Reservations Phone: 519/941-7633

Phone Hours: 8 a.m. to midnight daily (no collect calls)
Price Range of Homes: $30 ($22 U.S.) single, $35 ($26 U.S.) to $45 ($33 U.S.) double
Breakfast Included in Price: Full American (juice or fruit in season, bacon or sausage, eggs, toast, coffee; real maple syrup, Canadian bacon and hot muffins, often served (lunches and dinners available in some homes if requested in advance)
Brochure Available: No—send for personal answer, including stamped, self-addressed envelope
Reservations Should Be Made: At least 1 week in advance (last-minute reservations accepted if possible)

Scenic Attractions Near the B&B Homes: Bruce Trail, conservation areas, swimming, fishing, golfing, skiing, ice-fishing, snowmobiling, antiques and craft shops, wildflowers and hundreds of bird species

B&B Bonuses

A really unique service of this B&B is "car-jockey service"—when a guest is hiking on the trail, the first host will drive the guest's car to the second host home with the guest's overnight gear, change of clothing, bandages for his blisters, "maybe even a bottle of wine for evening relaxation." On Day 2, the second host will likewise move the car to the third host home, etc. Women in particular like this service, which, for a very nominal fee, saves carrying anything other than a compass, lunch, binoculars, and camera, while on the famous Bruce Trail. Or guests will be transported to and from the Bruce Trail by the host, making a car unnecessary for hikers.

The Bruce Trail, where many birds are found, is on the Niagara Escarpment and stretches from Niagara to Tobermory on the tip of Bruce Peninsula, a distance of 430 miles, or 712.7 kilometers.

STRATFORD & AREA BED & BREAKFAST
c/o 30 SHREWSBURY ST., STRATFORD, ON N5A 2V5, CANADA

Offers B&B Homes In: City and rural Stratford area (an easy day trip to Toronto and Niagara Falls)
Reservations Phone: 519/271-8520
Phone Hours: 9 a.m. to 10 p.m. daily
Price Range of Homes: $20 ($15 U.S.) to $35 ($26 U.S.) single, $25 ($18.50 U.S.) to $50 ($37 U.S.) double
Breakfast Included in Price: Continental (juice, roll or toast, coffee); many homes give fresh fruit in season, and scones or muffins

Brochure Available: Free
Reservations Should Be Made: As soon as possible (last-minute reservations accepted if possible)

Scenic Attractions Near the B&B Homes: Wildwood Conservation Park, Avon Valley Hiking Trail, Stratford Shakespearean Theater, sandy beaches of Lake Huron
Major Schools, Universities Near the B&B Homes: U. of Western Ontario at London, U. of Waterloo, Sir Wilfred Laurier U.

B&B Bonuses ─────────────────────────────

One spacious, century-old home, with grounds gently sloping to the water, is filled with art and antiques. A stone farmhouse offers home-grown fruit and vegetables, fresh eggs, and homemade smoked hams, breads, and jams.

QUÉBEC

B&B Reservation Services

MONTRÉAL BED AND BREAKFAST

4912 VICTORIA, MONTRÉAL, PQ H3W 2N1, CANADA

Offers B&B Homes In: Montréal and nearby communities (Dorval, where Dorval Airport is located; the Eastern Townships; Laurentian Mountains area)
Reservations Phone: 514/738-9410 or 514/738-3859
Phone Hours: 9 a.m. to 9 p.m. daily
Price Range of Homes: $30 ($22 U.S.) to $40 ($30 U.S.) single, $40 ($30 U.S.) to $70 ($52 U.S.) double
Breakfast Included in Price: Full American (juice, eggs, bacon, toast, coffee), plus regional specialties
Brochure Available: For $1
Reservations Should Be Made: 3 weeks in advance, if by mail; telephone reservations accepted; deposit by VISA or Mastercard

Scenic Attractions Near the B&B Homes: Mount Royal Park, Olympic Stadium, St. Joseph Oratory, Botanical Gardens, Place des Arts, Old Montréal, Museum of Fine Arts
Major Schools, Universities Near the B&B Homes: McGill, U. de Montréal

B&B Bonuses

As a guest of Montréal B&B, you qualify for a 15% discount on any Grey Line tour in Montréal.

Homes range from an apartment in a magnificent compound opposite Mount Royal Park, five minutes to downtown, to an unusual rowhouse in Montréal's Latin Quarter area, which features an indoor courtyard, skylighting, and wrought-iron spiral staircase.

Hosts offer good conversation, good suggestions, sometimes ironing and laundry facilities, sometimes lifts to the nearest Métro or even to the bus or train station. One hostess was able to arrange a day of sailing for her guests with a friend, a member of a local yacht club. When hosts know people in the same line of work as their guests, they sometimes organize a get-together.

GITE QUÉBEC BED & BREAKFAST
3729 AVE. LE CORBUSIER, STE-FOY, PQ G1W 4R8, CANADA

Offers B&B Homes In: Québec City and area
Reservations Phone: 418/651-1860
Phone Hours: 8 a.m. to 9 p.m. daily
Price Range of Homes:
$25 ($18.50 U.S.) to $30 ($22 U.S.) single, $50 ($37 U.S.) double
Breakfast Included in Price: Full American (juice, eggs, bacon, toast, coffee)
Brochure Available: Free
Reservations Should Be Made: 2 weeks in advance (last-minute reservations accepted if possible)

Scenic Attractions Near the B&B Homes: Château Frontenac, the Citadel and Governors' Promenade, Dufferin Terrace, the Plains of Abraham, Ste. Anne de Beaupré, Winter Carnival, Montmorency Falls, Île d'Orléans, Fort Museum Artillery Park, Chevalier House, Place d'Armes, Ursuline Convent and Museum

B&B Bonuses

Tour Québec City, the nearest thing to Europe in our hemisphere, staying at accommodations in private homes offering comfortable rooms, a complete breakfast, and warm hospitality.

"All of our listings have been personally inspected for their comfort and cleanliness. All are convenient to the city's attractions via excellent public transportation."

The 100 Best B&B Homes in North America

In the Depression era bed-and-breakfast may have only been a sparsely furnished room and a thin cup of coffee in a modest frame house somehwere along the highway. But today the B&B movement has become the Cinderella of the U.S. travel industry, and the accommodations, services, and thoughtfulness of hosts have created a delightful new way to travel. To help honor these new standards, *Frommer's Bed & Breakfast North America* guide-book has created a new category "The Best B&B Homes in North America."

In making these selections I have relied heavily on the recommendations of the bed-and-breakfast reservation services. Each was invited to nominate just one home, the best home on its list. The men and women who operate these services may see and judge hundreds of homes and are in a unique position to point with pride at a home that rises above the rest in their areas. I have also selected certain individual homes that are not connected with any reservation service, based on recommendations of travel writer colleagues, published reviews in the media, photographs, and written comments of guests who have stayed in the homes.

Of course, I couldn't resist selecting a home where the host is a professional magician who entertains his guests with magic tricks after breakfast. Or the B&B home that takes guests on a stage-coach tour of California's wine country. Or the granddaughter of a famous American artist who welcomes guests to the artist's studio home and serves them "ethereal eggs" with sour cream and cheese.

Some homes are truly spectacular southern mansions that rival *Gone with the Wind*'s Tara. Others are beautiful apartments with skyline views. Still others are more modest rural dwellings with a spectacular mountain or ocean view, unbelievable gourmet breakfasts, or a hostess who babysits and leaves a glass of sherry and cheeses on a bedstand at night.

Is each a perfect "10"? No, but I think each offers something really special to guests.

There is one confusing element. Some of the B&B homes I have selected call themselves "inns." But I have arbitrarily decided that any B&B operation in a private home is a "B&B home," to distinguish it from the larger commercial inns which are basically small hotels that serve breakfast and also call themselves "B&B inns."

Homes change owners and standards can change. If you stay at any of these homes and are disappointed—or find what you believe is a superior B&B in the same area—you're invited to become one of our "B&B Critics" and write to me with your evaluations and discoveries. The collective judgment of our readers will play a major part in future selections of the "100 Best."

But meanwhile you can use this list to help plan a wonderful B&B vacation for yourself and your family all across North America.

Note: In the case of homes nominated by reservations services, I have given only partial addresses. Please contact the service at the phone number listed. Some hosts prefer not to be contacted directly. For homes not listed by reservation services I have provided complete addresses and each host's phone number.

NEUBAUER HOUSE
FAIRBANKS, ALASKA

(Nominated by Fairbanks Bed & Breakfast)

This is a new two-story frame house with a large yard and deck. It's located in a quiet residential neighborhood, close to local historic houses and eight blocks from the downtown area. For breakfast the host serves juice, rolls, and cereal. In the summertime there will be fresh fruit, honeydew melons, and pancakes. There is a TV in the room. Guests (for a donation) can use the laundry facilities.

Rates: $48 to $58 double, May to September; $30 double, October to April
Reservations: 907/452-4567

EPLE HOME
SCOTTSDALE, ARIZONA

(Nominated by Bed & Breakfast Scottsdale)

Do you long to stay in a Territorial adobe where motion-picture stars once escaped to in the early days of the movies? This B&B is set at the base of a mountain in a canyon of villa homes. You have a choice of balcony or terrace rooms. "The host, Ann, is a wonderful cook and bakes fresh rolls and breads. Breakfast includes juice, fruit, and cheeses—sometimes soups or chili. The Eples are special people whose guests become instant friends."

Rates: $75 double, January 1 to April 30; $65 double May 1 to December 31
Reservations: 602/998-7044

CURTIS HOME
TEMPE, ARIZONA

(Nominated by Valley O' the Sun B&B)

This modern ranch has its own private pool. It's located near Arizona State University, the Phoenix Zoo, two city parks, a golf course, and Grady Gammage Auditorium. The hostess serves a full Arizona breakfast. Complimentary juice, coffee, and tea are available during the day. The hostess will take care of airport pickup and theater reservations.

Rates: $25 to $35 double
Reservations: 602/941-1281

TEMPE HOME
TEMPE, ARIZONA

(Nominated by Mi Casa–Su Casa)

This is a convenient and attractive home near major schools such as Arizona State University and Mesa Community College. It's close to shopping, numerous restaurants, and churches. The home has a tranquil, pleasant atmosphere with a swimming pool and fireplace. Guests have light cooking privileges. For breakfast they can dine on fresh fruit, bacon, sausage, and eggs. Ask for Room 1; it has its own private entrance to the outside pool through arcadia doors. Your hostess enjoys cooking and makes superior bagels. She also can arrange to pick you up at the airport and obtain tickets for local theater and music events.

Rates: $35 to $45 double
Reservations: 602/990-0682

THE RILEY HOUSE
420 QUAPAW AVE., HOT SPRINGS NATIONAL PARK, AR 71901

What about a romantic step into the past? Try this 1890 Victorian brownstone and brick retreat, nationally registered. From the exceptional woodwork, light fixtures, antiques, and black marble fireplace in the reception hall, this house takes you back decades. There are six rooms, four with private bath. A fruit bowl is provided in each, and mineral water and iced tea are always available. You can relax on the wicker chairs on upper wrap-around porches shielded by treetops. You can practice on the baby grand piano, watch cable TV, or use the game room. This home is centrally located within walking distance of Bathhouse Row and park headquarters. You will be surrounded by 50- to 80-year-old trees. Airport pickup is provided on advance notice.

Rates: $49 to $69 double
Reservations: 501/624-4275

FOOTHILL HOUSE
3037 FOOTHILL BLVD., CALISTOGA, CA 94515

This turn-of-the-century farmhouse is set among the trees, with views of valley and hills. Each room has a private entrance, four-poster bed, small refrigerator, and fireplace. Guests bubble over with compliments about the special touches—such as homemade cookies and a decanter of sherry on your bedside table, and all the fixings for a perfect fire arranged in the fireplace (all you have to do is light the match). The warm hospitality of the hosts makes you feel as if they are "best friends," as one couple put it. A generous breakfast includes freshly squeezed orange juice and two different kinds of delicious home-baked goods. The hosts will help you plan a complete tour of Napa Valley, including winery tours, picnics, and spa and restaurant reservations.

Rates: $75 to $95 double
Reservations: 707/942-6933

CARTER HOUSE
1033 3RD ST., EUREKA, CA 95501

Carter House has been much-honored in books and magazines. It looks like a bed-and-breakfast house that might have been designed by an 18th-century Walt Disney. Breakfast is really special: four gourmet courses including such surprises as baked apples in caramel sauce, eggs Benedict, baked ham, and muffins. Said the host, "Often guests come for the sole purpose of enjoying our breakfast." Cheese and fruit are served every evening, with wine, before a roaring fire in a marble fireplace. Airport pickups can be arranged and they're classy—you're met by a 1958 Bentley.

Rates: $45 to $150 double (the higher price for the suite)
Reservations: 707/445-1390

THE HOPE-BOSWORTH HOUSE
P.O. BOX 42, GEYERVILLE, CA 95441

Bob and Rosalite Hope purchased this house in 1980 and brought it back to its early Victorian life. All of the wallpapers and trim bring back the full sense of the period. The house was once an early stagecoach stop. The hosts go out of their way to welcome guests, with a glass of wine at the end of the day and a home-cooked breakfast at the beginning. They have also created a unique diversion for guests, "Stage a Picnic," an idea which was featured recently on national TV. Guests are taken by horse-drawn stage to wineries in Sonoma County, followed by a picnic: smoked meats, poultry, fresh garden vegetables, local cheeses, and—of course—some good California wine.

Rates: $55 to $75 double
Reservations: 707/857-3356

SANTA NELLA HOUSE
12130 HWY. 16, GUERNEVILLE, CA 95446

This 1870 Italian-Victorian-style farmhouse with a white circular veranda and artistic latticework is the perfect hideaway in the redwood Russian River wine country. It's located on the site of the first olive and lumber mills in the area, and was the main dwelling of the Santa Nella winery, established in 1880. The house is heated with wood-burning stoves. Turn-of-the-century furnishings, high ceilings, and deep red carpets are featured. Each bedroom has special character. The genial innkeepers serve what one guest praised as "almost sinful" breakfasts, including freshly ground coffee, eggs (Benedict on Sunday), omelets, homemade date-nut bread and jams, large fresh-fruit plates of mango, papaya, kiwi, melon, pineapple, etc., in season. Santa Nella House is within 2$\frac{1}{2}$ miles of Redwood Grove State Park, and there are 25 wineries to visit within 25 miles.

Rates: $65 double on weekends and holidays; $60 on weekdays
Reservations: 707/869-9488

THE BRADY HOME
LAGUNA BEACH, CALIFORNIA

(Nominated by Bed and Breakfast of Southern California)

This three-level, custom-built home (designed by the owners)is perched on a hill with magnificent views of Victoria Beach, the loveliest beach in Laguna. Guest facilities include a sauna and whirlpool, TV, fireplace, and laundry. A full breakfast includes homemade muffins or breads. The town of Laguna Beach makes for interesting strolling—many artists live here, and there is an assortment of galleries and shops. The Pageant of the Masters takes place here.

Rates: $55 double
Reservations: 714/738-8361

SPILLMAN HOME
1353 ALVARADO TERRACE, LOS ANGELES, CA 90006

A pleasant way to stay right in the midst of downtown L.A., this 1902 home is a registered National Historic Landmark and has original stained-glass windows and oak paneling. Period furnishings, unusual collectibles, and a gallery of artwork complete the early-century mood. This home and five other landmark homes surround a small park, yet the Los Angeles Convention Center is only eight blocks away. You're approximately one mile from downtown businesses and shopping areas. For breakfast, strawberries and cream, eggs Florentine, peach flan pie, fried bananas, lemon mousse with berries, and melon with piña colada yogurt dressing are just some of the surprises. The host is a professional magician who performs for guests after breakfast or during the afternoon social hour, when wine and refreshments are served. Arrangements can be made for guests to attend the exclusive "Magic Castle," a private club for magicians and their guests.

Rates: $55 to $85 double
Reservations: 213/381-1478

THE MILCAN HOME
PASADENA, CALIFORNIA

(Nominated by Eye Openers Bed & Breakfast Reservations)

Imagine living in a Spanish-style stucco home with a walled garden, patio, and swimming pool. Then think about being on a lovely boulevard in Pasadena, a small charming city known for its gracious homes and cultural offerings—just 15 miles northeast of Los Angeles. The home is only a mile from the Huntington Library and two miles from museums and numerous good restaurants. The hostess serves a full breakfast of cheese, meat, eggs, coffee, tea, and breads.

Rates: $40 to $50 double
Reservations: 213/684-4428 or 818/797-2055

CHAMBERS HOME
SAN FRANCISCO, CALIFORNIA

(Nominated by Bed & Breakfast International)

"Jack is an airline pilot and wine importer. Barbara imports fine copper cookware. Both enjoy welcoming guests from all over the world and are world travelers themselves. They have two dogs." Their B&B home is an 1890 Queen Anne Victorian. It has been carefully restored, right down to the parquetry floors and Lycrista wallpaper. (Because of the care taken in restoration, smoking is not permitted in the house.) It's right across from historic Buena Vista Park. Each B&B room is individually decorated. Guests are invited to share the living room, parlor, and grounds.

Rates: $75 to $125 double
Reservations: 415/525-4569

LYONS HOME
SAN FRANCISCO, CALIFORNIA

(Nominated by American Family Inn / Bed & Breakfast San Francisco)

This modern three-level home and garden are perched high up on a San Francisco hill. It has terrific views of the city. It's near all the sights, yet is in a quiet neighborhood. The hostess serves Swedish pancakes with homemade orange syrup, fancy omelets, and other specialties for breakfast. A number of her recipes have been published.

Rates: $55 double
Reservations: 415/931-3083

THE WILSON HOME
3995 SPRING MOUNTAIN RD., ST. HELENA, CA 94574

This "lodge" nestled in a forest, a rustic gem on four acres, has two guest units in the main residence. Each has a private entrance and bath, and one has a fireplace. Rooms are decorated with antiques, and fully carpeted. All possible amenities for total comfort are stressed. Breakfast consists of half a cantelope filled with fresh-grown strawberries/raspberries; fresh-ground coffee; homemade nut and fruit breads; orange juice; jams, jellies, and hand-pressed butter; muffins, and croissants. The Wilson Home is just minutes from major wineries, restaurants, spas, balloon rides. Private wineries accept Wilson Home guests, including the "Falcon Crest" location for the TV series. You can swim in the pool on the property, walk mountain paths, or picnic on the grounds.

Rates: $66 to $77 double
Reservations: 707/963-3794

AUSTRIAN GUEST HOUSE
SAN LUIS OBISPO AREA, CALIFORNIA

(Nominated by Megan's Friends Bed & Breakfast Reservation Service)

This unusual Austrian-decorated guesthouse has pegged oak floors, electric baseboard heat, and large windows with a beach and ocean view. It's located in a rural setting on the ocean bluff with deer and racoons for neighbors, near Montana de Oro State Park. A full breakfast is provided in the kitchen unit of the guesthouse for a self-catered breakfast. "This is a honeymoon and anniversary favorite because the guesthouse is a separate unit in a secluded spot."

Rates: $50 double (plus a $10 membership fee to join Megan's Friends Bed & Breakfast Reservation Service)
Reservations: 805/544-4406

LAKESIDE HOUSE
P.O. BOX 7108, TAHOE CITY, CA 95730

The Lakeside House is like many other B&B homes—in an attractive setting (on a lakefront). Guests have access to a private beach in the summer and can ski at 14 ski areas nearby in the winter. They are served a full American breakfast including fresh fruit and such specialties as corn-apple cakes. The house was built in 1916, and it's filled with many antiques and framed photographs and prints—like many other B&Bs. But the notes from the guests show how much extra attention they get from their hosts, Jim and Suni Kreft. "Everything was absolutely wonderful," wrote one. "Chris and I both really feel at home." Another wrote, "Your hospitality and warmth helped make our weekend extra-special." Said another, "Can't remember ever having fun with more charming hosts."

Rates: $65 to $95 double
Reservations: 916/583-8796

HOWARD CREEK RANCH INN
40501 N. HWY. 1, (P.O. 121), WESTPORT, CA 95488

You can stay either in the main house or in one of the cottages. The house, which dates from 1871, is built of virgin California redwood and is furnished with antiques, collectibles, and memorabilia. It is set in a private valley on the Mendocino Coast, 100 feet from miles of beach and near undeveloped redwood forests. A wood-heated hot tub, pool, and sauna set in the mountainside form a unique spa with dramatic views. Breakfast offerings include bacon and sausage, banana pancakes (with blackberries, in season) and "exotic" omelets, which combine sour cream, avocado, green onions, tomatoes, and cheese.

Rates: $40 to $75 double (according to season)
Reservations: 707/964-6725

DAVIS HOME
WHITTIER, CALIFORNIA

(Nominated by CoHost, America's Bed & Breakfast)

Want to take your children or grandchildren to Disneyland, Knott's Berry Farm, and Universal Studios—and then return to a luxurious home surrounded by exotic plants? All bedrooms here are decorator-designed with elegant private baths. From the deck you can see Los Angeles, Long Beach, and Catalina Island. Cooking is southern style, with bacon, sausage or ham, eggs, potatoes or grits, fresh fruit, and juice. Regional California dishes such as huevos rancheros, frijoles refritos, and fresh fruit, or pancakes, waffles, and popovers, are also served. The host will pick you up at the airport (for about what you'd pay a local bus service). The host will also plan and escort tours of the area, provide babysitting, and even host patio brunches or dinners for guests. Golf or tennis can also be arranged.

Rates: $50 to $60 double, May to September; $45 to $55 double, October to April
Reservations: 213/699-8427

THE FALLEN HOME
COLORADO SPRINGS, COLORADO

(Nominated by B&B Rocky Mountains)

No better views of mountain and city can be experienced than through the large windows of this special residence. You can relax, as well, in a hot tub on a deck overlooking a terrific view of Colorado Springs. A bar, refrigerator, fireplace, and television, even a dance floor, are provided for guests. Thick terrycloth robes are furnished for the hot-tubbing. You can walk to tennis or a hiking trail in the nearby park. A full gourmet breakfast with fresh-ground coffee is offered, and a champagne brunch on Sunday. The gregarious hostess is a retired business woman very knowledgeable about local events, restaurants, etc.

Rates: $65 double
Reservations: 303/630-3433

THE VIRGIEN HOME
BLOOMFIELD, CONNECTICUT

(Nominated by Nutmeg B&B)

This quiet country home is on 5.6 acres adjoining Penwood State Forest. It has 200 varieties of daffodils, and 11 goats that know their names and mow the lawn! Cross-country skiing is available just out the door. The host will arrange ski and bike rentals. A full breakfast is served.

Rates: $55 to $65 double
Reservations: 203/236-6698

HOUSE OF QUILTS
DENVER, COLORADO

(Nominated by B&B Colorado)

You sleep under homemade quilts in the House of Quilts, a 1909 "Denver Square" home located in one of the city's oldest and most prestigious neighborhoods. This spacious home is filled with natural light, colorfully decorated with family heirlooms and period antiques. It's just two blocks to City Park, a major museum, planetarium, theater, and zoo. The home is centrally located to all major points in the city, and downtown Denver is just ten minutes away. Public transportation is within two blocks. Before starting off to sightsee you are offered a hearty breakfast. It might be two eggs cooked in English porcelain coddlers with cheese or meat and herbs from the garden, served with juice or fresh fruit and homemade bran muffins wrapped in a quilt to keep them warm, and homemade jelly. Or it could be French toast cut from French bread filled with strawberry preserves and dusted with powder sugar.

Rates: $38 single, $42 double
Reservations: 303/333-3340

MANOR HOUSE
NORFOLK, CONNECTICUT

(Nominated by Covered Bridge Bed & Breakfast)

The Manor House is a mansion with wood-paneled walls and a large stone fireplace. Guests who have stayed here are very enthusiastic. Wrote one, "I felt the need to tell you again what a lovely time we had while staying with you. You have created such a comfortable, friendly atmosphere in your home, making one feel part of a family." Another waxed poetic: "A peaceful wind blows gently around the Victorian palace." Still another said, "Simply breathtaking and charming." Norfolk is a lovely little town surrounded by pine trees and a center of music during the summer.

Rates: $55 to $120 double
Reservations: 203/542-5690

TREMBLAY HOME
NORFOLK, CONNECTICUT

(Nominated by Covered Bridge B&B)

This 1898 Victorian English Tudor estate with Tiffany windows is surrounded by five park-like acres. "Our guests are welcome to use our home as theirs," say the hosts. Breakfast dishes include blueberry pancakes, orange waffles, poached eggs with lemon chive sauce, homemade breads and muffins, stuffed grapefruit, Norfolk maple syrup, and honey from the hosts' own hives.

Rates: $45 to $120 double (according to season)
Reservations: 203/542-5944

THE CAMPANELLA-ANDERSON HOUSE
WASHINGTON, D.C.

(Nominated by the Bed & Breakfast League Ltd.)

The innkeepers describe their brick-and-stone B&B as a "detached, bowfront Romanesque Revival–style" house. Conveniently located in the heart of Washington, the home is very near the zoo and within two miles of the Smithsonian and the White House. Dozens of restaurants, shops, and art galleries are within walking distance. Ice, a corkscrew, and daily fresh cookies are provided in your room.

Rates: $50 to $65 double
Reservations: 202/363-7767

RAMIREZ HOME
WASHINGTON, D.C.

(Nominated by Sweet Dreams & Toast, Inc.)

This contemporary English-style town house adjoins a private park in the exclusive Chevy Chase section of Washington. It is notable for its formal dining room, fine antique furniture, displays of Spanish art, and outstanding collection of Lladro figurines. Guests prepare their own continental breakfast on weekdays. There is a private patio. The city's monuments are easily accessible by car (recommended for this location).

Rates: $60 double
Reservations: 202/483-9191

FLORIDA HOME
MIAMI, FLORIDA

(Nominated by B&B Co.–Tropical Florida)

This rambling, two-story home, surrounded by lush tropical trees and foliage, is within walking distance of the unique, casual, upscale community of Coconut Grove. The home was originally an inn for travelers; later it was a well-known dining spot for travelers to Miami and locals. Today the downstairs rooms, with huge fireplaces, reflect the history. Two bedrooms upstairs are available for travelers. For history buffs, a tour of the home, including kitchen and gardens, is arranged. The continental breakfast includes native tropical fruits such as citrus or mangos, and food from the owner's organic garden.

Rates: $50 to $55 double, December 26 to April 30; $45 to $50 double, May 1 to December 25
Reservations: 305/661-3270

THE BERNARD HOME
ST. PETERSBURG BEACH, FLORIDA

(Nominated by B&B Suncoast Accommodations)

This one-story, five-bedroom Spanish home on a waterway with dock, hot tub, and rooftop deck is located on the Paradise Island of St. Petersburg Beach, overlooking milky-white sand beaches in the Gulf of Mexico. Each room has a refrigerator, television, air conditioning, heating unit, and separate entrance. Additional rooms are available for children. Guests are invited to use the kitchen, laundry, horseshoe pit, and gas grill. Breakfast consists of fruit in season, coffee, danish, muffins, juice, and jams. You're invited to "help yourself" to bacon and eggs as well. The home is less than an hour from Busch Gardens, Dale Museum, and Sunken Gardens, and two hours from Disneyland. As one guest recently summed it up: "We always felt at home and that makes a vacation something special and unforgettable." The hosts will take you on local tours as well.

Rates: $55 double, December 1 to April 30; $45 double, May 1 to November 30
Reservations: 813/360-1753

THE BEERS HOME
ATLANTA, GEORGIA

(Nominated by B&B Atlanta)

In this two-story, gray-shingled residence with light-green shutters, the host and hostess really care about your comfort. From the warmest of welcomes you are treated as family. Their well-appointed home, complete with residential elevator, is located on an old city street within walking distance of Atlanta's best-known street, Peachtree. On public transportation it's an easy hop from here south to the city and north to quality shopping areas. From the moment you wake up you are cared for. In summer breakfast is served in the garden; in winter, by the fire. It includes fresh fruit if available, good coffee, choice of teas, crisp bacon, hot muffins, cheese grits, and steamed apples. Guests can stay a week and never have a repeat breakfast. The individual attention even extends to a drive through residential areas, if desired.

Rates: $44 to $48 double
Reservations: 404/875-0525

REMSHART-BROOKS HOUSE
106 W. JONES ST., SAVANNAH, GA 31401

The Remshart-Brooks House was built in 1853–1854, the second house of a four-house row. Authentically restored, this row is now the focal point of many historic tours. Take a closer look at the bricks on the front, for you may never see their like again; the source of the clay and the formula for these lovely handmade Savannah gray bricks have been lost. You can stay in a suite furnished with country antiques. There's a fireplace in the living room, the original cooking fireplace of the home. Breakfast is provided in the suite, and guests can dine at their leisure on such items as sour cream coffee cake, molasses and rum muffins and sausage-cheese biscuits, all home-baked by your hostess, Anne Barnett.

Rates: $60 double
Reservations: 912/234-6928

WEBB-ABE HOUSE
HONOLULU, HAWAII

(Nominated by Bed & Breakfast Hawaii)

The lanai (patio) of this home commands a sweeping view of the ocean and the Honolulu area. The hostesses are a mother-and-daughter team who come from England. They serve a continental breakfast, either on the lanai or in the dining room. The house is located very near Hanauma Bay, a golf course, and Sea Life Park; there are also beaches and picnic areas nearby. Your hostesses will provide mats and coolers for the beach.

Rates: $49.50 double
Reservations: 808/822-7771

HAAGEN HOUSE
617 STATE ST., ALTON, IL 62002

This Victorian-style home with Italian influence was built by Bavarian immigrant and dry-goods store owner, Louis Haagen, in 1855. The one-room studio suite with private bath, kitchenette, fireplace, four-poster queen-size bed, and period antiques has a private entrance. A second suite is in the planning stages. Haagen House is located in the heart of the Christian Hill historic district, just 25 minutes from downtown St. Louis, 20 minutes from Père Marquette State Park, and 10 minutes from the village of Elsah, first to be listed in the National Register of Historic Places. It is within walking distance of bicycle and walking paths. Continental breakfast is left in the guest refrigerator to be prepared at leisure. A full breakfast (for $5 per guest) consists of bacon, sausage, eggs, English muffin, fresh fruit; there's also a $15-per-couple champagne breakfast. Free transportation is offered from the train station, and transportation for the airport for an extra charge.

Rates: $80 double
Reservations: 314/965-4328

KIMBLE CLIFF
R.R. 1, BOX 139, MANHATTAN, KS 66502

This limestone landmark, built in 1895, is on the north side of old U.S. 24. It was constructed of hand-fashioned decorated stone from a nearby quarry and has walnut-tree beams. The house has ten rooms with an attic. A choice of continental or farm breakfast is offered in a dining room overlooking Wildcat Valley. A recent guest wrote to the hosts afterward: "The beautiful setting of your home and the cordiality of your family was without question the highlight of our trip."

Rates: $30 double (also special family rates)
Reservations: 913/539-3816

BARNARD HALL
LOUISVILLE, KENTUCKY

(Nominated by Kentucky Homes Bed & Breakfast)

First, a bit of history. The house was built in 1912 for Louisville's best-known hotelier. "It's an elaborate example of the Georgian architecture of the period. At the same time, the portico and the balustrades relate the structure to the elegant formalized beaux arts style which dominated American architecture early in this century. It is still toured by students of architecture. Now you can stay in this incredible mansion in antiques-furnished double- or twin-bedded rooms with baths. You can even choose a waterbed room. Breakfast may be served in the formal dining room or the glassed-in porches. After touring Louisville, you may want to do what the original owners did. Retire to the billiard room for a few games.

Rates: $60 to $65 double
Reservations: 502/635-7341

CLASSIC GEORGIAN MANSION
LOUISVILLE, KENTUCKY

(Nominated by Kentucky Home B&B, Inc.)

This famous 1912 mansion, located in a neighborhood of the city's most outstanding homes, an exclusive suburb, is a local showplace. It's furnished with the richest antiques and woodwork, and a billiard room is open to guests. There are two large guest double bedrooms located in a separate wing. The mansion is near the campuses of Baptist and Presbyterian seminaries. It's ten minutes to Churchill Downs (of Kentucky Derby fame) and downtown cultural attractions. The area is ideal for walking and running. Breakfasts include fresh fruit according to season, sausage-and-egg casserole with speckled-heart grits, and homemade biscuits, jams, and jellies.

Rates: $75 double
Reservations: 502/635-7341

WELCOME HALL
VERSAILLES, KENTUCKY

(Nominated by Bluegrass B&B)

This handsome 1792 stone house and grounds are a perfect example of that period's self-sufficient country estate. It's set in the gently rolling pastures of Kentucky's famous bluegrass region, an area devoted to thoroughbred horses, with some 400 farms producing most of the world's supply of race horses. Four-poster beds, fireplaces, and delicious breakfasts are the specialties. You awake to a breakfast of fresh strawberries in season, biscuits with country ham, and eggs just plucked from beneath the hen. It's all served in an atmosphere of charm and grace nearly two centuries old. A brick-floored summer house in the middle of an extensive walled garden provides a pleasant retreat to read or converse.

Rates: $60 double
Reservations: 606/873-3208

GRIEST HOME
NEW ORLEANS, LOUISIANA

(Nominated by New Orleans Bed and Breakfast and Bed & Breakfast, Inc.)

This is a somewhat unusual situation in that two separate B&B reservation services selected the Griest Home as their best—so it must be something special. It's an elegant Greek Revival home refurbished with modern touches by the host (an architect) and the hostess (a furniture designer and interior decorator). Breakfast can include homemade sweet-potato muffins and other regional specialties. It's served on china with silver. Guests' requests for particular foods are always considered. The home is located near the French Quarter, world-famous restaurants, jazz clubs, and riverboat rides. It's also close to the historic St. Charles Avenue streetcar.

Rates: $55 to $85 double
Reservations: 504/525-4640 (Bed & Breakfast, Inc.) or 504/949-6705 (New Orleans Bed and Breakfast)

THE GOTT HOUSE
KENNEBUNKPORT, MAINE

(Nominated by Bed & Breakfast of Maine)

This is a historic home of Dutch colonial architecture, with antiques, sundecks, a swimming dock, a storage area for guests' bicycles, in a quiet country setting in a pine grove by a river. A full gourmet breakfast with a view includes homemade breads and fresh fruit. Private bath is available. The house is located near museums, amusement parks, day cruises to offshore islands, and charter sailing or fishing boats. And it's less than two hours from Boston.

Rates: $30 to $60 double (depending on the season)
Reservations: 207/781-4528

THE IVES HOME
BALTIMORE, MARYLAND

(Nominated by the Traveller in Maryland, Inc.)

This townhouse has an enclosed, landscaped garden and a deck with an unbeatable view of Baltimore. It's located in the Fells Point area, just 1 1/2 blocks from where the tugs come in. You can take a boat shuttle from Fells Point to the Baltimore Inner Harbor (May to October).

Rates: $60 double
Reservations: 301/269-6232

THE HERITAGE HOUSE
GRAFTON, MASSACHUSETTS

(Nominated by Folkstone B&B Reservation Service)

This Federal Period home (1795) has been restored to all of its original grace. It's located just off the Common in Grafton Center. There are four bedrooms decorated with antiques. Guests can also use several common rooms, including a library and a music room with a grand piano. The hostess serves a full country breakfast and provides nice extra touches—such as terrycloth bathrobes in the bedroom.

Rates: $68 double
Reservations: 617/869-2687

THE O'TOOLE HOME
AUBURN, MASSACHUSETTS

(Nominated by Folkstone B&B Reservation Service)

This 1765 colonial home with period furnishings is about 15 minutes from Sturbridge Village. The owners are proud of their herb garden, geese, and ducks. The herbs grace the breakfast table in the form of homemade herb bread. Crêpes (cheese, tarragon and chives, or bacon and spinach), eggs Benedict, and raspberry pop-overs (in season) are other mouthwatering breakfast specialties.

Rates: $48 double
Reservations: 617/869-2687

THE EDDY HOUSE
BARNSTABLE, MASSACHUSETTS

(Nominated by Bed & Breakfast Cape Cod)

This 275-year-old Cape Cod house has antique furnishings, a parlor, working fireplaces, and a flower garden. The guest rooms have canopy beds and private baths. You breakfast by a ten-foot fireplace on fruit, juice, eggs, bacon or sausage, French toast, banana pancakes, Cape Cod cranberry muffins, and Swedish coffee cake. The house is located in a historic district within walking distance of Cape Cod Bay. The mid-Cape area offers whale-watching, summer theater, beaches, antique shops, and many restaurants. The Nantucket ferry is nearby.

Rates: $55 to $75 double (according to season)
Reservations: 617/775-2772

1883 TOWNHOUSE
BOSTON, MASSACHUSETTS

*(Nominated by Bed and Breakfast Associates
Bay Colony, Ltd.)*

This five-story brick row-style town house is located in one of Boston's most historic and quietest residential neighborhoods (an area that contains the largest number of "row" houses in the U.S.). The two guest rooms are on the third floor and each has a fireplace. Breakfast may consist of juice, eggs Benedict, crêpes, and muffins. Your hosts are an interesting couple—Dominic, a professional interior painter and amateur chef, and Denis, who is an amateur architect and philosopher.

Rates: $60 double, March to November; $55 double, December to February
Reservations: 617/449-5302

VICTORIAN HOME
BOSTON, MASSACHUSETTS

(Nominated by the Bed & Breakfast Registry, Ltd.)

You can be the guest in a renovated Victorian town house located in a 19th-century landmark district adjacent to Back Bay. The three guest rooms have lovely furnishings which include an antique bed with a large oak headboard, overstuffed chairs, and sitting area. Symphony Hall is a two-block stroll, and you're only six blocks from the Boston Museum of Fine Arts. For breakfast you may get the host's favorite—"Uncle Willie's Yam Hash with poached eggs." You may often find cut flowers or a complementary sherry in your room when you arrive home.

Rates: $55 to $65 double
Reservations: 617/646-4238

THE LERMAN HOME
BROOKLINE, MASSACHUSETTS

(Nominated by Greater Boston Hospitality)

This red-brick, slate-roofed 1920 carriage house has a city location but a country setting. The immaculately kept rooms are amply furnished with antiques. Guest rooms are spacious; guests also have access to a den, 2,000-square-foot patio, and a piano. A full breakfast—including juice and/or fruit, eggs with bacon or sausage, and homemade muffins—is served. Brookline is located across the Charles River from Cambridge and is accessible to all the cultural wealth of the area.

Rates: $55 double
Reservations: 617/277-5430

THE KOPKE HOUSE
DUXBURY, MASSACHUSETTS

(Nominated by Christian Hospitality)

A 1708 historic house furnished with antiques. Guest rooms have easy chairs and TV. You can also use the large living room, which has a fireplace. The host serves "special scrambled eggs" for breakfast, as well as muffins, French toast, and blueberry pancakes. The house is a short ride from beautiful beaches.

Rates: $35 to $45 double (according to season)
Reservations: 617/834-8528

THE KOOMEY HOME
GRAFTON, MASSACHUSETTS

(Nominated by Folkstone Bed & Breakfast)

This is a 1795 Federal-period home, restored and furnished with antiques. There is a garden and patio area, and common rooms which include a music room with a grand piano. The house is located on a country road just out of the center of Grafton and a short drive to the Willard Clock Museum and the museums and concert halls of Worcester, also near ten colleges and universities and Sturbridge Village. You can dine on a full country breakfast including fresh fruit, roast beef or chicken hash, omelets, and blueberry pancakes. There is turn-down service at night. The host provides terrycloth robes to guests, and wine and cheese.

Rates: $50 double
Reservations: 617/869-2687

WALLWORK HOUSE
NEWTON, MASSACHUSETTS

(Nominated by New England Bed & Breakfast)

This gray stucco house, rather ordinary on the outside, radiates great warmth within. It's a short walk to the "T"—a mass-transit system that takes you to downtown Boston in 20 minutes. The hostess serves continental breakfast with homemade muffins.

Rates: $46 double
Reservations: 617/498-9819

JO-ELS HOME
PLYMOUTH, MASSACHUSETTS

(Nominated by Around Plymouth Bay)

You can vacation in an executive colonial garrison located on a huge pond filled with swans and ducks. Although in a country setting, you're close to all of Plymouth's historical sites, and you're also within an easy drive of Boston. For breakfast you'll be served a full American breakfast, starting with juice, then muffins, eggs any style, bacon, home-fries, and coffee, tea, or milk. The hosts can arrange to pick up guests at the Plymouth bus terminal and provide them with complete tour information. Each B&B room is exceptionally large, and guests can make use of two recreation rooms.

Rates: $55 double, May 1 to October 1
Reservations: 617/747-5075

THE GILLIS HOME
SCITUATE, MASSACHUSETTS

(Nominated by Be Our Guest Bed & Breakfast, Ltd.)

This 1743 carriage house has the original beams and carriage sliders. It's set on two well-manicured acres, with a stone wall and 100-foot blue spruce trees. Special amenities include an enclosed screened porch, a separate TV room (with cable and VCR), and a fireplace in the living room. Breakfast—served with fresh flowers and candles on a Queen Anne dining room set—includes fresh fruit, cereal, bacon or sausage, eggs or pancakes, and homemade pumpkin rolls.

Rates: $45 double, May to November
Reservations: 617/837-9867

WISNOWSKI HOUSE
WESTFORD, MASSACHUSETTS

(Nominated by the Bed an' Breakfast Folks)

You can enjoy a unique B&B experience in a country home with large bedrooms and full bath. There is a solar breakfast room overlooking the swimming pool and the extensive yard and gardens. It's located 35 miles from Boston, near historic Concord. The full breakfast includes cereal, juice or melon, and fresh-picked home-grown blueberries, blackberries, or raspberries in season; your choice of pancakes, French toast, omelet, eggs, bacon or sausage; plus bagels, muffins, or toast. And, yes, guests are welcome to browse in the garden and dip into the swimming pool.

Rates: $45 double
Reservations: 617/692-3232 Or 617/692-2700

HEBERT HOUSE
WILLIAMSBURG, MASSACHUSETTS

(Nominated by Berkshire Bed & Breakfast Homes)

This 200-year-old restored farmhouse is set on 27 acres of fields and woodlands overlooking Unquemonk Mountain. It has a large country kitchen with a fireplace and Dutch oven, a screened porch and dining room for breakfast, and a private sitting room with a TV, games, and wood-burning stove. Guest rooms have antique brass and iron beds. Flowers in the room and mints on the pillow are extra touches. Breakfast goodies include homemade applesauce, rhubarb sauce, bacon and eggs, freshly baked breads, buttermilk pancakes, and homemade jams. Snowshoes and sleds are available.

Rates: $40 double
Reservations: 413/268-7244

WOODS INN
ANN ARBOR, MICHIGAN

(Nominated by Betsy Ross B&B)

This fine Victorian home, decorated with the best antiques, has four rooms for guests—three doubles and one single—and a guest den and extensive screened porch. So superior are the antiques, wicker furniture, paintings, and other ornaments that Woods Inn is open as well for antiques tours. Breakfast is hearty and features Michigan produce served on antique dishes and in the 1800s mode. This historic inn is ideally located to enjoy the sports, art, theater, music, and other attractions of Ann Arbor. It is described as the "All American" city, and one of the ten best in which to retire or start a new business. The Henry Ford Museum is only 30 minutes away.

Rates: $35 to $45 double
Reservations: 313/561-6041

HIDDEN POND FARM
P.O. BOX 461, FENNVILLE, MI 49408

A friend told Edward X. Kennedy, "Have a dream, but don't be a dreamer. Make your dream into a reality." That's exactly what Mr. Kennedy did when he bought and completely restored a Michigan farm near the Lake Michigan beaches, Saugatauk and Fennville. There are two B&B bedrooms upstairs, but guests have access to seven rooms of the 13-room house, including a living room with fireplace, and a den. An outside deck overlooks the hidden pond. Guests can hike over woodland trails or cross-country ski. Mr. Kennedy offers his own special brew of coffee in the morning. He is a practical dreamer.

Rates: $75 to $85 double
Reservations: 615/561-2491

THE BALL HOUSE
GRAND RAPIDS, MICHIGAN

(Nominated by B&B of Grand Rapids)

This 20-room 1880s Georgian Revival home is located in the Heritage Hill district of Grand Rapids, the largest urban district featuring 62 different styles of architecture. The Ball House is also listed on the National Register of Historic Places. Featured inside are a two-story bay window, a two-story semicircular window, and a circular staircase. For breakfast you're served a deluxe continental that includes sweet breads and fruits. Tourist packages for dinners and local entertainment can be arranged as well.

Rates: $55 double
Reservations: 616/451-4849 or 616/456-7121

KEMAH GUEST HOUSE
663 PLEASANT ST., SAUGATUCK, MI 49453

Here's how the Travel Bureau of the Michigan Department of Commerce describes this unusual home: "Built in 1906, the Kemah Guest House radiates the elegance of yesterday with its blend of period decor—stained-glass windows, carved panels in the half-circle solarium, imported Dutch lace curtains beamed ceilings, and French doors. Each guest room is furnished with unusual antiques to create a charming historic atmosphere. All guests are welcome to enjoy the fireplace in the sunken den." I visited this home a year ago and noted, "The house has a tremendous feeling of space and warmth—a truly elegant B&B home."

Rates: $65 to $85 double
Reservations: 616/857-2919

WILLIAMSBURG-STYLE HOME
MERIDIAN, MISSISSIPPI

(Nominated by Lincoln Ltd. B&B; Mississippi Reservation Service)

Mississippi hospitality in every sense of the word is extended in this turn-of-the-century Victorian-style home. Gracious hosts offer a welcome beverage and genial conversation if desired. They share a wonderful collection of antiques from around the world that decorate the home. They are noted gourmet cooks and will include guests for dinner as well as breakfast by prior arrangement. For breakfast, southern cheese grits, ham, eggs, homemade muffins, omelets, Mississippi Muscidine Jellies, and "much, much more" are offered. There is plenty of acreage to jog, walk, or just relax in. Dogs are welcome, but children cannot be accommodated. There's plenty to see in this cultural, medical, industrial, and retail center of eastern Mississippi, with antebellum homes to tour. Among other things to do in Meridian are fishing and boating on beautiful lakes, or attending the Jimmie Rodgers Festival every May, the Lively Arts Festival in April, the symphony, art museum, and Little Theater.

Rates: $65 double
Reservations: 601/482-5483

DUNLEITH
NATCHEZ, MISSISSIPPI

(Nominated by Natchez Pilgrimage Tours)

This is considered one of the most classically beautiful Greek Revival homes in Natchez and is circa 1856. It is surrounded by 26 Tuscan columns, and is located on 40 acres of land. Furnishings are 18th and 19th century, French and English. A fruit basket, and in season, fresh flowers, are placed in each room. Guests have the use of private bath, a central stereo, local phone, and television, and are invited to tour the home. Breakfasts are nourishing, with bacon, ham, sausage, eggs, grits, muffins, biscuits, fruit in season, juice, and coffee. From here you can enjoy the Natchez State Park, Natchez Bluffs (overlooking the Mississippi River), Natchez under the Hill, and 500 antebellum historic structures and 30 antebellum historic tour homes.

Rates: $85 (plus tax) double
Reservations: 601/446-6631

RIVER'S ARM
FLORISSANT, MISSOURI

(Nominated by River Country B&B)

River's Arm is a B&B with a marvelous view, on a hill in northwestern St. Louis County overlooking the Missouri River. The host says, "On a clear day in the distance one can see the limestone bluffs along the Mississippi River." The home has had an unusual history, beginning as a farmhouse. Then it became a retreat home for nuns before being acquired by the present owners. The breakfast is served in the dining room, or on sunny days, on the sun porch. After breakfast guests can take a stroll to see the abundance of wildflowers and birds. There are also many animals that may be glimpsed—pheasant, wild turkey, and even occasionally a bald eagle (no hunting permitted). Guests can stay in a room with a comfortable 100-year-old rope bed. The house is furnished with numerous antiques.

Rates: $60 double
Reservations: 314/965-4328

WALTER HOUSE
INDEPENDENCE, MISSOURI

(Nominated by Truman Country B&B)

This turn-of-the-century middle-class Victorian home from the 1850s overwhelms with the feeling of generations past. Added to the basic setting are antique walnut furnishings, rugs, and period lighting. All reflects the Victorian era. The home is filled with century-old books sporting antique bookmarks, antique medicine bottles, and shaving paraphernalia in bathrooms. Just a few doors down is the Harry S. Truman home and library. Minutes away are amusement parks, malls, eating establishments, and Kansas City. A breakfast casserole of bread, eggs, meat, cheese, and mushrooms is served along with assorted nut breads, seasonal fruits, spiced winter fruits, juices, coffee, and tea. Airport pickup is offered, and bicycles are loaned for cycling, and information provided on historic sites.

Rates: $42.50 single, $45 double
Reservations: 816/254-6657

WILLIAMS HOME
KIMBERLING CITY, MISSOURI

(Nominated by Ozark Mountain Country B&B)

Located ten miles south of Kimberling on Williams Mountain in the heart of the Ozark mountain country, the home features two bedrooms. Each is furnished with double beds and private bath, and each opens onto a private patio. There is exclusive use of the sitting room there, and a game room and library. A small refrigerator is provided in the rooms. There is a spectacular view of Table Rock Lake. It's an area of seclusion, peace, and quiet. It is located within 15 to 20 miles of Silver Dollar City–White Water, Shepherd of the Hills, and Teather. A full gourmet breakfast with specialties of the house is served featuring Ozark sausage and blueberry pancakes. A complimentary snack is offered on arrival.

Rates: $50 double, April to October and in February and November
Reservations: 417/334-5077 and 417/334-4720

JOHN F. PETO STUDIO
102 CEDAR AVE., ISLAND HEIGHTS, NJ 08732

John F. Peto was a 19th-century artist who really began to receive recognition and fame many years after his death. Today he is considered one of the major painters of his era. You can stay in the home studio he built for himself, now occupied by his granddaughter, Joy Peto Smiley. There are reproductions of his most famous paintings throughout the house. Mrs. Smiley has operated the house as a B&B for the last five years. "It has been a wonderful human experience," said Mrs. Smiley, "especially meeting so many interesting people." She makes them welcome by serving what she calls "ethereal eggs"—two eggs with bacon, cheese, and sour cream. Many guests come to go sailing or walk around the three beaches of Island Heights.

Rates: $65 double
Reservations: 201/270-6058

GATES HILL HOMESTEAD
BROOKFIELD, NEW YORK

(Nominated by Leatherstocking Bed & Breakfast)

Beamed ceilings, a free-standing fieldstone fireplace, plank flooring, and hand-stenciled walls help create a great feeling of the 18th century when this house was born. There are antique furnishings which include a 19th-century piano and ladderback chairs. The rooms have braided rag rugs and quilts. Full American breakfasts include French toast, sausage, and homemade muffins. The hosts offer guests both sleigh and stagecoach rides through settlements almost 200 years old. You can hike or cross-country ski through the wooded farm.

Rates: $40 double; a suite is available for $60.
Reservations: 315/733-0040

THE INN AT BROOK WILLOW FARM
COOPERSTOWN, NEW YORK

(Nominated by American Country Collection)

This early 1900s Victorian cottage house shares 14 acres with a pond, a roaring brook, meadows and woods, and nesting birds. An authentic Victorian parlor with fireplace provides a cozy place to relax. A full country breakfast includes eggs from a nearby farm, juice, meats, and "the best blueberry muffins in the entire world." On arrival, guests find fruit, candy, and freshly cut wildflowers in their rooms. Barbecue facilities and guest privileges at the country club are available.

Rates: $48 double, June to October
Reservations: 518/370-4948

THE KLEIN HOUSE
CROTON-ON-HUDSON, NEW YORK

(Nominated by Bed & Breakfast USA, Ltd.)

This 1889 Victorian home has a 20th-century swimming pool, which guests are invited to use. Cheese strata, berry pancakes, cheese blintzes with jam, and coddled eggs are among the breakfast specialties. The house is located near the village, and it's possible to get there from New York City without using a car. (You take a 50-minute train ride, which affords scenic views of the Hudson). The hosts will arrange a tour of the historic and architecturally interesting parts of their old Hudson River town. Historic Van Cortlandt Manor is a short ride away. Racquet sports enthusiasts will be happy to know that tennis courts are only a short walk away, and you also have the use of a racquetball club.

Rates: $50 double
Reservations: 914/271-6228

NIELSEN APARTMENT
NEW YORK, NEW YORK

(Nominated by City Lights Bed & Breakfast Ltd.)

Stay in a huge, bright room furnished with antiques, including a Queen Anne desk and a bed with a hand-carved Victorian headboard. The East Side apartment has a 24-hour doorman and manned elevators, and is convenient to major museums and excellent restaurants. The hostess tries to satisfy the guests' preferences for breakfast. Always available are cereal, preserves, muffins, croissants, juice, and fruits. On occasion there's a special brunch of bagels and assorted cheeses. The hostess is a teacher at a well-known theater institute and published author. She is helpful in obtaining theater tickets and providing guests with local information. Guests may even be invited to special parties.

Rates: $55 to $60 double
Reservations: 212/877-3235

NEW YORK CITY APARTMENT
NEW YORK, NEW YORK

(Nominated by Urban Ventures)

In the sedate Gramercy Park section of Manhattan (16th Street and Third Avenue), this apartment has two terraces and excellent views of the city. The hostess is a native Mississippian, who has re-created the lushness of her native state in the decor. She has been described as "an incredibly caring person, who does everything to make guests feel at home."

Rates: $58 double
Reservations: 212/594-5650

THE FORD HOME
29 CRAVEN ST., BEAUFORT, NC 28516

Located in historic "Beaufort by the Sea," this gracious old Victorian home offers three spacious guest rooms. Guests celebrating anniversaries and newlyweds are given a box of Godiva chocolates. When the beds are turned down at night, chocolates are also left on the pillows. The breakfast includes bacon, eggs, fruit, hot tea or coffee, juice, croissants, muffins, apple pie, and blueberry jelly. The home is within walking distance of the Maritime Museum and excellent restaurants and shops. It is about eight miles to Fort Mason State Park at Atlantic Beach.

Rates: $55 double, April to November: $45 double, December to March
Reservations: 919/728-6031 or 919/945-5259

THE HOMEPLACE
CHARLOTTE, NORTH CAROLINA

(Nominated by Charlotte B&B)

Located in a 2½-acre country setting in southeast Charlotte, the Homeplace offers very personalized service. Upstairs rooms are provided with men's robes for the business traveler, since the bath is in the hall. A coffee/tea service is available at all times, as are soft drinks and juices. Evening appetizers and desserts are offered. Laundry service is provided. Ice, fruit, and flowers are put in the rooms. A small refrigerator on the screened porch is for guest use, as is the phone downstairs. Stamps and stationery are placed in all guest rooms. Homemade breakfast, featuring egg dishes with sausage, bacon, or ham, biscuits, muffins, date-nut or strawberry bread, bagels with cheese, danish, and sometimes crêpes, is served according to the guest schedule. The Homeplace is just ten minutes from major shopping centers, historical sights, cultural activities, and antique and country shops.

Rates: $50 to $60 double
Reservations: 704/366-0979 or 704/365-1936

THE SOWASH HOME
72 FITTING AVE., BELLVILLE, OH 44813

This magnificent 1863 Victorian home on a quiet street in a small village has a free-standing spiral staircase and 11-foot ceilings. Rooms are furnished with area antiques, including a piano and a 3,000-book library. The food policy is to offer only items that can be had nowhere else, and all items are homemade by the host, described as "more than a competent amateur chef." A full breakfast, always including fruit and pastry or eggs, is served on elegant china in the gazebo on the back lawn in a flower garden, or in cold weather in a hand-stencilled dining room. You can walk to the village, to the historic bandstand on the square, down maple-lined streets. Nearby are Malabar farm, Mohican State Park, Mansfield's Kingwood Center horticultural gardens, the Mid-Ohio Sports Car Race Track, and three colleges. You can canoe, bicycle, play the piano, read books, jog, and savor the mints on the pillow at night. Careful guidance is provided on dining spots, shops, and recreational opportunities.

Rates: $40 double
Reservations: 419/886-4283

THE JENKINS HOUSE
CINCINNATI, OHIO

(Nominated by Ohio Valley B&B)

This stone Victorian home in one of the oldest, most exclusive of Cincinnati's neighborhoods is convenient to downtown and to shopping. It's the last house on a private street. An iron gate leads to a double-door entry and into a large hall. Stained glass and natural woodwork, plus a grand stairway and fireplaces, reflect another era. The bedroom has inlaid Wedgwood near the ceiling, and the decor is all art deco. Other perks include an outside deck, a gourmet kitchen, and a fountain in the yard large enough to wade in. The hostess asks what guests desire for breakfast and tries "to meet their needs." She will also pick up guests at the airport.

Rates: $50 double for one night, $40 double for two or more nights
Reservations: 606/356-7865

THE CIDER MILL
2ND STREET (P.O. BOX 441), ZOAR VILLAGE, OH 44697

Built in 1863 and refurbished in 1972, the Cider Mill, located in the famed religious communal village of Zoar, offers comfort and serenity. Private guest rooms have exposed ceiling beams and select antiques. Shared baths provide complete, modern comfort. A spiral staircase links each level of the house. The living room brick wall has survived more than a century. A complimentary breakfast features broiled grapefruit, sausage-and-egg soufflé, and apple taffy coffee cake. Complimentary wine or hot-spiced cider is served on arrival. There's plenty to do in Zoar all day long: tour antique, craft, and gift shops; play golf; canoe on the river; cycle or hike on scenic paths along the old Ohio-Erie Canal. Airport pickup is offered.

Rates: $50 double
Reservations: 216/874-3133

STRAUMFJORD HOUSE
ASTORIA, OREGON

(Nominated by Northwest B&B Travel Unlimited)

This spacious home, built in 1909 high on a hill overlooking the Columbia River, is in the center of major attractions. A living history of frontier life is offered at Fort Clatsop National Memorial, once a Lewis and Clark headquarters. Remains of an 1806 shipwreck are in Fort Stevens State Park, largest in the state. Straumfjord House is decorated with fine antiques. From the sitting room, adjoining the large, comfortable bedroom, you can see wonderful views of freighters plying the river and rolling hills. A full American breakfast features such regional specialties as clam fritters, sourdough pancakes, English scones, and home-grown fruit platters. Guests can be picked up at the airport and taken on sightseeing tours in the western U.S. and British Columbia.

Rates: $22 to $40 single; $26 to $60 double
Reservations: 503/243-7616

THE JOHNSON HOUSE
216 MAPLE ST., FLORENCE, OR 97439

Just ask for the Johnson House when you drive into town—it's the oldest house in Florence. Of Victorian Italianate design, it was built in 1892 by Dr. O. J. Kennedy, the town's first resident physician. The building and grounds have been perfectly restored by the Fraeses, the current owners. Furnishings and decor are original—there are no reproductions in the house. The town is located on Oregon's spectacular central coast, part of the Oregon Dunes National Monument. For breakfast you can expect fresh juice and fruit in season (home-grown strawberries, blackberries, blueberries, cherries). And there are home-baked muffins (banana muffins are a house specialty). The main course might be frittata, soufflé, or eggs Benedict, served with freshly ground coffee. The owners will pick up guests at the nearby airport. Bicycles are available at no charge.

Rates: $45 to $55 double
Reservations: 503/997-8000

CORBETT HOUSE
7533 S.W. CORBETT AVE., PORTLAND, OR 97219

When you stay in this attractive home, you can look out your window at the lights of Portland, Mount St. Helens, and Mount Hood. There are three guest rooms upstairs and guests are provided with such amenities as robes, hair dryers, and picnic baskets. Breakfast includes fresh fruits, cereals, and home-baked whole-wheat breads and muffins. "I doubt that I will ever want to stay in a hotel again," one guest wrote.

Rates: $50 to $55 (plus local tax) double
Reservations: 503/245-2580

SPRING HOUSE
MUDDY CREEK FORKS, AIRVILLE, PA 17302

This 1798 stone house is tucked away in a quiet country village not far from York, Lancaster, and Gettysburg. The house is furnished throughout with antiques: one bedroom has an early Pennsylvania quilt; another, original stenciling. It all makes you feel as if you've taken a step back into the past. The library and the porch provide cozy areas where you can meet other guests or retire into a private corner to read. The house has a piano. The innkeeper serves two- or three-course breakfasts, which might include such specialties as coriander sausage, zucchini frittatas, and blackberry cobbler. She grows most of the fruit, vegetables, and herbs, and makes her own preserves. The Spring House is an excellent place to escape to. In the area, you can poke around antique shops, wineries, and galleries, and wander along country roads. More traveled areas, such as Lancaster County, are nearby, if you prefer.

Rates: $50 to $75 double (10% extra for one-night stay)
Reservations: 717/927-6906

THE FOSTER HOUSE
ALLENTOWN, PENNSYLVANIA

(Nominated by Bed & Breakfast of Southeast Pennsylvania)

This home has its own swimming pool, and you're invited to use it. You can also take advantage of two nearby parks for walking and jogging. The hostess serves a full breakfast, and you can request vegetarian or macrobiotic dishes, if you like. The location is convenient to three festivals—Kutztown (July), Musikfest in Bethlehem, and Bras Awkscht Fescht (antique cars, in August).

Rates: $40 to $45 double
Reservations: 215/845-3526

WEIDLEIN FARMHOUSE
GREENBURG, PENNSYLVANIA

(Nominated by Pittsburgh Bed & Breakfast)

This 1884 farmhouse (about 45 minutes from Pittsburgh) was picked by the reservation service as one of their best "because it is such a quiet retreat in the country." The home is surrounded by working farms and offers guests gardens for strolling. It's on the Historic Register and furnished with many antiques. This is a good base for people who want to ski in the nearby Laurel Highlands, and it's also close to numerous antique shops. You can expect a full American breakfast served with the house specialty, homemade tomato marmalade.

Rates: $50 to $65 double
Reservations: 412/367-8080

THE GATHERING PLACE
MIDDLETOWN, PENNSYLVANIA

(Nominated by Hershey B&B Reservation Service)

This family home (with children grown and gone) has an interesting collection of things from round-the-world travels. It's set on nine acres and has a large deck facing the woods. Area attractions include Hershey Park (7 miles), Lancaster County (20 miles), and Gettysburg (about 45 minutes). You can have a continental or full breakfast with some fresh fruits, homemade breads, sourdough pancakes, and hot apple dumplings.

Rates: $45 double
Reservations: 717/533-2928

GROSSMAN HOUSE
NEWPORTVILLE, PENNSYLVANIA

(Nominated by Bed & Breakfast of Philadelphia)

This house is located in Lower Bucks County, an area with much to see and do—historic towns, horse farms, flea markets, and much more. A fortifying five-course breakfast includes a selection of fresh fruits, homemade breads, cereal, eggs, and "exotic" coffee. If you want to pamper yourself, ask for the room that has the sauna and whirlpool.

Rates: $60 to $80 double
Reservations: 215/688-1633

THE VARS HOME
NEWPORT, RHODE ISLAND

(Nominated by Bed & Breakfast of Rhode Island)

This 1850 home is located in Newport's historic Point Section, a neighborhood of 18th- and 19th-century houses, two blocks away from the harbor and a five-minute walk from the center of town. A brick walk banked with ivy and a colorful flower bed welcome you into this cheerful home, where great effort has gone into even the table settings. Breakfast comes complete with china, stemware, and fresh flowers. The hostess serves fresh fruits (peaches, strawberries, blueberries, melon, kiwi), homemade banana breads, German pancakes with fresh apples, blueberry pancakes (always on Sunday), and a variety of other delights. Guests are invited to use the piano and to relax in the glider in the yard. You'll find the fixings for tea, coffee, and bouillon, as well as an electric coffee pot, in your room.

Rates: $55 to $70 double (according to season)
Reservations: 401/849-1298

CAPERS MOTTE HOUSE
69 CHURCH ST., CHARLESTON, SC 29401

This is considered one of Charleston's greatest early Georgian town houses, and is associated with prominent families in local and state history. Four rooms are provided for guests, each with fireplace and spacious bath, and access to the drawing room. Guests are usually invited to use the swimming pool in the yard. They meet other guests at tea time or cocktail hour in the drawing room on the second floor. This historic home is filled with antiques, original Georgian paneling, wing chairs, drop-leaf table, and wig stand. Breakfast is served in the dining room downstairs. Hominy surprise is a specialty, along with banana bread, cranberry-nut bread, and blueberry pancakes with blueberry syrup. Located on historic Church Street, it's just a block from the Battery, close to the Market area and outstanding restaurants and shops.

Rates: $75 to $80 double, February to June 15; $70 to $75 double, June 16 to January 31
Reservations: 803/722-2263

THE OLDE TOWNE INN AND GUEST HOUSE
184 ASHLEY AVE., CHARLESTON, SC 29403

This Charleston home, complete with side porches, is located near the city's historic district. Each room is equipped with a television and a small refrigerator. A help-yourself pot of coffee is always perking in the kitchen. At breakfast, you're likely to sample the cheese-baked grits, coconut-orange juice, and Mississippi muffins. Writes one guest, "Afraid you spoiled me with your wonderful breakfasts, not to be confused with the sparse meal I fix for myself in the morning."

Rates: $30 to $45 double (according to season)
Reservations: 803/723-8572

THE THOMAS HOME
CHARLESTON, SOUTH CAROLINA

(Nominated by Historic Charleston B&B)

Right in the center of Charleston's historic district in this unique home, a national historic landmark and Category I building. There are two bedrooms, study and bath, living room, dining room, and kitchen. The home is decorated with antiques and reproductions. A large patio is encircled by a flourishing garden. Stables and kitchen lead to the main house. This home was featured in the July-August 1986 *Southern Accents* magazine. Daily maid service is provided and fresh flowers decorate the guest rooms. Breakfast consists of fresh fruit, juice, croissants or pastries, and coffee and tea. Many historic homes, quaint shops, museums, parks, and restaurants are nearby; beaches are ten miles away, and Fort Sumter where the Civil War began.

Rates: $110 double, March to June; $100 double, July to February; and $175 for four people
Reservations: 803/722-6606

THE 1790 HOUSE
630 HIGHMARKET, GEORGETOWN, SC 29440

Right in the middle of Georgetown's Historic District is this 200-year-old historic home. Eight guests in four rooms with private bath can be accommodated at one time. Decanted sherry and fresh fruit and flowers are provided in the rooms. Four public rooms are available for chatting, reading, or relaxing. This classic colonial home with mansard roof is three stories tall. It has a handmade English brick foundation and coral stone porch. A full breakfast is served with juice, fruit, bacon, ham, sausage, fresh muffins, biscuits, eggs or custard French toast (a house specialty), grits, and pancakes. Guests are treated as part of the family, not as customers. It's just two blocks to the revitalized downtown Front Street on the Sampit River, 15 minutes to Brookgreen Gardens and Huntington State Beach, one hour to Charleston, 35 minutes to Myrtle Beach, and walking distance to restaurants.

Rates: $40 to $45 single, $50 to $55 double
Reservations: 803/546-4821

CANYON LAKE B&B
RAPID CITY, SOUTH DAKOTA

(Nominated by South Dakota B&B)

This ranch-style home is ideally located. In a matter of five minutes you walk to an 18-hole municipal golf course, cast your line into Canyon Lake or Rapid Creek for trout, stroll through the park for a leisurely dinner at Canyon Lake Supper Club, or drive to Star Kirke, the peaceful Norwegian "Chapel in the Hills." In addition, Mount Rushmore is a half-hour drive with many attractions along the way. In a little over an hour you can enjoy the Badlands or tour scenic Custer State Park. And in winter there are the Deer Mountain and Terry Park ski areas. Accommodations include two double rooms, one queen-size, two twins, and one special single. Homemade muffins and jam are served for breakfast along with scrambled eggs, sausage or bacon, juice, fruit, or a continental breakfast. On request there is airport pickup. You can also relax in a sitting room with TV and a fireplace.

Rates: $30 double
Reservations: 605/528-6571 or 605/339-0759

SIMMONS HOUSE
HOUSTON, TEXAS

(Nominated by the Bed & Breakfast Society of Texas)

You can stay in an attractive two-story colonial-style house near I-45 South, the Gulf Freeway. The house is decorated with antique furnishings. The hostess is a musician who also loves to cook. She offers a full breakfast which may include eggs cooked to order, bacon or sausage, blueberry muffins, and fresh-fruit compotes. She can arrange to pick up guests at Hobby Airport and can also transport them to bus stops, etc. A crib is available for babies. She can also take guests on tours of the Gulf Coast area. There is a wooded backyard, and an abundance of flowers.

Rates: $30 double
Reservations: 713/868-4654

PRIDE HOUSE
409 E. BROADWAY, JEFFERSON, TX 75657

Women's Day magazine named this gingerbread Victorian confection "one of the 23 most romantic spots in America." You'll see why when you visit. The Blue Room has stained-glass windows and antique white furniture. The Green Room has a brass double bed and fireplace. Breakfast is an elaborate continental with such specialties as poached pears in crème fraîche and apple dumplings. The owner, Ruth Jordan, reports, "Pride House was the first B&B home in Texas."

Rates: $75 to $110 double
Reservations: 214/665-2675

NIEMANN HOME
BOYCE, VIRGINIA

(Nominated by Blue Ridge Bed & Breakfast)

Choose this B&B and stay in a lovely country stone mansion on the Shenandoah River. There are five B&B rooms. Since four have working fireplaces, be sure to ask for one when you make your reservations. You are located nearby the Skyline Drive, and about one hour's drive to Washington, D.C., close to Dulles Airport. You'll be served a full country breakfast. This home is equipped for handicapped travelers, and guests have use of recreational equipment.

Rates: $45 to $65 double
Reservations: 703/955-1246

THORNROSE HOUSE
STAUNTON, VIRGINIA

(Nominated by Shenandoah Valley B&B)

Southern hospitality prevails in this modified Georgian Revival brick residence, circa 1912. It's located in a historic Victorian town adjacent to a 300-acre park with tennis, golf, lakes with ducks and swans, and swimming. Three guest rooms are tastefully decorated, furnished with antiques. All rooms have air conditioners and bathrooms. You can watch television or play the grand piano by a working fireplace in the guest sitting room. Or you can read books and play games. You can linger on a wrap-around veranda among vine-covered colonnades or sit on park benches on spacious, shaded grounds. Breakfast is varied with the specialty "Birchermuesli," a popular concoction of oats, raisins, fruits, nuts, and whipped cream. Afternoon tea is provided and a decanter of sherry. Literature on many local historic sites is provided. The hosts cater to nonsmokers.

Rates: $35 single (plus 6¼% total tax); $45 to $50 double (plus 6¼% total tax)
Reservations: 703/885-7026

CREGAR HOUSE
835 E. CHRISTENSON RD., GREENBANK, WA 98253

This guesthouse complex on Whidbey Island, amid historic towns, near the nation's first historic land preserve and five state parks, is close to Seattle yet light-years away in peace, quiet, and beauty. Included are a luxurious log home just for two, three cottages, plus the Wildflower Suite in a 1920s farmhouse. All are equipped with kitchenettes, fireplaces, stained-glass windows, country antiques, microwave ovens, video players, color television, and small libraries. The hosts describe it as the "fun and romance" spot. As many as five honeymoons have gone on at one time here. Breakfasts include omelets, quiches, eggs Benedict, shirred eggs, biscuits, blueberry muffins, strawberry waffles, ham, bacon, sausage, juices, and fresh fruits among the choices. Special amenities include a spa and swimming pool, rowboating on a wildlife pond, badminton, horseshoes, hammocks, barbecues, and picnics—all on 25 acres of woods and pasture.

Rates: $65 double in cottages, $60 double in the Wildflower Suite, and $120 double in the lodge
Reservations: 206/678-3115

THE OGLE HOUSE
1307 DOGWOOD HILL, PORT ORCHARD, WA 98366

This hillside contemporary house has a view of the water. It also has a deck, gardens, and orchard. In Port Orchard (located about 12 miles west of Seattle) you can browse through antique stores and art galleries. It's also right on Puget Sound waters and the gateway to the Olympic National Forest. Guests have a breakfast choice (including fresh-squeezed orange juice, home-baked sweet rolls), served by a view window on china and linen. Guests are encouraged to make themselves at home in the living room, den, deck, and library, and use the TV or VCR. The hosts will pick up guests coming into the marina.

Rates: $38 double
Reservations: 206/876-9170

"CEDARYM"
1011 240TH AVE., NE, REDMOND, WA 98053

This authentic colonial Cape Cod reproduction with its pine floors, large cooking fireplace, wrought-iron lift latches, and bull's-eye glass above the front door, offers true tranquility. Grounds are extensive with rolling lawns, natural-wood walks, a formal rose garden, and two cottage gardens. A gazebo comes complete with hot tub. In the barn is a Model T car used for sightseeing jaunts. Located within minutes of Seattle, guests can enjoy major Northwest sights. Beds are turned down in the evening and homemade mint fudge is left on the pillows. In each room are fresh flowers and a fruitbasket. In case of chilly weather, fires are lit in fireplaces. The inn hosts respect the privacy of guests, but conduct tours for those interested in colonial lifestyle or antiques.

Rates: $30 single, $40 double (plus tax)
Reservations: 206/868-4159

WEAVER HOUSE
SEATTLE, WASHINGTON

(Nominated by Mrs. Irmgard Castleberry, Pacific B&B Reservation Service)

This Tudor-style home, built in 1904 of large timbered cedar, overlooks the most spectacular city and water views of Seattle. There are four bedrooms and several common rooms, including a solarium, game room, and hot tub area. Located in the prestigious West Seattle Admiral district, it's only 12 minutes from the heart of downtown, the Space Needle, Kingdome, and Pike Place Market, four minutes from tennis courts and a golf course, a bit more to indoor and outdoor swimming pools. Mini-parks are within walking or jogging distance, and boating, fishing, and waterskiing are just down the hill in Elliott Bay. Breakfast is an expanded "continental" of fresh juice, fruit, croissants, bran/blueberry muffins, cold cereal and cream, and coffee, tea, or hot chocolate. Airport/Amtrak pickup or delivery, rental cars, and Grey Line tours can be arranged.

Rates: $60 double
Reservations: 206/784-0539

THE BRETL HOME
MAPLEWOOD, WISCONSIN

(Nominated by B&B Guest Homes)

This colonial-style family home is situated in a tiny town at the south end of Door County. It is farm country and a favorite vacation destination in the Middle West. The home is beautifully maintained, with two guest rooms plus a hide-a-bed for a child or children and a shared bath. A full farmer-type breakfast of eggs, sausage, home-made baked goods, and fresh fruit is provided. You'll find plenty to do in the five nearby state parks, at summer theater, musical festivals with artists in residence, and both winter and summer sporting events. The hostesses go out of their way to serve guests. They have been known to wash guests' cars.

Rates: $40 double
Reservations: 414/743-9742

PENTHOUSE APARTMENT
MILWAUKEE, WISCONSIN

(Nominated by B&B of Milwaukee, Inc.)

This newly constructed ninth-floor apartment atop a warehouse is located in the historic Third Ward district of old Milwaukee. The area is undergoing dynamic change with condominium conversion within warehouses. The professional talents of the hostess, an interior designer, is reflected in the furnishings of the living area, kitchen, full bath, and bedroom. A king-size bed converts to twin beds and a queen-size hide-a-bed is in the living area. The skyline view is spectacular. A solarium, spa, and deck are at the disposal of guests. Current newspapers, books, and magazines are provided, along with Scrabble, Trivial Pursuit, chess, and cards. It is described as the perfect setting for a honeymoon or true getaway. A continental breakfast of fresh-squeezed orange juice, cinnamon-sugar rolls, and a carafe of freshly roasted ground coffee is provided. Downtown, the fruit and vegetable district, several excellent restaurants, and the lakefront are within walking distance.

Rates: $60 single, $75 double
Reservations: 414/544-0060

TETON TREE HOUSE
WILSON, WYOMING

This unique house perched on the side of a mountain is only about eight miles from Jackson. It's an ideal base for skiing or touring the area, including the Grand Tetons. The house is being built in stages by a very friendly couple, Chris and Denny Becker. The rooms are spacious and most have great mountain views. In warm weather you can even sit out on the deck and have oatmeal with granola, fresh fruit, and delicious muffins made with oats and sunflower seeds. The hosts know the area thoroughly and can help plan your hiking, skiing, or white-water rafting expeditions. The area is so remote that in the winter peeping-tom mooses have been known to appear at the windows. They have two young children who will soon make you part of the family. I had a wonderful visit with them and I'm pleased to nominate this B&B as one of the 100 Best.

Rates: $50 to $75 double
Reservations: 303/630-3433 (Bed & Breakfast Rocky Mountains)

SPRUCE HAUS
1183 FORGE WALK, VANCOUVER, BC CANADA V68 3R1

This European-style B&B, on the waterfront across from the Expo '86 site, features picturesque views of marinas, quaint walks on carless cobbled lanes, and lush floral deck gardens. There is a choice of the Blue Room with twin beds or the Garden Room with a king-size bed and accompanying view of a garden and the water. Both are equipped with cable TV. Also offered are a washer/dryer service, refrigerator, coffee and tea service, and underground parking. It's three minutes on the ferry from Granville Island to the city side of Vancouver, and a five-minute ride to the city center by bus. Healthy breakfasts include fresh fruits and breads, homemade preserves, muffins, scones, crêpes, omelets, and soufflés. "This has been unbelievable. The best B&B we've ever stayed in," one guest recently wrote.

Rates: $55 ($40 U.S.) to $65 ($48 U.S.) double in high season, $45 ($33 U.S.) to $55 ($40 U.S.) double in low season
Reservations: 604/738-8589

POWELL HOUSE
ONTARIO, CANADA

(Nominated by Country Host)

The ducks quack, the sheep and cows bleat, and the little goats are birthed and bottle-raised on this 109–acre farm complete with an 80-year-old refurbished farmhouse. Inside are antiques galore, plus original pine floors and wainscotting. Located in a rolling countryside farm community, Powell House is accessible to hiking trails, fishing, fairs, and festivals, with guest transportation provided. All summer sports are featured on Georgian Bay; it has the best downhill skiing in winter in Ontario, and 20 miles of cross-country skiing on groomed trails. Breakfasts are plentiful, with fruits in season, fresh juice, eggs according to choice with ham, bacon, or sausage, topped off with hot muffins or toast, homemade jams and jellies, or pancakes and maple syrup.

Rates: $40 ($30 U.S.) double (higher in February); lunch for hikers is $3.50 ($2.60 U.S.) each; dinner, $8 ($5.90 U.S.) each.
Reservations: 519/941-7633

JOHANNE HARRELLE HOUSE
MONTRÉAL, QUÉBEC, CANADA

(Nominated by Montréal B&B)

In this most unusual renovated rowhouse in Montréal's Latin Quarter, guests have the first level of the house for themselves—double bedroom with private bath, living area, courtyard patio, and quaint dining area. This two-story B&B has an interior courtyard, skylight, and wrought-iron spiral staircase. It's located one street parallel to St. Denis Street, the heart of the Latin Quarter district with cafés, restaurants, shops, Métro. It's an easy walk to St. Louis

Square, a park haven, and to Old Montréal and everything downtown. This is considered an ideal setup for honeymoon couples, but "appreciated by all guests." Breakfasts include choice of juices, yogurts, pancakes, eggs, crêpes, and superior coffee.

Rates: $70 ($52 U.S.) double
Reservations: 514/738-9410

Would You Like To Become
One of Our B&B Critics-at-Large?

Have you discovered a great bed-and-breakfast home that belongs in our list of "100 Best"? Have you stayed in an elegant B&B inn that should be featured in this book?

Or have you been dissatisfied in any way with any of the homes and inns mentioned in this book?

You're invited to become one of our secret B&B critics. Just complete and send in the attached B&B home or B&B inn rating forms. There's no need to tear up the book—just photocopy as many forms as you need right from the book.

If you have been dissatisfied in any way with a B&B home, inn, or reservation service currently featured in this book, please let me know with a short note explaining the problem.

If you have really been pleased with your B&B experience, one of the nicest things you could do is send a copy of your evaluation to your host. They would be delighted to know that you thought enough of them and their home or inn to nominate them as "one of the best in North America."

Mail the completed form to:

B&B Critics
c/o Bed & Breakfast North America
Frommer Books
Prentice Hall Press
One Gulf + Western Plaza
New York, NY 10023

Reader Nomination for "One of the Best B&B <u>Homes</u> in North America"

Name of B&B Hosts _____

Address _____

City _____ State _____ ZIP _____

Phone _____

Criteria

(Please check one box for each category)

	Excellent	Good	Fair	Poor
1. Quality of room and furnishings	☐	☐	☐	☐
2. Quality of breakfast	☐	☐	☐	☐
3. Housekeeping	☐	☐	☐	☐
4. Friendliness/helpfulness of host and hostess	☐	☐	☐	☐

Why do you believe this home qualifies as one of the 100 best in North America? _____
_____
_____
_____

Your name _____
Address _____
City _____ State _____ ZIP _____

May we quote you by name in the next edition of this book if your nominee is selected as one of the 100 best?

☐ Yes　　☐ No

Reader Nomination for One of the Better B&B Inns in North America
(*Note:* Many B&B homes also call themselves "inns." But this category is primarily for the large commercial establishments of eight rooms or more and closer in feeling to a hotel than to a private home.)

Name of B&B Inn _____
Address _____
City _____ State _____ ZIP _____
Phone _____

Criteria

(Please check one box for each category)

	Excellent	Good	Fair	Poor
1. Quality of room and furnishings	☐	☐	☐	☐
2. Quality of breakfast	☐	☐	☐	☐
3. Housekeeping	☐	☐	☐	☐
4. Friendliness/helpfulness of the innkeeper and the personnel of the inn	☐	☐	☐	☐
5. Quality of the public rooms	☐	☐	☐	☐

Why do you believe this home qualifies as one of the better B&B inns in North America? _____
_____
_____
_____

Your Name _____
Address _____
City _____ State _____ ZIP _____

May we quote you by name in the next edition of this book if your nominee is selected as one of the 100 best?

☐ Yes   ☐ No

Index

GENERAL

Alabama, 23, 199–201
Alaska, 23, 269–271, 285
American Automobile Association (AAA), 22
Antigua, 43
Arizona, 23, 245–248, 285–286
Arkansas, 23, 221, 286–287
Aruba, 43
Australia, 34–36, 43
Austria, 33, 36, 43

Bahamas, 44
Barbados, 44
B & B guests, 27–29
B & B hosts, 14–15, 49–58
B & Bs abroad, 30–48, 61–62, 63–64
B & Bs, cost of, 13–14, 17–18
B & Bs, definition of, 19
B & Bs, finding, 21–26
B & Bs, history of, 18
B & Bs, 100 best, North America, 283–333
Bed & Breakfast, see B & B
Belgium, 44
Bermuda, 36–37, 44
Bolivia, 44
Bonaire, 44
Brazil, 44
British Columbia, 275, 331–332
British Virgin Islands, 44
Bulgaria, 37, 44
Business travel, 19

California, 14, 23, 248–264, 287–293

Canada, 44, 275–281, 331–333
Cape Cod, 16, 82, 84, 86, 88, 92–95, 304
Cayman Islands, 44
Chile, 44
China, 44
Colombia, 44
Colorado, 23, 222–228, 294–295
Connecticut, 23, 69–72, 294–296
Cost, B & Bs, 13–14, 17–18
Costa Rica, 44
Curaçao, 44
Cyprus, 37–38, 45
Czechoslovakia, 38, 45

Delaware, 23, 131
Denmark, 38, 45
District of Columbia, 26, 132, 296; see also Washington, D.C.
Dominica, 45
Dominican Republic, 45

Egypt, 33, 38, 45
England, see Great Britain

Finland, 45
Florida, 24, 202–206, 297
France, 30–32, 45
French West Indies, 39, 45

Georgia, 16–17, 24, 206–210, 298
Germany, 33, 39–40, 45
Great Britain, 32–33, 40, 44
Greece, 33, 45
Guadeloupe, 39

Guam, 26
Guatemala, 45

Haiti, 45
Hawaii, 24, 271-272, 299
Hong Kong, 45
Hosts, B & B, 14–15, 49–58
Hungary, 45

Idaho, 24, 181–182
Illinois, 24, 169, 299
India, 40, 45
Indiana, 24
Indonesia, 45
Iowa, 24, 182–183
Ireland, 41, 45
Israel, 41, 46
Italy, 33, 46

Jamaica, 46
Japan, 34, 41, 46
Jordan, 46

Kansas, 24, 228–229, 300
Kentucky, 24, 211–213, 300–301
Kenya, 46
Korea, 46

Laundry facilities, 14, 28
Liberia, 46
Louisiana, 16, 24, 229–233, 302
Luxembourg, 46

Maine, 24, 72–79, 302–303
Malaysia, 46
Mariana Islands, 26
Martinique, 39
Maryland, 24, 133–135, 303
Massachusetts, 16, 24, 80–95, 303–308
Mauritius, 46
Mexico, 46
Michigan, 24, 170–172, 309–310
Minnesota, 24, 184
Mississippi, 24, 213–214, 311–312
Missouri, 24, 234–235, 312–313
Monaco, 46

Montana, 25, 185–186
Morocco, 46

National Historic Register, 15
Nebraska, 25
Netherlands, 46
Nevada, 25
New Hampshire, 25, 95–100
New Jersey, 25, 135–136, 313–314
New Mexico, 25, 236–237
New Zealand, 33–35, 42, 46
New York, 25, 101–113, 314–316
North Carolina, 25, 137–142, 316–317
North Dakota, 25, 186–187
Northern Ireland, 46
Norway, 42, 47
Nova Scotia, 276–277

Ohio, 25, 173–175, 317–318
Oklahoma, 25, 238
Ontario, 277–280, 332
Oregon, 25, 187–191, 319–320

Pakistan, 47
Panama, 47
Pennsylvania, 17, 25, 142–151, 320–322
Peru, 47
Pets, 19–20
Philippines, 42, 47
Poland, 47
Portugal, 47
Puerto Rico, 26

Quebec, 280–281, 332–333

Reservation services, national and regional, 61–66; see also individual states
Reservations, 19, 27–28
Rhode Island, 25, 113–116, 322–323
Romania, 47

Senegal, 47
Singapore, 47

South Carolina, 25, 151–158, 323–325
South Dakota, 25, 191–192, 325
Soviet Union, *see* U.S.S.R.
Spain, 47
Sweden, 47
Switzerland, 47

Tanzania, 47
Tennessee, 26, 214–217
Texas, 26, 239–242, 326
Thailand, 47
Togo, 47
Tourist offices, foreign, 34–48
Tourist offices, states and territories, 23–26
Trinidad and Tobago, 47
Turkey, 48
Turks and Caicos Island, 48

United Kingdom, *see* Great Britain
Uruguay, 48
U.S.S.R., 48
Utah, 26, 265

Venezuela, 48
Vermont, 26, 116–128
Virginia, 26, 158–164, 327
Virgin Islands, 26

Washington, 26, 192–195, 329
Washington, D.C., 26, 132, 296
West Virginia, 26, 164–165
Wisconsin, 15, 26, 175–177, 330
Wyoming, 26, 331

Yugoslavia, 43, 48

Zambia, 48

ATTRACTIONS

Acadia National Park (ME), 73, 75
Acadian country (LA), 231
Adirondack Museum (NY), 110
Adirondack State Park (NY), 103, 110
Aiken Triple Crown (SC), 153
Alabama Shakespeare Theater (AL), 199
Alaskaland (AK), 270
Alaska Oil Pipeline (AK), 269
Alaska Railroad (AK), 269
Alaska Salmon Bake (AK), 270
Alpine Slide (VT), 120, 122, 124, 126
Alpine Village (GA), 209
American Frontier Museum (VA), 159
American Royal (KS), 228
Amicalola Falls (GA), 209, 210
Amish country (PA), 143–146
Amish Homestead (PA), 144
Anderson Historic District (SC), 153
Angeles National Forest (CA), 249
Annual Indian Market (NM), 236
Antique Automobile Club of America (PA), 144
Appalachian Trail (GA), 208
Appalachian Trail (CT), 71
Appalachian Trail (NC), 139
Appalachian Trail (VA), 160
Appalachian Trail (VT), 123
Appomattox National Park (VA), 161
April Historic Garden Week (VA), 160
April Rose Festival (GA), 209
Aransas Wildlife Refuge (TX), 239
Arlington National Cemetery (D.C.), 132
Ashland Shakespeare Theater (OR), 190
Ash Lawn (VA), 160

Asia Pacific Museum (CA), 249
Aspen Highlands (CO), 226
Astrodome (TX), 241
Atlanta Historical Society (GA), 207
Audubon Center (WI), 176
Audubon Park and Zoo (LA), 229–231
Audubon Sanctuary (MA), 88
Audubon Society Nature Center (VT), 126
Avon Valley Hiking Trail (ON), 280
Azalea Trails (TX), 240

Baalsburg (PA), 146
Badlands (ND), 186
Bahai Temple (IL), 169
Bahia Honda State Park (FL), 203
Balboa (CA), 249
Bald Mountain (ME), 78
Baltimore Aquarium (MD), 134
Baltimore Inner Harbor (MD), 133, 134
Baltimore Museum of Art (MD), 134
Baltimore Zoo (MD), 134
Bardstown (KY), 212
Bar Harbor (ME), 73
Baseball Hall of Fame (NY), 101, 103, 109
Basketball Hall of Fame (MA), 89
Bath (NC), 137
Battery (SC), 155, 156
Beacon Hill (MA), 82
Beacon Hill Park (BC), 275
Beale Street (TN), 215
Beall Greenhouses (WA), 195
Beaver Creek ski area (CO), 225
Belle Grave Plantation (VA), 159
Belleville Amish Market (PA), 147
Bellefield Nature Center (SC), 157
Bellingrath Gardens (AL), 200

Bell Museum (NS), 276
Bennington Museum (VT), 116
Bennington Museum and Battle-field (NY), 109
Berkshire Playhouse (MA), 93, 123
Berkshire Theater (MA), 91–92, 94
Bethpage Recreation Village (NY), 108
Big South Fork National Park (TN), 217
Big Sur (CA), 258
Billings Farm (VT), 123
Biltmore House (NC), 138, 140
"Bird City" (ON), 277
Black Forest (PA), 149
Black Hills (SD), 192
Black River Museum (VT), 122
Blackwater Falls State Park (WV), 165
Blue Hill Fair (ME), 75
Blue Mountain Museum (NY), 111
Blue Ribbon Downs (OK), 238
Blue Ridge Mountains (NC), 140
Blue Ridge Parkway (NC), 141
Blue Ridge Parkway (VA), 159–161, 163
Bodega Bay (CA), 255
Boothbay Dinner Theater (ME), 75
Boscobel Mansion (NY), 101
Boston Ballet (MA), 82
Boston Harbor (MA), 82
Boston Pops (MA), 82
Boston Symphony (MA), 82, 84
Boundary Waters Canoe Wilderness Area (MN), 184
Brackenridge Park and Zoo (TX), 242
Brandywine Battlefield (PA), 145
Brandywine River Museum (DE), 131
Brandywine River Museum (PA), 143, 145
Bras d'Or lakes (NS), 276
Bretton Woods ski area (NH), 98
Brevard Music Center (NC), 138, 140

Brevard Music Festival (NC), 140
British Art Museum (CT), 70
British Cemetery (NC), 140
Britt Garden Music Festival (OR), 188; Peter Britt Music Festival (OR), 190
Broadmoor Zoo (CO), 224
Bromley (VT), 120
Bromley Mountain (VT), 128
Brown House, Molly (CO), 224
Bruce Trail (ON), 279
Bryant Homestead, William Cullen (MA), 90
Buena Vista (CO), 224
Bureau of Printing and Engraving (D.C.), 132
Burke ski area (NH), 98
Busch Gardens (FL), 204
Busch Gardens (VA), 162–164
Busch Stadium (MO), 235
Butchart Gardens (BC), 193, 275
Buttermilk (CO), 226

Cabot Trail (NS), 276
Calhoun home, John (SC), 156
Calistoga mud and mineral baths (CA), 252
Campobello Island (ME), 76
Canaan State Park (WV), 165
Canal Museum (PA), 142
Cannon Mountain Tramway (NH), 98
Cannon ski area (NH), 98
Cape Cod (MA), 16, 82, 84, 86, 88, 92–95, 304
Cape Cod National Seashore (MA), 86
Cape Playhouse (MA), 88
Captiva Island (FL), 205
Caramoor Music Festival (NY), 101
Carousel Music Theater (ME), 75
Carson Wildlife Preserve, Rachel (ME), 78
Carthage Home (TX), 240
Catskill Game Farm (NY), 109
Casco Bay (ME), 76

Casey State Park (WA), 194
Castle Museum (MT), 186
Castle Town (MT), 186
Cathedral State Park (WV), 165
Central Park (NY), 104, 105
Chalmette National Historic Site (LA), 233
Champoeg Park (OR), 191
Chappaquiddick (MA), 92
Charles Town Races (WV), 164
Château Frontenac (PQ), 281
Chattahoochie National Forest (GA), 208
Chattahoochie State Park (GA), 210
Cherokee Indian Reservation (NC), 138
Cherokee National Forest (TN), 216
Chesapeake Bay (MD), 133
Chesterfield Gorge (MA), 90
Chesterwood (MA), 93
Chevalier House (PQ), 281
Children's Museum (D.C.), 132
Chinatown (CA), 254, 263
Chinatown (MA), 82
Chocolate World (PA), 144
Christian Science Church (MA), 82
Chrysler Museum (VA), 161
Churchill Downs (KY), 212
Cincinnati Opera/Zoo (OH), 174
Citadel (PQ), 281
Civil War monuments (GA), 207
Clay home, Henry (KY), 212
Cleveland Museum of Art (OH), 173
Cleveland Natural History Museum (OH), 173
Cleveland Zoo (OH), 173
Cliff Walk (RI), 115, 116
Coast Guard Station (NC), 140
Cobscook State Park (ME), 76
Coconut Grove Village (FL), 203
Cohutta Wilderness (GA), 208
Cold Spring (NY), 101
Cold Spring Village (NJ), 136
College Football Hall of Fame (KY), 211

Colonial Parkway (VA), 164
Colossal Cave (AZ), 247
Colt State Park (RI), 114
Columbia (SC), 156
Columbus Pilgrimage (MS), 213
Commonwealth Winery (MA), 87
Concord (MA), 84, 89
Concord River (MA), 83
Confederate Museum (SC), 155
Connecticut River (VT), 118
Continental Divide (CO), 227
Coolidge birthplace, Calvin (VT), 122, 123
Cooper-Hewitt Museum (NY), 104
Coors International Bicycle Race (CO), 222
Coral Castle (FL), 202
Corning Glass Museum (NY), 101, 111
Corpus Christi Art Museum (TX), 239
Covenant Presbyterian Seminary (MO), 235
Craigdarroch Castle (BC), 275
Cranberry World (MA), 87
Cranbrook Art Museum (MI), 170
Crater Lake Park (OR), 188, 189
Crawford Auto Museum (OH), 173
Crested Butte (CO), 227
Crocker Art Museum (CA), 253
Croton Clearwater Revival (NY), 101
Crown Center (MO), 228
Crystal Speedway (MI), 172
Cumberland Falls (KY), 212
Cumberland Gap (KY), 212
Governor Curtin Mansion Village (PA), 147
Cyclorama (GA), 207
Cypress Gardens (FL), 204

Dahlonega Gold Museum (GA), 210
Dale Hollow Lake (KY), 212
Dali Museum (FL), 205
Dania Jai-Alai (FL), 203

DAR State Park (MA), 90
Dauphin Islands (AL), 200
Deerfield Village (MA), 89–91
Delaware Natural History Museum (PA), 145
Del Coronado Hotel (CA), 250
Denver Art Museum (CO), 224
Denver Zoo (CO), 224
Desert Botanical Gardens (AZ), 246, 247
Detroit Convention Center (MI), 170
Detroit Zoo (MI), 170
Devon Horse Show (PA), 148
Diamond City ghost town (MT), 186
Discovery cruise (AK), 270
Disneyland (CA), 250–252, 257, 262
Disney World, Walt (FL), 14, 204, 205
Dixon Gallery and Gardens (TN), 215
Dockery Lake (GA), 210
Dodger Stadium (CA), 249, 257
Dollywood (TN), 216
Dorney Park Velodrome and Art Museum (PA), 142
Dorset Playhouse (VT), 116, 120
Drayton Hall (VT), 117
Drew Theater, John (NY), 108
Dubuque Greyhound Park (IA), 183
Dufferin Terrace (PQ), 281
Durango Silverton Narrow-Gauge Railroad (CA), 225
Dutch Wonderland (PA), 144

Eastman House of Photography (NY), 102
Edaville Railroad (MA), 87
Edenton (NC), 137
Elizabeth City Historic District (NC), 137
Elliot House Museum (SC), 154
Emerson Home, Ralph Waldo (MA), 83
Empire State Plaza (NY), 109, 112

Empress Hotel (WA), 193
Enchanted Forest (NY), 111
Endless Taverns (VA), 159
EPCOT (FL), 204
Equestrian Center (CA), 257
Essex (CT), 71
Estes Park (CO), 224, 227
Everglades National Park (FL), 203

Fairbanks Museum and Planetarium (VT), 118
Fairmount Park (PA), 146
Falcon State Park (TX), 242
Fall Foliage Festival (ME), 76
Falmouth Playhouse (MA), 88
Faneuil Hall (MA), 82, 84
Farmer's Museum (NY), 103
Farnsworth Art Museum (ME), 79
Fatima Shrine (NY), 107
Faulkner Home, William (MS), 213
Fenelon Place Elevator (IA), 183
Fenelon Rivers Hall of Fame (IA), 183
Fenway Park (MA), 81
Finger Lakes (NY), 111
Fire Island National Seashore (NY), 108
Fisherman's Wharf (CA), 254, 263
Fisher Theater (MI), 170
Flagler Museum (FL), 203
Flatrock Playhouse (NC), 140
The Flume (NH), 100
Fogg Museum (MA), 82
Fontbonne (MO), 235
Ford Museum, Gerald R. (MI), 171
Ford Museum, Henry (MI), 170
Forest Park Zoo (MO), 235
Fort Conde (AL), 200
Fort Museum Artillery Park (PQ), 281
Fort Niagara (NY), 107
Fortress Louisburg (NS), 276
Fort Ross (CA), 260
Fort Sam Houston (TX), 242
Fort Stanwick (NY), 103

Fort Sumter (SC), 155, 156
Fort Vancouver (OR), 187
Fort Worden State Park (WA), 195
Fox Theater (MO), 235
Franconia ski area (NH), 98
Franklin Museum (PA), 145
Freedom Trail (MA), 82, 84, 85
French Creek State Park (PA), 142–143
French Market (LA), 233
French Quarter (LA), 229–231

Galveston Bay (TX), 240, 241
Garden District (LA), 231
Garden of the Gods (CO), 224
Gardner Museum (MA), 81, 82
Gateway Arch (MO), 235
Gatlinburg (TN), 216
Gay Head (MA), 92
Genesee County Museum (NY), 102
German Village (OH), 174
Gillette Castle (CT), 71
Glacier Bay National Monument (AK), 271
Glacier Bay National Park (AK), 270
Glencoe Botanic Garden (IL), 169
Glencoe Historic Hotel (WA), 192
Golden Gate Park (CA), 249, 254
Gold Museum (GA), 210
Goodspeed Opera House (CT), 71
Governor's Promenade (PQ), 281
Grand Avenue Mall (WI), 176
Grand Canyon (AZ), 245–247
Grand Prix (MI), 170
Great Bear Wilderness (MT), 185
Great Smoky Mountains (NC), 141
Great Smoky Mountains National Park (NC), 138, 139
Great Smoky Mountains National Park (TN), 216
Greek Theater (CA), 257
Greenfield State Park (NH), 100
Greenfield Village (MI), 170
Green Mountain Forest (VT), 118
Green Mountain National Park (VT), 123

Green Mountains (VT), 83, 119, 128
Greenwich Village (NY), 104
Griffith Park Observatory (CA), 257
Guild Hall Art Exhibits (NY), 108
Gulf Coast (CA), 229, 231
Gulf of Mexico (TX), 240
Gulf Shores (AL), 200
Gunflint Trail (MN), 184

Hagley Museum (DE), 131
Hagley Museum (PA), 143
Halsey Homestead (NY), 108
Hammondsport Wineries (NY), 111
Hamptons (NY), 102
Hapgood Pond (VT), 120
Harbor Springs (MI), 171
Hargreaves Vineyard (NY), 108
Harper's Ferry National Park (WV), 164
Hartwell Park, Jane (SC), 153
Hawthorne home, Nathaniel (MA), 83
Hazen's Notch Cross-Country Ski Center (VT), 120
Hemingway home, Ernest (FL), 202, 203
Henry home, Patrick (VA), 161
Heritage Hill District (MI), 171
Heritage Plantation (MA), 88, 91
Hershey Museum of American Life (PA), 144
Hershey Park (PA), 144
Hershey Rose Gardens (PA), 144
Hialeah Racetrack (FL), 203
Hidden Valley ski area (CO), 227
Higgins Armor Museum (MA), 80
Highlands Playhouse (NC), 139
High Museum (GA), 206
High Museum of Art (GA), 207
Hildene (VT), 120, 122
Hilton Head Island (SC), 154, 156
Hither Hills State Park (NY), 108
Holland Tulip Festival (MI), 171
Holly Springs Pilgrimage (MS), 213

Hollywood (CA), 252
Hollywood Bowl (CA), 257
Hollywood Race Track (CA), 257
Holmes State Park (NC), 140
Home Sweet Home Museum
  (NY), 108
Hopeland Gardens (SC), 153
Hope Plantation (NC), 137
Hopewell Village (PA), 143
Horticultural Society (MA), 80
Hot Springs (AR), 221
Hot Sulphur Springs (CO), 224
Howe Caverns (NY), 101, 103
Hudson River (NY), 11
Hunter Mountain (NY), 113
Hunting Island State Park (SC),
  154
Huntington Beach (SC), 157
Huntington Library and Gardens
  (CA), 249
Hyde Park (NY), 101, 109, 113

Île d'Orleans (PQ), 281
Illinois River (OR), 189
Independence Hall and National
  Park (PA), 143, 146
Indian Archeological Institute
  (CT), 71
Indian Caverns (PA), 147
Indian Mountain Gunnery (CT),
  71
Indiantown (FL), 206
Intracoastal Waterway (FL), 205
Iowa Great Lakes (IA), 182
Irish Hills (MI), 170
Irvine Meadows (CA), 251

Jackson Laboratory (ME), 73
Jackson headquarters, Stonewall
  (VA), 159
Jackson house, Stonewall (VA),
  159
Jackson Square (LA), 230, 232
Jacob's Pillow (CT), 70
Jacob's Pillow (MA), 89–94
James River Plantation (VA), 162
Jamestown (VA), 163, 164
Japanese Art Museum (TX), 239

Japanese Botanical Gardens (TX),
  240
Jay Peak (VT), 120
Jazz Halls (LA), 230
Jefferson home, Joseph (LA), 233
Jefferson summer home, Thomas
  (VA), 161
Jimmy Rodgers Festival (MS), 213
Jones Beach (NY), 108
Jones Memorial Library (VA), 161
Jungle Garden (LA), 233
Junior Miss Pageant (AL), 200

Kansas City Zoo (MO), 234
Kennebec River (ME), 76
Kennedy Center (D.C.), 132
Kennedy Compound (MA), 93
Kennedy Library (MA), 82
Kennedy Memorial (MA), 93
Kentucky Horse Park (KY), 212
Killington (VT), 118
Kilmer Memorial Forest, Joyce
  (NC), 141
King Memorial Site, Martin Luther
  (GA), 206
King of Prussia (PA), 148
King Ranch (TX), 239
King's Dominion (VA), 162
Kings Island (OH), 174
Kings Island Park (KY), 211
Kitt Peak Observatory (AZ), 245,
  247
Kleinhans Music Hall (NY), 107
Kneisel Music Camp (ME), 75
Knott's Berry Farm (CA), 251,
  252, 257
Kootznahoo Inlet Archipelago
  (AL), 200
Kutztown Folk Festival (PA), 143

Laclede's Landing (MO), 235
Lafitte National Park, Jean (LA),
  233
Lake Blue Ridge (GA), 208
Lake Champlain (VT), 125
Lake Cleone (CA), 260
Lake Cumberland (KY), 212
Lake Dunmore (VT), 122

Lake Erie (PA), 147
Lake Havasu (AZ), 245
Lake Huron (ON), 280
Lake Michigan (IL), 169, 171
Lake Okeechobee (FL), 206
Lake Ontario (NY), 102
Lake Powell (AZ), 245, 247
Lake Sunapee (NH), 95, 97
Lake Tahoe (CA), 262, 264
Lake Waramaug (CT), 71
Lake Winnipesaukee (NH), 95
Langley (WA), 194
LBJ Ranch (TX), 242
Leavenworth (WA), 194
Lemon Dam (CO), 225
Lenox (MA), 109
Letchworth Park (NY), 102
Lewistown Art Park (NY), 107
Lexington (KY), 212
Lexington (MA), 84, 89
Liberty Bell (PA), 146
Lighthouse (NC), 140
Lime Rock car racing (CT), 71
Lincoln Center (NY), 104
Lincoln home, Robert Todd (VT),
  122
Lincoln house, Mary Todd (KY),
  212
Lincoln Park Zoo (OK), 238
Lion Country Safari (CA), 252
Little Brown Jug (OH), 174
L. L. Bean (ME), 76
London House and Museum, Jack
  (CA), 255
Longfellow home (MA), 82
Long Trail (VT), 123, 127
Longvue Gardens (LA), 231
Long Wharf Theater (CT), 70
Longwood Gardens (DE), 131
Longwood Gardens (PA), 143,
  145, 148
Los Angeles Art Museum (CA),
  257
Los Angeles Zoo (CA), 249
Louisiana State Park (LA), 221
Lowell Observatory (AZ), 245,
  247
Lowndesboro (AL), 199

Luther Burbank Gardens (CA),
  255
Lyndhurst Castle (NY), 101
Lost River (NH), 100

MacArthur Memorial (VA), 161
Macaulay House (ON), 277
MacKerricher State Park (CA), 260
Mag Glen (VT), 126, 127
Magazine Street antique shops
  (LA), 231
Magic Mountain (VT), 120, 128
Magnolia Gardens (VT), 117
Mammoth Cave (KY), 212
Maple Grove Museum and Factory
  (VT), 118
Mardi Gras (AL), 200
Marginal Way (ME), 78
Marietta River Festival (OH), 174
Marineland (CA), 252
Marlboro Music Center (VT), 128
Marlboro Music Festival (VT), 128
Marshall Homes Tour (MI), 170
Marshall house, John (VA), 162
Marshall Museum and Library,
  George C. (VA), 159
Marshall Wilderness, Bob (MT),
  185
Martha's Vineyard (MA), 88, 92,
  93
Master's Golf Tournament (SC),
  153
Mayflower (MA), 87
McCormick Place (IL), 169
McFaddens Wharf (CA), 262
Meadow Brook Hall (MI), 170
Meadowlands Sports Complex
  (NJ), 135
Meeker Park (CO), 224
Melody Tent (MA), 88
Memphis Convention Center (TN),
  215
Mendocino (CA), 260
Mennonite country (PA), 143, 145
Merrimack Valley (NH), 95
Mesa Verde National Park (CO),
  224, 225
Meteor Crater (AZ), 246, 247

Metro Zoo (FL), 202
Miami Seaquarium (FL), 202, 203
Miccosukee Indian Village (FL), 203
Michigan Space Center (MI), 170
Middleton Place (VT), 117
Miller Outdoor Theater (TX), 241
Million Dollar Drive (RI), 115
Miner's Museum (NS), 276
Minithorn House (OR), 191
Mission San Xavier del Bac (AZ), 247, 248
Mississippi Fly Way (MS), 221
Mississippi (LA), 230, 233
Mobile Bay (AL), 200
Mobile Greyhound Park (AL), 200
Mohawk River (NY), 111
Mohawk Trail (MA), 89
Monadnock State Park (NH), 100
Monkey Jungle (FL), 202, 203
Monroe Hot Springs (UT), 265
Montauk Lighthouse (NY), 108
Monticello (VA), 160
Montmorency Falls (PQ), 281
Montpelier (ME), 78
Moosehorn National Wildlife Refuge (ME), 76
Morelands Moto-Cross (MI), 172
Morgan horse farm (VT), 127
Moscone Convention Center (CA), 254
Mound Builder's Sites (OH), 174
The Mount (MA), 91–92
Mountain Music Shows (MO), 234
Mount Blue (ME), 78
Mount Mansfield (VT), 124, 125
Mount Ranier National Park (WA), 192
Mount Royal Park (PQ), 280
Mount Rushmore (SD), 192
Mount St. Helena tours (WA), 193
Mount St. Helens (WA), 187
Mount Vernon (VA), 132, 158
Mount Washington (NH), 98
Mount Zirkel Wilderness Area (CO), 227
Movieland Wax Museum (CA), 251

Mud Island (TN), 215
Muirfield Golf Course (OH), 174
Muny Outdoor Opera Theater (MO), 235
Murcoot Park (NY), 101
Museum of the Albermarle (NC), 137
Museum of American Frontier Culture (VA), 163
Museum of Appalachia (TN), 216
Museum of the Confederacy (VA), 162
Museum of Fine Arts (MA), 81, 82, 84
Museum of Science (MA), 82, 84
Museum Row (NY), 104
Mystic Seaport (CT), 69, 70

Nantahala National Forest (NC), 141
Nantahala River (NC), 138
Nantucket (MA), 88, 93–95
Nantucket Wahling Museum (MA), 94
Napa Valley wineries (CA), 261
NASA Space Center (TX), 241
Natchez Bluffs (MS), 214
Natchez State Park (MS), 214
Natchez Under the Hill (MS), 214
National Archives (D.C.), 132
National Bird Sanctuary (OR), 189
National Civil War Park (MS), 213
National Cowboy Hall of Fame (OK), 238
National Historic Preservation of Old Louisville (KY), 212
National Horse Racing Hall of Fame (SC), 153
National Rivers Hall of Fame (IA), 183
National Wildlife Refuge (TX), 242
National Zoo (D.C.), 132
NBC—TV Studios (CA), 249, 257
N.E. Aquarium (MA), 82
Nelson Art Gallery (MO), 228
Nevada City Museum (MT), 185
Newfoundland ferry (NS), 276
New Haven Coliseum (CT), 70

New London Barn (NH), 98
New London Playhouse (NH), 98
New Orleans Museum of Art (LA), 230
Newport (RI), 114–116
Newport Folk Festival (RI), 115
New York City (NY), 101
Niagara Falls (NY), 107
Nob Hill (CA), 263
Norfolk Naval Base and Air Station (VA), 161
North Carolina State Theater (NC), 138
Northington Plantation (TX), 242
Norton Simon Museum (CA), 249

Oak Bluffs (MA), 92
Oakleigh (AL), 200
Ocean Drive (RI), 116
Ocoee River (GA), 108
Ogunquit Playhouse (ME), 78
Ohio Historical Center (OH), 174
Old Army Museum (TX), 242
Old Canal Mission (CA), 258
Old Forge (NY), 111
Old Kentucky Home (KY), 212
Old Man of the Mountain (NH), 98, 100
Old New Castle (DE), 131
Old Slave Market (SC), 155
Old Stone House Museum (VT), 121
Oldtown (CA), 253
Oldtown (IL), 169
Old Tucson (AZ), 248
Olvera Street (CA), 257
Olympia Brewery (WA), 195
Olympic Stadium (PQ), 280
Oregon Caves (OR), 188, 190
Orkney Springs Open Air Concerts (VA), 159
Owls Head Transportation (ME), 79

Padre Island (TX), 239
Pageant of the Masters (CA), 251
Pali Lookout (HI), 272

Pamlico Sound (NC), 140
Parrish Museum (NY), 108
Parrot Jungle (FL), 202, 203
Patriot's Point Museum (SC), 156
Peabody Museum (CT), 70
Pearl Lakes State Park (CO), 227
Pennekamp Coral Reef (FL), 203
Pennekamp State Park (FL), 203
Penn Museum, William (PA), 144
Penns Cave (PA), 147
Pennsylvania Dutch Country (PA), 143, 145, 146, 148, 149
Pennsylvania Farm Museum (PA), 144
Pebble Hill Plantation Museum (GA), 209, 210
Perkin's Cove (ME), 78
Petrified Forest (AZ), 246, 247
Philadelphia (PA), 131
Philadelphia Museum of Art (PA), 143, 146
Philadelphia Zoo (PA), 146
Philbrook Art Museum (OK), 238
Phillips Mushroom Museum (PA), 145
Phoenix Zoo (AZ), 245–247
Physick House Victorian Museum (NJ), 136
Pike's Peak (CO), 224
Pine Creek (PA), 149
Pink Palace Museum of Natural History (TN), 215
Pisgah National Forest (NC), 138, 140
Place d'Armes (PQ), 281
Place des Artes (PQ), 280
Plains of Abraham (PQ), 281
Plant Ocean (FL), 202, 203
Point Lobos State Reserve (CA), 258
Point Robinson Lighthouse (WA), 195
Polar Caves (NH), 100
Ports O'Call (CA), 252
Prairie Edge Museum (TX), 242
Pierce home, Franklin (NH), 96, 97

Plimoth Plantation (MA), 87, 95
Plymouth Rock (MA), 87, 95
Plymouth (MA), 82
Plymouth Wax Museum (MA), 87
Poe Museum, Edgar Allan (VA), 162
Powder Ridge ski area (CT), 70
Provincial Museum (BC), 275
Purgatory ski area (CO), 225

Queechee Gorge (VT), 122, 123
Queen Emma Summer Palace (HI), 272
Queen Mary (CA), 252
Quincy Market (MA), 82, 84

Rangeley Lake State Park (ME), 78
Ravinia Festival (IL), 169
Rawhide (AZ), 246
Reading shopping outlets (PA), 143, 148
Recreation Path (VT), 124
Red Rocks (CO), 224
Redwood Forest (CA), 255
Redwood National Park (OR), 189
Reid State Park (ME), 75
Reversing Falls (ME), 76
Reynolds Dinner Theater, Burt (FL), 203
Rice Museum (SC), 157
Richards Oar House (AL), 201
Rideau Canal (ON), 278
Ringling Museums (FL), 203
Riverfront (MO), 235
Robert Trent Jones golf course (ME), 77
Rock of Ages Quarries (VT), 125
Rockport Art Colony (TX), 239
Rockwell Museum, Norman (MA), 93, 94
Rockwell Museum, Norman (VT), 123
Rockwell Museum of Western Art (NY), 111
Rocky Mountain National Park (CO), 222, 224, 227
Rodin Museum (PA), 143, 146

Rogue River (OR), 189, 190
Rollins State Park (NH), 97
Roosevelt Estate (NY), 109
Roosevelt International Park (ME), 76
Rose Bowl (CA), 249
Rose Test Gardens (GA), 210
Ross house, Betsy (PA), 146
Ruby Falls, Anna (GA), 210
Russian River resorts (CA), 255
Rye Playland (NY), 101

Sabino Canyon (AZ), 248
Saddleback Mountain (ME), 78
Sagamore Hill (NY), 108
Sag Harbor Customs House (NY), 107–108
Sag Harbor Whaling Museum (NY), 108
Saguaro National Monument (AZ), 248
St. Charles Avenue streetcar (LA), 230, 231
St. John's Church (VA), 162
St. Joseph Oratory (PQ), 280
Ste. Anne de Beaupre (PQ), 281
Salmon Locks (WA), 192
Salmon River (ID), 181, 182
San Antonio Art Museum (TX), 242
San Antonio Riverwalk (TX), 241
Sandburg house, Carl (NC), 140
San Diego Zoo (CA), 249, 250, 252
Sandwich Glass Museum (MA), 88, 91
San Francisco (CA), 260, 264
Sanibel Island (FL), 205
San Jacinto Monument (TX), 241
San Juan Capistrano (CA), 252
Santa Anita Race Track (CA), 249, 257
Santa Barbara Mission (CA), 264
Santa's Village (NH), 98, 100
Saratoga (NY), 101
Saratoga Race Course (NY), 109
Savoy Theater (NS), 276

Sawtooth National Fish Hatchery (ID), 182
Sawtooth Recreation Area (ID), 182
Science Center (MD), 134
Science Museum of Virginia (VA), 162
Scripps Aquarium (CA), 250
Scripps Institute of Oceanography (CA), 250
Seal Island Bridge (NS), 276
Seattle Center (WA), 192
Sea World (CA), 250, 252
Sea World (FL), 204, 205
Serpentarium (FL), 202, 203
Sesame Place (PA), 143
Seven Mile Bridge (FL), 203
17-Mile Drive (CA), 258
1796 Patterson Museum (NY), 111
Severance Hall (OH), 173
Shaker Museum (NY), 109
Shakertown (KY), 212
Shaker Village (NH), 99
Shakespeare Festival (CO), 222
Shakespeare Festival Theater (OR), 188, 190
Shark Valley (FL), 202
Sharon Playhouse (CT), 70
Shawmet National Park (MA), 91
Shelburne Museum (VT), 117, 121, 125–127
Shenandoah National Park (VA), 160
Shenandoah Summer Music Theater (VA), 159
Shinnecock Indian Reservation (NY), 108
Shipyard Museum (NY), 110
Shubert Theater (CT), 70
Silver Dollar City (MO), 234
Silver Lake Harbor (NC), 140
Silver Springs (FL), 204
Silverton (CO), 228
Six Flags (GA), 207
Skippack Village (PA), 143
Skyline Drive (VA), 160, 163
Skyline Drive (VT), 116

Slate Mill (RI), 114
Sleeping Bear Dunes National Park (MI), 170
Sleepy Hollow Restoration (NY), 101
Smithsonian (D.C.), 132
Smuggler's Notch (VT), 125
Snowmass (CO), 226
Soho (NY), 104
Sonnenberg Gardens (NY), 102
Sonoma Old Spanish Mission (CA), 255
Sonora Desert Museum (AZ), 247, 248
Southern Vermont Art Center (VT), 116
South Ferry (NY), 104
South Street Seaport (NY), 104
Spanish Missions National Park (TX), 242
Squam Lake (NH), 100
Squaw Valley Ski Resort (CA), 262
Stanley Park (WA), 193
Stark Trail, Molly (VT), 128
State Archives (VA), 162
Steamboat State Park (CO), 227
Steam Town (NH), 96
Sterling Clark Museum (MA), 90
Stone Mountain Park (GA), 206, 207
Stony Brook Museum Complex (NY), 108
Stowe (VT), 121, 125
Strasburg Railroad (PA), 144
Stratford Festival (ON), 22
Stratford Shakespeare Theater (ON), 280
Stratton Mountain (VT), 120, 128
Strawberry Banke Capitol Complex (NH), 99
Strong Toy Museum (NY), 102
Sturbridge Village (MA), 69, 80, 84, 89
Sugarbush (VT), 126, 127
Sugarloaf (ME), 77
Suislaw Forest (OR), 191
Summerville (VT), 117

Summit Point Raceway (WV), 164
Sunapee (NH), 97
Sunken Garden (FL), 205
Sunken Meadow State Park (NY), 108
Sunrise Theater (FL), 202
Sunset Center (CA), 258
Sunset Rock (NC), 139
Superdome (LA), 230
Sutter's Fort (CA), 253

The Tabernacle (MA), 92
Tampa Bay Football Stadium (FL), 204
Tanglewood (MA), 89–94, 109
Tanglewood Music Festival (MA), 70
Texas Falls (VT), 122
Texas Hill Country (TX), 240
Texas Safari Wild Game Park (TX), 240
Texas Stadium (TX), 240
Theater District (NY), 104
Theater of the Sea (FL), 203
Thoreau Lyceum (MA), 83
1000 Islands Craft School and Textile Museum (NY), 110
Tite Flume (NH), 98
Toccoa River (GA), 208
The Tor (CA), 258
Torrey Pines Golf Course (CA), 250
Town Hall Museum (NY), 110
Townshend State Park (VT), 128
Trapp Family Lodge (VT), 121, 125
Trolley Museum (ME), 77
Truman home, Harry S. (MO), 234
Truman Library (MO), 228
Tumbledown Mountain (ME), 78
Topiary Gardens (RI), 114
Touro Synagogue (RI), 115
Tucson Zoo (AZ), 245
T. V. A. (GA), 208
28th Division Military Shrine and Museum (PA), 147

Ulysses ghost town (ID), 181
Union Square (CA), 263
Union Theological Seminary (VA), 162
United Nations (NY), 104
Universal City (CA), 252, 257
Universal Studios (CA), 249, 257, 262
Ursuline Convent and Museum (PQ), 281
U.S. Capitol (D.C.), 132
U.S. Mint (CO), 224
U.S.S. *Alabama* (AL), 200
U.S.S. *Drum* (AL), 200
Utica Brewery (NY), 103

Vail (CO), 225
Valleoto Lake (CO), 225
Valley Forge National Park (PA), 143, 145, 148
Vandalia Trap Shoot (OH), 174
Vanderbilt Mansion (NY), 101, 113
Vanderbilt Planetarium (NY), 108
Verdier Museum (SC), 154
Vicksburg (MS), 213
Vineyard Haven (MA), 92
Virginia Beach (VA), 161
Virginia Historical Society (VA), 162
Virginia Museum (VA), 162
Virginia Ten Miler Road Race (VA), 161
Virginia Theater for the Performing Arts (VA), 162
Vizcaya (FL), 202, 203
Vogel State Park (GA), 210
Volvo International Tennis Tournament (VT), 128

Waitsfield Village (VT), 127
Walden Pond (MA), 84, 89
Wall Street (NY), 104
Washington birthplace, Booker T. (VA), 161
Washington Center for the Performing Arts (WA), 195

Washington's Headquarters (NJ), 135
Waterloo Village (NJ), 135
Watermill Old Mill Museum and Windmill (NY), 108
Waterside Festival Marketplace (VA), 161
Watkins Glen (NY), 111
Wax Orchard fruit juice factory (WA), 195
Wayside Theater (VA), 159
Westbury Music Fair (NY), 108
West End Yacht Club (LA), 231–232
Weston Theater (VT), 120
White Chapel Meeting House (ON), 277
White Flower Farm (CT), 71
White Mountain National Forest (NH), 98, 100
White Mountains (NH), 83, 95, 99
White Point Gardens (SC), 156
Whiteside Rock (NC), 139
Whitewater Falls (SC), 158
White Water Fun Park (MO), 234
Wild Animal Park (CA), 252
Wilder Pageant, Laura Ingalls (SD),192
Wildwood Conservation Park (ON), 280
Williamsburg (VA), 162–164
Williams home, Tennessee (FL), 202, 203
Williamstown Theater (MA), 70, 90
Wilson birthplace, Woodrow (VA), 159, 163

Winslow (NH), 97
Winter Carnival (PQ), 281
Winter Park (CO), 224
Winterthur Museum and Gardens (PA), 131, 143, 145
Woodburn Plantation (SC), 157
Woodland Zoo (WA), 192
Woodstock (VT), 122
Woodward Cave (PA), 147
Woodward Riverboat Museum (IA), 183
Worcester Science Center (MA), 80
World Affairs Conference (CO), 222
World Congress Center (GA), 207
Worlds of Fun (KS), 228
World Trade Center (NY), 104
World War I Aerodrome (NY), 113
Wright Foundation, Frank Lloyd (AZ), 245
Wyeth Art Museum, Andrew (PA), 148

Xootsnoowu Island (AL), 200

Yellow Rock Mountain (NC), 139
Yellowstone National Park (MT), 185, 186
Yorktown (VA), 163, 164
York Village (ME), 79
Yosemite (CA), 249

Zane Grey house (AZ), 245
Zoo America (PA), 144

SCHOOLS AND COLLEGES

Adelphi (NY), 108
Agnes Scott (GA), 207
Alaska Pacific University (AK), 269
Albertus Magnus (CT), 70
Albion (MI), 170
Albright (PA), 143
Algonquin College (ON), 278
Allentown (PA), 143
Alvernia (PA), 143
American College of Physicians
  (PA), 143
American Graduate School of
  Business (AZ), 245
American Graduate School of
  International Management (AZ),
  247
American River College (CA), 253
Amherst (MA), 89–90
Anna Maria College (MA), 80
Antioch (OH), 174
Arizona State University (AZ),
  245, 246, 247
Art Center College of Design
  (CA), 249
Atlantic Union College (MA), 80
Atlanta University (GA), 21, 206,
  207
Auburn (AL), 199
Augustana (SD), 192
Austin Peay (TN), 216
Avila College (KS), 228

Babson (MA), 82, 83
Baptist College (SC), 151
Barry College (FL), 202
Baruch (NY), 104
Bates (ME), 73
Baylor College of Medicine (TX),
  241
Bay Pines VA Hospital (FL), 205
Beaver (PA), 143
Belhaven (MS), 213
Bellarmine (KY), 212

Bennington (VT), 71, 109
Bentley (MA), 84
Berkeley School of Music (MA), 84
Berkshire (CT), 71
Biscayne College (FL), 202
Black Hills State (SD), 192
Boston College (MA), 82, 83, 84
Boston University (MA), 81, 82,
  83, 84
Bowling College (NY), 108
Bowdoin (ME), 73
Brandeis (MA), 82, 83, 84
Brewster Academy (NH), 96
Bridgewater (VA), 159
Bridgewater State College (MA),
  87
Brockport (NY), 102–103
Brown (RI), 114
Bryant (RI), 114
Bryn Mawr (PA), 143, 148
Bucknell (PA), 147
Buffalo State (NY), 107

Cabrini (PA), 143
Cal College Long Beach (CA), 257
California Institute of Technology
  (CA), 249, 259
California State University (CA),
  250, 251, 253, 257
Calvin College (MI), 171
Cambridge (MA), 83
Camosun College (BC), 275
Canisius (NY), 107
Cape Cod Community College
  (MA), 88
Cape Cod Conservatory of Music
  and Art (MA), 88
Capital (OH), 174
Capitol Campus of Penn State
  (PA), 144
Carleton University (ON), 278
Carnegie-Mellon (PA), 147
Case Western Reserve (OH), 173

Catholic University (D.C.), 132
Cedar Crest (PA), 143
Central Missouri State (MO), 278
Central State (OK), 238
Choate (CT), 69, 70
The Citadel (SC), 151, 152
Chowan (NC), 137
City College (NY), 105, 106
Claremont Colleges (CA), 249,
   259
Clark University (MA), 80
Clemson University (SC), 157,
   158
Cleveland State (OH), 173
Coast Guard Academy (CT), 69,
   70
Cobleskill (NY), 103
Colby (ME), 73
Colby-Sawyer (NH), 95–96
Colgate (NY), 103
The College of Charleston (SC),
   151, 152
College of the Albermarle (NC),
   137
College of William and Mary (VA),
   163
Colorado College (CO), 223, 224
Colorado Mountain College (CO),
   223, 224
Colorado School of Mines (CO),
   223, 224
Colorado State University (CO),
   223, 224
Columbia (NY), 101, 104, 105,
   106
Columbus (MS), 213
Columbus Tech (OH), 174
Concordia (MO), 235
Concordia College (OH), 174
Concord School (NH), 95–96
Cornell (NY), 101
Corpus Christi State (TX), 239
Cranbrook Schools (MI), 170
Cuyahoga Community College
   (OH), 173
C. W. Post (NY), 108
Cypress College (CA), 251

Dartmouth (NH), 95–96, 98
Davenport Business College (MI),
   171
Deerfield Academy (MA), 90
Delaware Law School (DE), 131
Del Mar Junior College (TX), 239
Dennison (OH), 174
De Paul (IL), 169
Dillard (LA), 229, 232
Dominican College (LA), 230
Domingas Hills (CA), 257
Drake (IA), 182
Drew (NJ), 135
Drexel Institute (PA), 143, 146
Dufreye Medical Center (PA), 143
Duquesne (PA), 147

Eaglebrook Prep (MA), 90
East Carolina University (NC), 137
Eastern (PA), 143, 148
Eastern Kentucky (KY), 212
Eastern Mennonite (VA), 159
Eastern Virginia Medical School
   (VA), 161
Eckard College (FL), 205
Elizabethtown College (PA), 144
Elmira College (NY), 101
Emmanuel (MA), 82
Emory (GA), 206, 207
Evergreen State College (WA), 195

Fairleigh Dickinson (NJ), 135
Florida Atlantic University (FL),
   203
Florida International University
   (FL), 202, 204
Florida Memorial (FL), 202
Florida State (GA), 209
Fordham (NY), 104, 105
Fort Lewis College (CO), 225
Franklin (OH), 174
Franklin Institute (PA), 143
Franklin and Marshall (PA), 144
Fuller Theological Seminary (CA),
   249
Fullerton College (CA), 251, 252,
   257

Fulton (NY), 103

Genesee (NY), 102–103
Georgia Institute of Technology (GA), 207
Georgia State (GA), 207
Georgetown (D.C.), 132
George Washington (D.C.), 132
Gordon (MA), 83
Gorham (ME), 73
Goucher (MD), 133
Grand Rapids Junior College (MI), 171
Grand Valley State (MI), 171
Grandview (IA), 182
Grinnell (IA), 182

Hamden Hall (CT), 70
Hamilton (NY), 101, 103
Hampshire (MA), 89–90
Harcum (PA), 148
Harrisburg Area Community College (PA), 144
Harvard (MA), 81–84
Haverford (PA), 143
Hawthorne College (NH), 96
Herkimer (NY), 103
Hofstra (NY), 108
Holderness (NH), 95–96
Hopkins (CT), 70
Hotchkiss (CT), 69, 71
Howard (D.C.), 132
Hunter (NY), 104, 105
Huntingdon College (AL), 199

Immaculate College (PA), 148
Institute of Texas Culture (TX), 242
Iona (NY), 101
Iowa State (IA), 182
Ithaca College (NY), 101

James Madison University (VA), 159
Jefferson Medical School (PA), 143
John Carroll University (OH), 173
John Jay (NY), 104

Johns Hopkins (MD), 133, 134
Johnson and Wales (RI), 114
Jopia-Lincoln Jr. College (MS), 214
Judson School (AZ), 245, 247

Keene State (NM), 95–96
Kendall School of Design (MI), 171
Kenrick Seminary (MO), 235
Kent (CT), 69, 71
Kenyon (OH), 174
King's Point Marine Academy (NY), 108
Kutztown University (PA), 143

Lafayette (PA), 143
Lake Forest (IL), 169
Lakevilla (CT), 69
La Salle (MA), 84
La Salle (PA), 143
Lebanon Valley College (PA), 144
Lehigh (PA), 143
Lesley (MA), 84
Lewiston (ME), 73
Liberty University (VA), 161
Lincoln (PA), 145
Logan Chiropractic College (MO), 235
Louisiana State (LA), 229
Loyola (IL), 169
Loyola (CA), 257
Loyola (LA), 229–232
Loyola (MD), 134
LSU Dental School (LA), 230
Lynchburg College (VA), 161

Maine Maritime (ME), 73
Manhattanville (NY), 101
Marietta (OH), 174
Marquette (WI), 176
Mary Baldwin (VA), 159
Marymount (CA), 257
Marymount (NY), 105
Massachusetts College of Art (MA), 82

Massachusetts Maritime Academy
(MA), 84
Massanutten Military Academy
(VA), 159
McGill (PQ), 280
Medical University of South
Carolina (SC), 152
Medical College of Virginia (VA),
162
Medical College of Wisconsin
(WI), 176
Memphis State (TN), 215, 216
Mercer (GA), 206
Metro State (CO), 224
Miami-Dade Community College
(FL), 202, 204
Michigan State (MI), 170
Middlebury (VT), 109
Milford Academy (CT), 70
Millersville (PA), 144
Millsaps (MS), 213
Mississippi College (MS), 213
Mississippi Southern (MS), 229
Mississippi State (MS), 213
Mississippi University for Women
(MS), 213
Miss Porter's Farmington Prep
School (CT), 69
M.I.T. (MA), 82–84
Mobile College (AL), 200
Montclair State (NJ), 135
Moore College of Art (PA), 146
Moravian (PA), 143
Morehead (KY), 212
Morningside (IA), 182
Mount Holyoke (MA), 89–90
Mount St. Joseph (KY), 211
M.S. Hershey Medical Center of
Penn State (PA), 144
Muckingum (OH), 174
Muhlenberg (PA), 143

Napa Jr. College (CA), 252
Naropa Institute (CO), 222
Naval War College (RI), 114, 115
Nazareth (NY), 102–103
New England Conservatory (MA),
82, 83

New Hampton School (NH),
95–96
New Orleans Baptist Seminary
(LA), 232
New School (NY), 106
New York Academy of Science
(NY), 104
New York University (NY),
104–106
Niagara University (NY), 107
North Adams State (MA), 89–90
Northeastern (MA), 82–84
Northeastern (ME), 73
Northern Arizona University (AZ),
245, 247
Northern Kentucky University
(KY), 211
Northridge (CA), 257
Northwestern (IL), 169

Oakland (MI), 170
Occidental (CA), 257
Oglethorpe (GA), 207
Ohio Dominican (OH), 174
Ohio State (OH), 174
Ohio University (OH), 174
Ohio Wesleyan (OH), 174
Oklahoma Christian (OK), 238
Oklahoma City University (OK),
238
Oklahoma State (OK), 238
Old Dominion (VA), 161
Orange Coast College (CA), 251
Orme School (AZ), 245, 247
Otterbein (OH), 174
Our Lady of the Lake (TX), 240

Pace (NY), 106, 105
Pacific Union College (CA), 252
Pasadena City College (CA), 257
Peabody (MD), 134
Penn State (PA), 147
Penn State Graduate School (PA),
148
Penn State at Lima (PA), 145
Pepperdine (CA), 257
Perkiomen School (PA), 143

Philadelphia Textile College (PA), 143
Picken Tech (GA), 208
Pine Manor (MA), 82, 83
Plymouth State (NH), 95–96
Polytech at Pomona (CA), 257
Pomfret (CT), 69
Portland (ME), 73
Portsmouth Abbey (RI), 114, 115
Presbyterian Hospital (PA), 143
Providence College (RI), 114

Randolph Macon (VA), 161, 162
Rosemary Hall (CT), 69
Rensselaer Polytechnic Institute (NY), 101
Rhode College (TN), 215
Rhode Island College (RI), 114
Rhode Island School of Design (RI), 114
Rice (TX), 240, 241
Roanoke Bible College (NC), 137
Rochester Institute of Technology (NY), 102–103
Roger Williams (RI), 114
Rosemont (PA), 143, 148
Rosenstile University (FL), 202
Russell Sage (NY), 101

Sacramento City College (CA), 253
St. Catherine's School (VA), 162
St. Christopher's School (VA), 162
St. Elizabeth School of Nursing (NY), 103
St. George's School (RI), 114, 115
St. John Fisher (NY), 102–103
St. John's (MD), 132, 133
St. Josephs (PA), 143
St. Louis University (MO), 235
St. Michael's (RI), 115
St. Paul's (NH), 95–96
St. Paul's University (ON), 278
St. Petersburg Jr. College (FL), 204, 205
Salisbury (CT), 71
Salve Regina (RI), 114, 115
San Diego State (CA), 252
San Francisco State (CA), 249, 254

Santa Rosa Jr. College (CA), 255
Sarah Lawrence (NY), 101
Scottsdale Artists School (AZ), 246
Scripps Institute of Oceanography (CA), 250
Seattle College (WA), 193
Seattle Pacific University (WA), 193
Shenandoah College (VA), 159
Shenandoah Valley Academy (VA), 157
Simmons (MA), 81–83
Simon's Rock at Bard (MA), 71
Simpson (IA), 182
Sioux Falls College (SD), 192
Sir Wilfred Laurier University (ON), 280
Skidmore (NY), 101, 109
Smith (MA), 89–90
Sonoma State (CA), 255
Southampton College (NY), 101, 108
South Dakota School of Mines (SD), 192
South Dakota State (SD), 192
Southern Connecticut State (CT), 70
Southern Methodist University (TX), 240
Southern Seminary (VA), 159
Southern University (LA), 229
South Florida University (FL), 204
Spalding (KY), 212
Stanford (CA), 254
Springhill College (AL), 200
Starkville (MS), 213
Stetson Law School (FL), 205
Stonehill (MA), 83
SUNY Albany (NY), 109
SUNY Cobleskill (NY), 109
SUNY at Marcy (NY), 103
SUNY Buffalo (NY), 107
SUNY New Paltz (NY), 101
SUNY Stony Brook (NY), 108
Swarthmore (PA), 143
Sweet Briar (VA), 161

Taft (CT), 70, 71

Tampa College (FL), 205
Temple (PA), 143, 146
Texas Christian University (TX), 240
Texas University (TX), 240
Thomas More (KY), 211
Tilton Academy (NH), 95–96
Trinity (CT), 69
Trinity (TX), 240
Tufts (MA), 81–83
Tulane (LA), 229–232
Tulane Medical School (LA), 230

Union College (NY), 109
Université de Montréal (PQ), 280
University of Alaska (AK), 269, 270
University of Arizona (AZ), 245, 247
University of British Columbia (BC), 193
University of California (CA), 251
University of California, Irvine (CA), 250, 252
University of California, Los Angeles (CA), 249, 250, 252, 257
University of California Medical Center (CA), 254
University of California, Riverside (CA), 257
University of California, San Diego (CA), 249, 250, 257
University of Chicago (IL), 169
University of Cincinnati (OH), 174, 211
University of Colorado (CO), 222, 223
University of Dayton (OH), 174
University of Delaware (DE), 131, 145
University of Denver (CO), 223, 224
University of District of Columbia (D.C.), 132
University of Hawaii (HI), 272
University of Houston (TX), 240, 241

University of Illinois at Chicago (IL), 169
University of Kansas (KS), 228
University of Kentucky (KY), 212
University of Louisville (KY), 212
University of Maine (ME), 73
University of Maryland (MD), 133
University of Massachusetts (MA), 89–90
University of Massachusetts Medical School (MA), 80
University of Miami (FL), 204
University of Miami Marine Laboratory (FL), 202
University of Michigan (MI), 170
University of Mississippi (MS), 213, 215, 229
University of Missouri (MO), 228, 235
University of Missouri/Kansas City Extension Center (MO), 235
University of Montgomery (NC), 199
University of New Mexico (NM), 229
University of New Orleans (LA), 230, 232
University of Northern Iowa (IA), 182
University of Oklahoma (OK), 238
University of Ottawa (ON), 278
University of Pennsylvania (PA), 143, 146
University of Pittsburgh (PA), 147
University of Puget Sound (WA), 193
University of Rhode Island (RI), 114
University of Richmond (VA), 162
University of Rochester (NY), 102–103
University of St. Thomas (TX), 241
University of San Diego (CA), 252
University of South Alabama (AL), 200
University of South Dakota (SD), 192

University of Southern California (CA), 249, 250, 252, 257
University of Southern Colorado (CO), 224
University of Southern Maine (ME), 73
University of Southern Mississippi (MS), 214
University of South Florida (FL), 204
University of Tampa (FL), 204
University of Tennessee (TN), 216
University of Tennessee Medical School (TN), 215
University of Vermont (VT), 109
University of Victoria (BC), 275
University of Virginia (VA), 160
University of Washington (WA), 193
University of Waterloo (ON), 280
University of Western Ontario (ON), 280
University of Wisconsin (WI), 176
Ursinus (PA), 148
U.S. Air Force Academy (CO), 223, 224
U.S. Naval Academy (MD), 132, 133
Utica College (NY), 103

Valley College (CA), 257
Verde Valley School (AZ), 247
Virginia Episcopal School (VA), 161
Valdosta State (GA), 209
Valley Forge Military Academy (PA), 148
Vanderbilt (TN), 216
Vassar (NY), 101
Villanova (PA), 143, 148
Virginia Commonwealth University (VA), 162

Virginia Military Institute (VA), 159
Virginia Wesleyan (VA), 161

Wallingford (CT), 69
Washington College (MD), 133
Washington and Lee (VA), 159
Washington University (MO), 235
Waterville (ME), 73
Wayne State (MI), 170
Wellesley (MA), 82, 83
Wesleyan (CT), 69, 70
Westbrook (ME), 73
Westchester Community College (NY), 101
West Chester University (PA), 131, 145, 148
Western Kentucky (KY), 212
Western New England (MA), 89–90
Western State College of Law (CA), 251
Wheaton (IL), 169
Wheelock (MA), 81
Whittier (CA), 257
William Penn (IA), 182
Williams College (MA), 71, 89–90, 109
Wills Eye Hospital (PA), 143
Wilmington (OH), 174
Wittenberg (OH), 174
Woods Hole Oceanographic Institute (MA), 88
Worcester Polytech (MA), 80
Wright State (OH), 174

Xavier (LA), 229
Xavier (OH), 211

Yale (CT), 69, 70
Yeshiva (NY), 105
Young Harris College (GA), 208

Date_____

PRENTICE HALL PRESS
ONE GULF + WESTERN PLAZA
NEW YORK, NY 10023

Friends:

Please send me the books checked below:

FROMMER'S $-A-DAY GUIDES™

(In-depth guides to sightseeing and low-cost tourist accommodations and facilities.)

☐ Europe on $25 a Day $12.95	☐ New Zealand on $25 a Day $10.95
☐ Australia on $25 a Day $10.95	☐ New York on $45 a Day.............. $9.95
☐ Eastern Europe on $25 a Day $10.95	☐ Scandinavia on $50 a Day........... $10.95
☐ England on $35 a Day.............. $10.95	☐ Scotland and Wales on $35 a Day..... $10.95
☐ Greece on $25 a Day................ $10.95	☐ South America on $30 a Day $10.95
☐ Hawaii on $45 a Day................ $10.95	☐ Spain and Morocco (plus the Canary
☐ India on $15 & $25 a Day........... $9.95	Is.) on $40 a Day $10.95
☐ Ireland on $30 a Day................ $10.95	☐ Turkey on $25 a Day (avail. Nov. '87) . $10.95
☐ Israel on $30 & $35 a Day $10.95	☐ Washington, D.C. on $40 a Day $10.95
☐ Mexico on $20 a Day $10.95	

FROMMER'S DOLLARWISE GUIDES™

(Guides to sightseeing and tourist accommodations and facilities from budget to deluxe with emphasis on the medium-priced.)

☐ Alaska (avail. Nov. '87) $12.95	☐ Cruises (incl. Alaska, Carib, Mex,
☐ Austria & Hungary $11.95	Hawaii, Panama, Canada, & US) $12.95
☐ Belgium, Holland, Luxembourg $11.95	☐ California & Las Vegas $11.95
☐ Egypt............................. $11.95	☐ Florida........................... $10.95
☐ England & Scotland $11.95	☐ Honeymoons (US, Canada, Mexico, &
☐ France $11.95	Carib) (avail. Nov. '87)............... $12.95
☐ Germany.......................... $11.95	☐ Mid-Atlantic (avail. Nov. '87) $12.95
☐ Italy.............................. $11.95	☐ New England...................... $11.95
☐ Japan & Hong Kong $12.95	☐ New York State (avail. Aug. '87)...... $11.95
☐ Portugal (incl. Madeira & the Azores) . $11.95	☐ Northwest $11.95
☐ South Pacific (avail. Oct. '87)........ $12.95	☐ Skiing in Europe $12.95
☐ Switzerland & Liechtenstein $11.95	☐ Skiing USA—East $10.95
☐ Bermuda & The Bahamas........... $10.95	☐ Skiing USA—West $10.95
☐ Canada $12.95	☐ Southeast & New Orleans $11.95
☐ Caribbean $12.95	☐ Southwest........................ $11.95
	☐ Texas............................ $11.95

TURN PAGE FOR ADDITIONAL BOOKS AND ORDER FORM.

THE ARTHUR FROMMER GUIDES™

(Pocket-size guides to sightseeing and tourist accommodations and facilities in all price ranges.)

☐ Amsterdam/Holland	$5.95	☐ Mexico City/Acapulco	$5.95
☐ Athens	$5.95	☐ Minneapolis/St. Paul (avail. Dec. '87)	$5.95
☐ Atlantic City/Cape May	$5.95	☐ Montreal/Quebec City	$5.95
☐ Boston	$5.95	☐ New Orleans	$5.95
☐ Cancun/Cozumel/Yucatán	$5.95	☐ New York	$5.95
☐ Dublin/Ireland	$5.95	☐ Orlando/Disney World/EPCOT	$5.95
☐ Hawaii	$5.95	☐ Paris	$5.95
☐ Las Vegas	$5.95	☐ Philadelphia	$5.95
☐ Lisbon/Madrid/Costa del Sol	$5.95	☐ Rome	$5.95
☐ London	$5.95	☐ San Francisco	$5.95
☐ Los Angeles	$5.95	☐ Washington, D.C.	$5.95

FROMMER'S TOURING GUIDES™

(Color illustrated guides that include walking tours, cultural & historic sites, and other vital travel information)

☐ Egypt	$8.95	☐ Paris	$8.95
☐ Florence	$8.95	☐ Venice	$8.95
☐ London	$8.95		

SPECIAL EDITIONS

☐ A Shopper's Guide to the Best Buys in England, Scotland, & Wales	$10.95	☐ Marilyn Wood's Wonderful Weekends (NY, Conn, Mass, RI, Vt, NJ, Del, Pa)	$10.95
☐ A Shopper's Guide to the Caribbean (avail. Aug. '87)	$10.95	☐ Motorist's Phrase Book (Fr/Ger/Sp)	$4.95
☐ Bed & Breakfast—N. America	$8.95	☐ Swap and Go (Home Exchanging)	$10.95
☐ Fast 'n' Easy Phrase Book (Fr/Ger/Ital/Sp in *one* vol.)	$6.95	☐ The Candy Apple (NY for kids)	$11.95
☐ How to Beat the High Cost of Travel	$4.95	☐ Travel Diary and Record Book	$5.95
		☐ Where to Stay USA (Lodging from $3 to $30 a night)	$9.95

ORDER NOW!

In U.S. include $1.50 shipping UPS for 1st book; 50¢ ea. add'l. book. Outside U.S. $2 and 50¢ respectively.

Enclosed is my check or money order for $_____

NAME_____

ADDRESS_____

CITY_____ STATE_____ ZIP_____